Britain finds itself in a radically new world in the 1990s. The events of the closing months of the 1980s in Eastern Europe and the move towards an economically and politically integrated Western Europe, have heralded a new stage in International Relations. Consequently, established policies and ways of thinking about Britain's external affairs are now being questioned. In this book, leading academics in the fields of political economy, foreign policy analysis, defence studies and political theory offer alternative approaches to the study of British foreign policy.

Each contributor surveys recent literature on his/her topic and then considers the major questions that any analysis of Britain in the world in the 1990s must face. To what extent can Britain insulate itself from the adverse consequences of interdependence? What is the appropriate political response to increased economic interdependence? What are the implications of the changing nature of the international security environment? And, how should sovereignty be defined in the 1990s?

This is the first book to examine the study of Britain in world politics and the academic perspectives that bear upon it. Its multidisciplinary approach will ensure it is read by all students and specialists interested in British, European and International Politics.

T0381873

BRITAIN IN THE WORLD

BRITAIN IN THE WORLD

Edited by

LAWRENCE FREEDMAN
Department of War Studies
King's College
LONDON

and

MICHAEL CLARKE
Centre for Defence Studies
King's College
LONDON

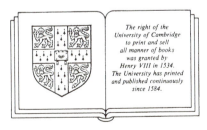

The right of the
University of Cambridge
to print and sell
all manner of books
was granted by
Henry VIII in 1534.
The University has printed
and published continuously
since 1584.

CAMBRIDGE UNIVERSITY PRESS

Cambridge
New York   Port Chester
Melbourne   Sydney

CAMBRIDGE UNIVERSITY PRESS
Cambridge, New York, Melbourne, Madrid, Cape Town, Singapore,
São Paulo, Delhi, Dubai, Tokyo

Cambridge University Press
The Edinburgh Building, Cambridge CB2 8RU, UK

Published in the United States of America by Cambridge University Press, New York

www.cambridge.org
Information on this title: www.cambridge.org/9780521130769

First published 1991
This digitally printed version 2010

A catalogue record for this publication is available from the British Library

Library of Congress Cataloguing in Publication data
  Britain in the world / edited by Lawrence Freedman and Michael Clarke.
    p.   cm.
  Papers presented at a conference held Nov. 12–13, 1987 at King's College London.
  Includes bibliographical references and index.
  ISBN 0 521 37566 5 (hardback)
  1. Great Britain – Foreign relations – 1945– – Congresses.
  2. World politics – 1985–1995 – Congresses.
  I. Freedman, Lawrence.   II. Clarke, Michael, 1950– ·
  DA589.8.B735   1990
  327.41 – dc20   90–38359   CIP

ISBN 978-0-521-37566-5 Hardback
ISBN 978-0-521-13076-9 Paperback

CONTENTS

PREFACE

On Thursday and Friday 12–13 November 1987 a group met at King's College London to discuss papers prepared in connection with a possible initiative on Britain in the World in the 1990s to be sponsored by the Economic and Social Research Council. A considerable amount of preparatory work had already gone into this initiative and the idea of the conference was to assess how different academic approaches might be brought together to help develop a fuller understanding of the issues facing this country.

Four papers were commissioned. The four papers were by Dr Ellen Kennedy (QMC) on 'The State and Sovereignty', Dr Steve Smith (UEA) on 'Foreign Policy Analysis', Dr Barry Buzan (Warwick) on 'Interdependence' and Professor Ron Smith (Birkbeck) on 'International Political Economy'. There were two discussants for each paper (see Appendix). Together the paper-givers, discussants and other participants made up a diverse group. The disciplines represented included Economics, International Law, Political Theory, Geography and History as well as International Relations. A former senior diplomat was present as was a director of a leading city firm.

In the event the initiative was lost in the process of reorganising the ESRC's Committee structure. However, the quality of the papers was such that we felt it worthwhile to publish them. To ensure a comprehensive coverage Michael Clarke has provided an extra chapter on the security dimension.

The editors wish to express their thanks to those who contributed so much to the seminar, including the staff of the ESRC.

I ~ Britain in the world
Lawrence Freedman

The events of the closing months of the 1980s in Eastern Europe heralded a new stage in international relations and so in British foreign policy. The familiar parameters of the cold war alliances, which set the terms for so much of the foreign policy debate, gave way to a much more complex set of relationships. The implosion of the communist world and the possible fragmentation of some its more prominent states, including the Soviet Union itself, and the prospect of German reunification suggested both the irrelevance of many of the preoccupations of the strategists while raising new security concerns developing out of chaos in the Eastern half of the continent.

For Britain the disorienting impact of these changes was magnified by anxieties as to the proper pace and direction of integration within Western Europe. The commitment to the European Community (EC) had become irreversible. The Commonwealth no longer provided an economic alternative while the special relationship with the United States mattered for far less as the United States itself came to matter for less, along with those nuclear and intelligence activities that had rendered the relationship special in the first place. But the commitment to Europe, which had extended into the Single European Act, was not necessarily of the sort that Europe sought from Britain. The Prime Minister argued that the economic and social assumptions behind much of the continental drive for integration were of the same nature as those she had spent a decade fighting within Britain. It was for precisely this reason that many of those who had opposed the European cause in the past, especially in the Labour Party, now embraced it. They were enthused rather than deterred by the corporatist and welfarist aspects of the EC.

Yet the EC had been able to make progress because it too worked within the cold war framework, able to take on the mantle of Europe even while it excluded much of Europe. As Hungary, Czechoslovakia, Poland and East Germany came in from the cold, a tension developed between the continuing drive for integration among the established members of the Community and the need to reach out to the fledgeling democracies of the East.

This book does not offer a formula for handling these problems nor even a full guide to their many aspects. It does not attempt to address the current foreign policy agenda. Rather it seeks to explore the analytical frameworks which shape so much of our thinking about Britain's external relations. Now more than before we need to question not only our established policies but also our established ways of thinking.

The traditional approach to foreign policy is state-centred. Relations between states are managed through 'high politics' with security the basic interest and armed force the ultimate arbiter. The study of foreign policy becomes the study of potential and actual threats to security – often by means of a guided tour of the world's trouble spots – and the alternative forms of response.

This approach has been criticised as being too narrow and unable to cope with substantial changes that have transformed the international system in recent decades. Among the powers of the first and second ranks, the number and type of disputes that can be considered soluble by military means has declined. For much foreign policy, the 'ultimate sanction' of armed force is quite irrelevant. Within Western Europe relations are no longer governed by armed force with the exception of the influence that may result from the extent of the contribution to collective defence, and this too may decline if the demands of collective defence are seen to be less pressing as a result of the collapse of communist power.

None the less, one cannot discard the traditional concern with the preservation of sovereignty in the face of military threats. It is impossible to preclude all threats in the future. Outside Europe many countries are acquiring formidable military capabilities. Within Europe Britain is one of three nuclear powers. However remote a possibility, the avoidance of war must be a prime responsibility of government. Furthermore, it may be that the reason why armed force appears so often to have so little utility and direct military threats to sovereignty appear so remote may be precisely because considerable attention has been devoted to these problems over the last few decades and successful security arrangements have been established which have helped reduce the importance of armed force in everyday political life. The implosion of the Warsaw Pact has been accompanied by a whole range of old rivalries coming to the fore in Eastern Europe which warn against taking anything for granted in security affairs.

So while the importance of the military dimension to international affairs cannot be ignored, this dimension is by no means as pre-eminent as it once was, and this must have consequences for the overall framework. Any framework for the study of international politics must take as its starting-point the state. The state would once have been defined in terms of military power. *Internally* it enjoyed a monopoly of organised violence. The capacity to monopolise violence was the basis of power and of international recognition. A loss of monopoly could lead to the disintegration of the state. *Externally* the power resources at its disposal would determine its place in the hierarchy of states. Drives in the eighteenth and nineteenth centuries to centralise state power and mobilise national resources reflected a belief that only through maximum state power could national interests be secured in a hostile world, a view reflected in the economic sphere in mercantilism.

It remains the case that one of the key properties of a state is its monopoly of military power, so that the loss of this monopoly threatens the very existence of the state and renders it vulnerable to secession or revolution. There is little tolerance for any pluralism in the military sphere or any loss of tight state control. However, beyond the military sphere the pre-eminence of the state has been challenged. In the economic and social spheres there is now great plurality. This creates enormous problems of integration. The rivalries and hostilities that may be found among the diverse regional, ethnic, religious and economic groupings that make up society at times threaten its cohesion.

In addition, these various groupings often have their own international networks and in consequence quite distinctive, and often opposing, pulls to those resulting from their membership of a particular nation state. An executive for a multinational company based in Scotland, a dealer in the Futures Market, a Sikh in Southall, a Jew in Manchester, a newspaperman in Northern Ireland, an academic in Oxford may all be aware of trans-national loyalties that in some cases may be more pressing than their national. Even government departments can sometimes feel a greater affinity with their counterparts in allied countries than other departments owing loyalty to the same government (defence versus finance ministries). London as a region is more cosmopolitan than other parts of Britain and therefore is likely to respond to international stimuli in quite different ways. The City of London often expects its special position in international financial markets to shape national fiscal policy. The Rushdie affair indicates how race relations in Britain can be influenced by an appeal from Iran to fundamental belief that creates a direct conflict between the sensitivities of a substantial minority and established political and legal conventions.

Meanwhile, external pressures impinge on many aspects of everyday life. It is not only that the budgetary, agricultural or energy policies of other states can constrain and shape British policy but that the activities of international companies, farmers and bankers also can. This is what has come to be known as 'interdependence' and provided the backdrop for much of our discussions. It may be that the concept of interdependence has become something of a cliché, but the phenomenon is very real and the term is evocative even if no longer innovative.

Thus while in strategic terms, the centrifugal forces in the world seem to be stronger than the centripetal, it is argued that in economic and resource terms the opposite is becoming the case. Interdependence results from the rapid increases in all forms of trade, with multinational business operations encouraged by improving communications and leading to the wider distribution of advanced technology. The increasingly diffuse nature of political power inhibits attempts to create international order, but it is suggested that a similar trend in economic power, making everyone dependent upon each other, creates incentives for co-operation and togetherness.

But it is also the case that this interdependence makes everyone vulnerable to collapse or malevolent behaviour in particular countries, such as the mineral producers of Southern Africa or the oil producers of the Gulf. Distortions in the workings of the larger economies, most recently with the United States, can dislocate the whole system. This puts a high premium on co-operative behaviour. So, it is argued, multinational institutions are needed to organise this behaviour, reminding all of the costs of failure and acting quickly to limit disruption resulting from particular failures.

The picture of interdependence needs qualification: patterns of trade are still largely determined by political and historical factors and inequalities in development. The intense interaction among members of the EC is not matched by the countries of Africa. Relations between developed and developing countries remain asymmetrical and when specific bilateral relations are examined in detail, there is often no real sense of mutual dependence.

Yet interdependence represents a genuine phenomenon for Britain and coming to terms with it complicates and creates major tests for foreign policy. The inter-penetration of the economies and societies of the Western world blurs the boundary between the domestic and the foreign. The political sphere must expand to accommodate the variety of factors that shape the nation's security and welfare. The modern state is expected to take a greater responsibility for feeding, housing and educating its population and for its health and prosperity than was expected of its predecessors (although of course the degree of responsibility has now become a matter for intense political debate). As all these tasks have a pronounced external dimension then so the requirements of external policy must grow proportionately.

Because of this governments have become more prepared to enter into institutionalised co-operative arrangements with other governments in order to ensure that they can all meet their domestic responsibilities more efficiently. This means that governments must take a view on the quality of international organisations such as the UN, EC, IMF, OECD, NATO and operate within them with a view to their overall worth as well as their specific value in particular issues. Any transnational phenomenon – such as acid rain or radioactive fallout or cocaine – can add to the demands on international organisations.

Yet this growth of the political sphere internally and externally, and thus in principle the remit of the state, has not been matched by a growth in the effective power of the state. The wide responsibilities of the state coupled with the tendency towards disaggregation within society and the sheer pace and intensity of interdependence render it impossible for even a relatively powerful state to be at all 'in control'.

The pursuit of domestic goals in the international environment requires a clear view on the nature of those goals, but these are often politically controversial at home and even within the government.

It is proving to be difficult to use multilateral forums for creative diplomacy, even in the economic sphere. The mechanisms of international co-operation work at speeds which fail to match those of the events they are seeking to control. Initiatives to solve international problems, for example related to the environment or poverty, or to improve the collective lot, by stabilising commodity prices or stimulating world economic growth, have foundered on the clumsy nature of multilateral institutions in conditions of decentralised power. The need to achieve consensus saps the strength from new initiatives. Laborious negotiations tend to be either overtaken by numerous and unco-ordinated unilateral actions, or else they result in an agreement to freeze matters in their existing form.

This has dampened enthusiasm for attempts to master international events and not be at their mercy. The inclination has come to be increasingly to disclaim responsibility in the face of external forces – the world economy can be blamed for all manner of problems within the domestic economy. In a world of multiple causation who is to blame for adverse outcomes? This has important consequences for democratic accountability as can be seen with the debate within Britain over the expanding remit of European institutions and the consequent downgrading of parliamentary government.

THE RELEVANCE FOR BRITAIN

Britain provides an interesting case study for those concerned with the general question of how a modern middle-range state can cope with the ambiguous and complex challenges of an interdependent world. The analysis of this set of problems however has relevance for those concerned more specifically with the quality of British policy.

In the past the study of British foreign policy has been shaped by a traditional approach that would have been recognised by Castlereagh and Palmerston, and even Eden, preoccupied with forming alliances, opposing aggression and participating in political affairs at every level throughout the world in pursuit of interests that were themselves distinctly 'overseas' in nature. For those who still cling to this tradition there is an increasingly desperate search for something unique and exceptional for Britain to contribute to the conduct of world affairs. The value of long traditions of diplomacy, and familiarity with all regions of the globe have been asserted to justify participation in attempts to settle a variety of the world's troubles. International systems have been designed in which Britain is at the centre, offering links with the English-speaking world, her old colonies and Europe, helping mutual understanding because of her empathy with all. For a country that no longer qualifies as a superpower in either the military or the economic spheres, a collection of excellent contacts may be the best there is to offer. It is unfortunately difficult to elevate this to a 'world role'. There are now many channels of communication in the world through which nations can speak to each other and Britain is necessary as an intermediary in very few of them.

The attempt to play a world role was mocked in the Berrill Report on the FCO in the 1970s. It is felt by many to be romantic and anachronistic. The recognition that Britain is no longer able to cultivate and police her own 'spheres of influence' can be used to suggest that Britain can no longer afford a foreign policy or at least that such a policy need be no more than an external expression of domestic interests.

It is important not to exaggerate Britain's former strengths or the contemporary strength of other major powers. The fact is that it is the world that has changed as much as Britain's capacity to operate within it. The withdrawal of British administrators and troops from Asia, the Middle East and Africa have left vacuums that have been filled in a variety of ways. It is true that the superpowers, particularly the United States, moved in when the old Imperial powers left, but their positions are not often as comfortable or secure as those of their predecessors and are rarely commanding. There has been a shift in power away from the industrialised world. The developing countries have achieved the attributes of sovereign states which gives them certain rights and leverage in international organisations. At times, some of their number have effective control over resources of vast importance to the industrial nations and have not hesitated to exploit them for economic and political benefit. They have accepted responsibility for their own defence and have bought large quantities of weapons for this purpose, thus reducing further their dependence on the major powers. New centres of power have emerged to complicate international life. The world is no longer conducive to the interference of the major powers as it was once. Whilst it is true that the superpowers can impose on others more than can countries of Britain's size and resources, even they are finding it difficult to order the world according to their preferences. Foreign policy, in the traditional sense, is becoming a much more unsatisfactory and tiresome activity.

In these circumstances it has been argued that rather than give up on a foreign policy, Britain can no longer afford *not* to have a foreign policy. The more Britain's well-being depends on the attitudes and activities of foreigners, and the less Britain is able to influence them by the exercise of military and economic power, the more we must rely on a skilful diplomacy, artful and persuasive, employing remaining sources of leverage with care and parsimony.

However, this may turn out to be little more than a reactive pragmatism, in which a clear, but short-term national interest usually serves as the easiest (and electorally popular) guide. Few attempts are made to develop international initiatives which integrate national needs with the greater good. The needs of the international system as a whole are an inherently lower priority as the system lacks a domestic political constituency. Instead of enlightened self-interest we get the enlightened presentation of self-interest.

What sort of attitude should we take towards the changing international system? From a security perspective interdependence can appear downright dangerous, something to be deplored and resisted. Too many people can let us down – and we can let them down. Traditionally dependence on others has been something to avoid rather than embrace. At times of war, key supplies can become vulnerable to interference, either at source or in transit. At times of peace, instabilities in supply or in price of key materials or the whims of financial markets can disrupt economic management. It is therefore not surprising to find signs of a hankering after greater independence in Britain.

One of the issues raised in this volume is therefore inevitably the extent to which a state such as Britain can insulate itself from the adverse consequences of interdependence even while enjoying its benefits elsewhere. Governments believing in free markets may still find 'security considerations' sufficient justification for active intervention.

Self-sufficiency normally has a cost. Security of supply involves premium prices, and the attempt to reduce one's vulnerability may only create new vulnerabilities elsewhere. And even if we could extend the areas of self-reliance, the fact that we would still need to import non-fuel minerals and to export manufactured goods, combined with our inability to defend ourselves, would still leave Britain extremely dependent upon the outside world.

It is impossible to come to grips with the incoherence of the international system – the mass of everyday transactions and their complex interrelationships – other than by reproducing this incoherence. We need to stand back sufficiently to see the patterns and then concentrate on the implications for the state.

How does the British public understand the international system of which Britain is a part and what implications does this have for national policy? What has been the character of elite debates on these issues? What is the significance of the relative weakness of federalist, mercantilist and corporatist traditions? To what extent are the international dimensions to some of the country's most distinctive features – its geography, physical resources, language, ethnic composition – appreciated? What does all this mean in terms of national identity and citizenship? To the extent that some distortions resulting from the working of the international system can only be tackled at an international level, can international institutions be reformed to make them more effective?

Lastly, what are the policy implications of all this? It would no doubt be nice to produce a coherent set of policies, translating the level of high abstraction – world peace, prosperity, human happiness and the rest – into concrete terms and linking the result to the level of practical administration and diplomacy, and laying down ways of getting from here to there. This would emphasize the importance of goal-setting, anticipation of significant movements in the international system and a clear strategy for achieving goals within this system.

This is a mode of policy-making advocated more often by the theorist than the practitioner. The practitioner notes the unpredictability of international life which can upset the best-laid plans. But then foreign policy comes to be no more than a set of manoeuvres, opportunistic or damage-limiting, that are essentially short-term reactions to the vicissitudes of international life. We should be paying more attention to unstated assumptions and sentiments, and addressing the confrontation between national interests and trends in the international system.

International life is inevitably full of surprises. Even when an event is predictable, as was the turmoil in the Shah's Iran or indeed the drive for reform in Eastern Europe, its timing, character and consequences can rarely be anticipated. We dare not base policy simply on crystal ball gazing. We can note general trends, problems that demand solution, irresistible pressures meeting immovable objects and so on, but an attempt at detailed prediction would be doomed to failure. Similarly with goal setting, the need is to demonstrate the range of choice in the future rather than make definite recommendations. This creates problems with 'coherence' as an objective in itself. Because of competing national interests and values, one goal can often be achieved only at the expense of another.

Thus the essays in this volume should be judged not simply in terms of the answers that they might suggest to the policy agenda of the moment but as part of an effort to develop the broad stances that might help us orient ourselves to the changing nature of our own society and the international system as a whole, and the sort of trades between different policy objectives that will need to be faced.

2 ~ Interdependence and Britain's external relations

Barry Buzan

The purpose of this study is to introduce the concept of interdependence as it has developed within the field of International Relations, and to survey its significance for Britain. The first and second sections examine the intellectual origins of the term, why it came into vogue during the 1970s, what its users seek to express about the international system and what levels of meaning the concept encompasses. The third section looks at the impact of interdependence on a state such as Britain. The argument is that this impact is very wide-ranging, carrying fundamental political implications not only for Britain's external relations, but also for how the country is governed. Any attempt to link interdependence to making decisions in respect of British policy has to involve major normative, and therefore political, choices. If the academic debate about interdependence has a use on the policy side, it is to clarify what these choices are.

THE ORIGINS AND SIGNIFICANCE OF THE TERM INTERDEPENDENCE

Any appreciation of the literature of International Relations reveals that the concept of interdependence became fashionable in the field of International Relations during the 1970s. A few late 1960s works by writers such as Richard Cooper (1968), Oran Young (1969) and Kenneth Waltz (1970) had, by the mid-1970s, burgeoned into a large and influential literature. The high point of this fashion was perhaps the widely circulated book *Power and Interdependence* (Keohane and Nye, 1977). During the 1980s, writing about interdependence has become more critical. Early enthusiasm for the idea has waned in the face of definitional and methodological difficulties in applying it to the study of real world events. Changes in the pattern of events that originally spurred interest in the idea, most notably the shift from détente to Cold War during the late 1970s, also sapped the force of the first wave. With the dramatic return of détente in the late 1980s, however, interdependence is once again back in fashion, most notably in the speeches of Mikhail Gorbachev. The term has become a firmly established part of the language of International Relations, both within the narrower academic community and the much broader media one. Whatever the theoretical difficulties it raises, interdependence is widely, and correctly, held to identify some important, durable and increasing qualities of the contemporary international system.

Interdependence is not a new idea in thinking about international relations. In both the security and economic sectors, there are well-established intellectual traditions supporting the idea that the fates of nations are deeply interlinked. In the security sector, the idea of the balance of power dates back at least to Thucydides, and is a clear statement that the security of individual nations rests not only on their own capabilities, but also on the patterns of capabilities and relationships in the system as a whole. Since the security of each state depends on it not being attacked by others, security interdependence has long been understood as a central feature of life in a system of independent sovereign states. An early work by Schelling actually conceives of strategy in terms of seeking to identify how 'mutual dependence can be exploited for unilateral gain' (Jones and Willets, 1984, pp. 118–21; Schelling, 1963, pp. 83–4). The contemporary system of nuclear deterrence is only a peculiarly intense version of this old idea. The two superpowers depend on nuclear restraint by the other for their very survival, and yet seek to exploit the fears of the other to their own advantage.

In the economic sector, the idea of interdependence is of more recent but no less potent, vintage. The liberal assault on classical mercantilism that began with Adam Smith was, among other things, an explicit attempt to *make* the world more interdependent by encouraging both free trade, and the specialisation of production along the lines of comparative advantage. Liberal economists argued that free trade would not only increase economic efficiency and welfare, but also entangle nations in a web of joint interests and mutual dependencies. That entanglement, they hoped, would reduce or even eliminate the incentives for war. The core logic of the classical liberal case for free trade and peace that was argued by great nineteenth-century polemicists like Richard Cobden is still central to the significance of interdependence today.

Under mercantilism, the pursuit of wealth tended to lead to war because of the close linkage between wealth and control of territory. With each state trying to close its economy against imports (except of gold), the resources and markets necessary to increase state power and domestic welfare could best be assured by direct control of the territory in which they were to be found. Mercantilism thus contained strong economic incentives towards competitive empire-building. The liberal solution was to break the association between wealth and territory by making both resources and markets available on economic terms. Free trade would thus remove the incentive to resort to force for economic reasons. The growing welfare interdependence that free trade would stimulate would also create inhibitions against the use of force by increasing the costs to states of doing so. War would disrupt the operation of the international economy on which the welfare of all would have come to depend. This basic idea was prominent in the American thinking that led to the creation of the Bretton Woods economic system after the Second World War. As Cordell Hull put it, 'If goods can't cross borders, soldiers will' (Gardner, 1980, pp. 7–9).

Given that the idea of interdependence is not new, why did it come into vogue during the 1970s? Two strong lines of explanation are readily apparent. The more immediate, but superficial, one is that the international position of the United States was undergoing major changes in both the military and economic sectors. The longer-term, and more durable, one arises from a growing awareness of the increasing density that characterises humankind's occupation of the planet. Woven into these two lines, but none the less distinct, is a third one to do with the rather arcane dynamics of the academic debate.

The position of the United States

During the late 1960s and early 1970s, the United States was visibly slipping from the extraordinary position of dominant power that it had held since the Second World War. In the military sector, it became vulnerable to large-scale Soviet nuclear bombardment, and also tasted serious defeat in Vietnam. In the economic sector, it lost its export dominance, was unable to maintain the strength of its currency, and so was forced to abandon the Bretton Woods system of fixed exchange rates. In 1973 it lost control of the price and the supply of oil to the OPEC cartel. The fact that the United States occupied such a central role in the international order meant that these changes were significant not only for America itself, but also for the international system as a whole. For the United States, the loss of power meant increased domestic exposure and vulnerability to the economic and military forces at play in the international system. While such exposure was a familiar fact of life for most countries, it was a disturbing novelty for the United States. Before the Second World War, the United States had been substantially insulated from the disruptions of world affairs by its relatively self-contained continental economy, its ocean buffers and its isolationist foreign policy. After the war, its extraordinary degree of economic, military, and even political and social, dominance within the Western system enabled it to engage itself worldwide without seeming to make itself vulnerable to external forces.

The events of the late 1960s and early 1970s reflected the reconstruction of war-damaged industrial societies in Western Europe, Japan and the Soviet Union. The natural resurgence of these centres of economic and/or military power inevitably reduced the relative dominance of the United States within the international system. In addition, the American economy became increasingly dependent not only on international patterns of trade and finance, but also on external supplies of key raw materials, most notably oil. During the 1980s, the American economy also became dependent on external supplies of capital to finance its huge deficits. In combination, these events imposed a major adjustment of perception on the United States. Americans now had to see their own welfare and security as much more immediately susceptible to the actions of others than had hitherto been the case. Interdependence was a useful and congenial concept for expressing this adjustment to a quite serious relative decline in both power and self-reliance.

This particularly American side of the interdependence story provides most of the explanation for why the concept surged into fashion when it did. The field of International Relations is heavily dominated by American writers, part of whose tradition involves an active interest in the policy problems of their own country. The take-up of interdependence by American scholars thus had a disproportionate effect on the field outside the United States, where the realities of interdependence were not new. What might be seen simply as kow-towing to American setting of the intellectual agenda did, however, have an additional justification. The decline of American power had implications not only for the United States, but also for all of those countries that had a stake in the international order led by the United States. To the extent that the decline of American power meant a loosening of central management in the system as a whole, all of the countries within the Western sphere faced the prospect of a more turbulent foreign policy environment.

In this sense, the rise of interest in interdependence reflected a weakening of the Western international order, particularly, but not exclusively, in the economic sector. For the countries within that order, the loss of exchange-rate stability, the rise in the price of oil, the problem of surplus capacity in industrial production, the intensification of trade rivalry, the debt crisis and other instabilities in the international financial system, and the growing pressures to indulge in protectionism, all presaged a period of more difficult economic relations. The seemingly effortless growth of the 1960s, which made co-operation relatively easy, was replaced by the inflation and recession of the 1970s, which made it difficult. More broadly, then, the focus on interdependence during the 1970s and 1980s signified awareness of a general management crisis within the Western international economy attendant on the declining power of the United States. If the United States could no longer play the role of hegemonic leader, it was not clear that sufficient management could be generated on a collective basis to sustain the relatively open international economy that had been the basis of 1960s prosperity (Keohane, 1984; Kindleberger, 1973, 1981). Interdependence already existed in the complex network of trade, production and finance that linked the capitalist economies of the Western states both to each other and to the countries of the Third World: the problem was how to prevent the whole structure from drifting into decay. The nightmare at the end of this line was a 1930s-style collapse of the whole international order, both economic and political.

Increasing density

The longer-term and more durable factor that underlies the potency of interdependence is what might be called the increasing *density* with which humankind occupied its planet. Density is defined by the intensity of interaction within the international system. Since a system is defined as a set of interacting parts, with no interaction there would be no system, only isolated parts. Density, in one sense, therefore *is* the systemic component. Rising density increases the importance of the system in relation to its parts.

Viewed in its simplest terms, density is a function of population size and level of activity. The mere fact that by the year 2,000 human numbers will have quadrupled from the 1.6 billion of a century earlier, and are highly likely to double again to 12 billion during the next century, speaks volumes about density. But this simple index is compounded by the rising levels of activity that each human being represents. This expanding activity is in turn explained by interrelated and continuing increases in human knowledge, productivity, mobility, education, consumption, wealth and organisation. Rising per capita activity adds a large multiplier effect to the raw impact of human numbers. The resulting picture is one in which more people are engaged in a widening sphere of increasingly intense activities. Since all of this expansion is confined to the more or less fixed space of the earth and its near environs, the probability that people's activities will impinge on each other increases. The inevitable multiplication of interactions – both positive and negative, wanted and unwanted – is the hallmark of an increasingly dense world society.

From this perspective, interdependence is about much more than the particular crisis created by the decline of American hegemony. That crisis is just a particular, immediate, manifestation of a broader historic trend that is transforming the conditions of human occupation of the planet. The basic hypothesis is that interdependence increases in direct proportion to density. As density rises, more and more human activities will have either intended or unintended impacts on all or part of the human community. Intended impacts range from the nuclear threats that the superpowers direct against each other's populations, to the successful marketing by the Japanese of consumer goods in North America and Western Europe. Unintended ones include pollution problems like acid rain, and currency instabilities resulting from the development of fast-moving financial markets. Higher density also means that human activity puts greater pressure on the physical environment. Demand for resources rises against an ultimately finite supply, and the planet's ecology is increasingly altered by human impact on both other life forms and on the various physical systems that govern the global climate. One predictable consequence of such developments is that more and more issues will become global in scale, whether they involve natural systems, like the various effects of gaseous and particulate pollutants on the insulating qualities of the planetary atmosphere, or elements of human society, like the cycles of growth and recession in the international economy.

The significance of interdependence in this context stems from the very rapid increase in density that marks the present historical era. During the twentieth century, the volume, speed and variety of human activities have accelerated with unprecedented speed, a trend that shows no sign of reversal bar a major war or an ecological catastrophe. As we approach the end of that century, human society is unquestionably global in a number of important respects. Putting the present into historical perspective, it does not seem unreasonable to say that human society is now in the middle of an historic transformation. In the past, the lives of most individual humans were largely dominated by events arising within their own locality. In the future, rising density seems bound to ensure that individual lives will be increasingly shaped by factors that permeate the whole international system. Under these conditions, interdependence must replace independence as the dominant feature of existence for the many nations and states into which humanity is divided.

This line of reasoning points to the long-term significance of interdependence, which is the apparent contradiction between a politically fragmented system of sovereign states on the one hand, and an international agenda increasingly dominated by issues that are collective and global in nature, on the other. The anarchic structure of international politics ('anarchy' used here strictly in its formal meaning of absence of central government) means that policy-making is territorially divided amongst more than 160 sovereign states. No government makes policy for more than a fraction of the planet despite the fact that issues and problems are increasingly global in character. The conclusion that rising density requires a shift from independent states towards world government is obvious but irrelevant. Neither an ideological consensus nor a concentration of power sufficient to support a world government is anywhere in sight. Almost everywhere, the sovereign state is firmly established as the preferred form of political organisation, even when, as for the Kurds, the Palestinians, the Eritreans, the Sikhs, the Tamils and many other ethnic groups, it is not the existing state that is preferred. The prospect is therefore of a future in which a politically fragmented system has to deal with an increasingly global agenda. In this sense, interdependence points to a situation in which individual states will simply be unable to deal effectively with an increasing range of issues unless they can co-ordinate policy with some, if seldom all, of the other states in the system. If the preferred political structure of sovereign states within an anarchic international society is maintained, as it almost certainly will be, then rising density will make states increasingly dependent on each other for effective political management of their affairs.

The theoretical work of Kenneth Waltz provides one interesting perspective on the tension between an anarchic system of sovereign states and rising levels of interdependence (Waltz, 1970, 1979). He argues that interdependence arises as a result of a division of labour. When individuals or units specialise their labour in relation to mutually necessary functions, then they become interdependent. A division of labour into blacksmiths and farmers, for example, makes each dependent on the other, respectively for supplies of food and tools. In order to manage a complex system of interdependent relations, some form of central political power and authority becomes necessary (in Waltz's terms a *hierarchic* political structure rather than an *anarchic* one). Hierarchic political structure and functional interdependence are mutually reinforcing, as illustrated by the increasingly specialised division of labour within most modern states.

By contrast, anarchic structure, in Waltz's view, both encourages and reflects the primacy of functionally similar units. In order to maintain sovereignty, fulfil the requirements of government and ensure reasonable chances of survival in the uncertain environment of anarchy, states tend to pursue similar functions and degrees of self-reliance across a broad range of activities. The imperative of anarchy thus pushes units to become functionally similar, as illustrated by the fact that most existing states are quite similar in many ways, though very different in both capability and style. A more specific illustration is the global accumulation of surplus production capacity that results from the widespread attempts of individual states to maintain or establish strategically significant industries like steel, ship-building and agriculture (Sen, 1984). Retaining such basic industries gives states a foundation of self-reliance that could be crucial in time of crisis or war, even though it makes little economic sense within a global market. The requirements of survival necessitate a certain copying of the most successful states. Failure to keep up with the most effective forms of organisation can result in such huge differentials of power that the weak become vulnerable to imperialism by the strong, a danger profoundly demonstrated by the history of European expansion from the fifteenth to the twentieth century.

Inasmuch as states pursue similarity, they thwart moves towards a functional division of labour. The anarchic system of sovereign states thus provides a fundamental counterpressure to the otherwise relentless political logic implied by increasing density and interdependence. The hard facts of environmental, security and economic interdependence cry out for central management on a scale that implies a shift towards a centralised, hierarchical world political structure. But the deeply rooted realities of myriad sovereign states as the only currently achievable form of govern-ment, makes even rather primitive levels of collective management at the global level extraordinarily difficult to achieve. Independent sovereign states are a poor instrument for collective management at the global level. Most of them are plagued with either parochial electorates or insecure ruling elites, neither of which condition allows much scope for consistent and responsible international behaviour.

Attempts by leading powers to create durable international orders have not proved stable. As the experience of both Britain and the United States illustrates, the role of hegemonic leader eventually exhausts the state undertaking it. Such leadership anyway invites challenges for the role of top country, and provides incentives for lesser powers to 'free ride' on the largesse and global interests of the hegemon, as Japan and Western Europe have been doing to the United States since the completion of their recovery from the Second World War. Even the most internationalist states guard the prerogatives of their sovereignty jealously, with the result that attempts at collective international decision-making are usually slow, intensely political, and seldom productive of more than lowest-common-denominator agreements lacking in both universal commitment and independent authority. Co-operation is possible, as illustrated by the vast and ever-expanding array of international organisations and agreements. The problem of is that both the pace of its development and the reach of its effects seem to lag behind the even more rapidly growing agenda of collective problems. Even in Europe, where levels of density and inter-dependence makes incentives for co-operation the highest on the planet, moves towards greater co-ordination and co-operation are painfully slow.

Academic debates

The third theme underlying the emergence of the vogue for inter-dependence during the 1970s has to do with the dynamics of academic debate within the field of International Studies. From this perspective, interest in interdepence is closely linked to the parallel resurgence in the study of International Political Economy (IPE). Both IPE and inter-dependence were part of a challenge to the orthodoxy of realism that dominated International Studies during the 1950s and most of the 1960s. Realism was about power politics, and reflected the experience of both the Second World War and the Cold War that followed. It focused primarily on states as the essential actors in the international system, and was centrally concerned with the dynamics of the struggle for power among states. In the realist perspective, the 'high politics' of ideological and military rivalry dominated the international agenda, and economic issues were largely relegated to the secondary status of 'low politics'.

The challenge to realism posed by IPE and interdependence reflected both the success of American economic hegemony during the 1950s and 1960s, and the decay of its leadership during the 1970s and 1980s. On the one hand, the success of the American-led liberal international economic order during the 1950s and 1960s had created a large and powerful group of states amongst which relations bore decreasing resemblance to the realist orthodoxies. Power politics within the Western group seemed to have become less important than collective economic and environmental issues. None of the major Western states seemed at all likely to use force against any of the others, and non-state actors like multinational companies played an increasingly important role in the dense network of transnational relations that penetrated through the ostensibly hard boundaries of the territorial state. For the Western states at least, realism seemed an increasingly inappropriate model for international relations. On the other hand, the conspicuous weakening of American hegemony during the 1970s greatly raised the salience of economic issues on the foreign policy agenda. Since all Western states had come to depend on the liberal international economic order for their prosperity, all were inevitably caught up in the leadership crisis that threatened the continuity of that order. In addition to these factors, the 1970s development of détente between the superpowers added momentum to the apparent retreat of realism. Détente seemed to herald an overall decline in the salience of 'high politics', with its emphasis on military security, and to pave the way for a world in which the 'low politics' of economic interdependence would move to centre stage.

By the late 1970s, the adversarial stage of this debate was well on the wane. Some of the advocates of interdependence had already begun to busy themselves with synthesising interdependence and realism (Keohane and Nye, 1977). On the other side, the neo-realists redeployed the logic of power politics on a more explicitly structuralist basis (Waltz, 1979) that was at least potentially less contradictory to interdependence reasoning than was classical realism. These moves were accompanied, and reinforced, by the demise of détente and the onset of the Second Cold War between the superpowers. The passions of antagonism that attended debates about interdependence during the 1970s have largely faded, but the concept remains firmly established as a central part of the vocabulary in which international relations have to be discussed.

It is also worth noting under this heading that the term interdependence came to play a central role in the arguments between those whose view of IPE derived from the liberal tradition, and those who took their cue more from marxian analysis. During the 1960s and 1970s, a marxian-derived school of so-called *dependency theorists* enjoyed a considerable vogue. Like the liberals, the dependency theorists took a systemic view of the international economy. Their purpose, however, was to argue that the operation of international capitalism bred and sustained large inequalities between industrialised states and the countries of the Third World. For the dependency theorists, the rise of a global capitalist economy produced systematic and serious disadvantages for the weaker states enmeshed within it. They saw underdevelopment, both political and economic, as a direct consequence of the capitalist international economy. For those within the liberal tradition, the concept of interdependence was a useful counter to the dependency line. Interdependence emphasised the mutuality of interests within a capitalist economy. It allowed the real problems identified by the dependency theorists to be addressed in a vocabulary that did not presuppose negative consquences.

THE MEANING OF THE TERM INTERDEPENDENCE

As the above discussion suggests, interdependence is a complex idea capable of being interpreted in different ways. It has two major threads of meaning, one unravelling through the broad agenda of density, and the other through the more specific domain of liberal international economic relations. Its economic sense relates strongly to the capitalist construction of the international economy. Indeed, in one important sense, inter-dependence is primarily a way of talking about the consequences of capitalism. Like many central concepts in the social sciences, it has no firmly accepted core definition, and no means by which it can be reliably measured. Instead, it is used in a variety of meanings, and for a variety of purposes, some of them distinctly normative and political.

The most basic meaning of interdependence is *mutual dependence*. The minimum conditions for mutual dependence require at least two actors, between which there are interactions which carry significant consequences for both. The necessity for two or more actors means that it is incorrect to use the term to describe the condition of a single state, unless the reference is only to the domestic structure of that state. Interdependence in the context of international relations can only be used correctly to describe the pattern of relations either within the system as a whole, or within some subset of the system containing at least two actors. *Dependence* is a strong term, implying matters that affect the basic economic, political, social or environmental well-being of society in some way. Interdependence is thus taken to be distinct from, and more than, mere *interconnectedness*. Britain and France may for example, be interconnected by a mutual passion for World Cup football without being interdependent.

The distinction between interconnectedness and interdependence implies a boundary that is defined by the level of consequences attached to the interactions between actors. Interconnectedness only becomes inter-dependence when consequences are significant. But since we have few objective ways of measuring interdependence, and since the evaluation of consequences is inherently subjective (e.g. not everyone would agree with my dismissive attitude towards the importance of World Cup football) this boundary is necessarily vague, as is any attempt to ascribe degrees of interdependence. Difficulties of measurement limit the scientific, or even systematic, use of the concept. But this problem is endemic in the social sciences and does not negate the general utility of the idea for describing and explaining aspects of international relations. We have no measure for *power* either, but that does not prevent the term from occupying a central place in a wide range of political discourse.

Keohane and Nye (1977, pp. 12–13) introduced a distinction between *sensitivity*, defined as the degree and speed of costs involved in breaking a dependency relationship, and *vulnerability*, indicating the degree of diffi-culty facing an actor in changing the policy context so as to escape the costs of sensitivity. Countries like Japan and the United States, for example, are sensitive to restrictions on the import of oil. They can reduce their sensitivity by stockpiling. If need be, they can reduce their vulnerability by using their industrial and technological capabilities to produce alternative sources of hydrocarbons (coal, shale oil, arctic methane) and/or energy (nuclear power). Cuba is also sensitive to oil supplies, but because it lacks the capital and technological resources, faces much greater difficulties in altering its vulnerability. This distinction has quite wide currency in the literature, though not all writers accept it. Baldwin (1980), for example, rejects the idea of sensitivity, arguing that dependence is essentially about vulnerability. Virtually all writers on the subject would agree, however, that interdependence is about relationships that are so costly to break that their existence imposes serious constraints on state policy. These relationships can be either positive, like mutual trade, or negative, like arms racing, but either way, ceasing to participate is likely to pose higher costs that continuing (Baldwin, 1980, pp. 482–3). A definition close to that used by Jones and Willetts (1984, p. 8) captures the political consequences of interdependence in these terms: interdependence exists when a satisfactory outcome on an issue of policy requires suitable developments elsewhere, and when this situation is mutual for two or more actors.

The simplest model for interdependence is where two actors share a reciprocal dependency on a single issue. Sweden and Finland, for example, have mutually dependent security policies. Sweden would find it much more difficult to maintain its policy of independent neutrality without the buffer of Finland between itself and Soviet military power. Finland would find it difficult to maintain the degree of freedom it now has from the deployment of Soviet forces on its territory unless Sweden continues with its policy of strict neutrality. This kind of interdependence is neat, clear and easy to understand.

Unfortunately, the interdependence that is of most interest in international relations is not of this type. Both the immediate imperatives of declining American hegemony, and the longer-term ones of increasing density, point towards patterns of interdependence that embrace either a large number of actors, or the international system as a whole. In the economic sector, for example, one does not get a clear picture of the significance of interdependence by looking at the patterns of dependency in trade, production and finance between pairs of states. The most important patterns of dependency in trade, production and finance are global in scope, and extremely complex in character. Consequently, the focus of dependency is much more on the operation not only of long chains of interactions involving many actors, but also on the interaction of the many such chains that combine to make up the international economic system. It may be true to say that China and Japan are interdependent because China depends on Japan for some of its investment and technology, while Japan depends on China for some of its markets and supplies of raw materials. But it is more significant that both depend in a much broader sense on the continuing smooth operation of global systems that support the large-scale transfer of people, goods, information and finance across international boundaries.

In this sense, interdependence is a characteristic of the whole system. All states are to some degree tied into an elaborate pattern of mutual dependencies. Within that pattern, some states will command more resources and leverage, and reap more benefits, than others. In systemic interdependence, as in the two-party form, interdependence can be asymmetrical, and therefore be a source of power for the better-placed party (Keohane and Nye, 1977, ch. 1). Countries like Japan, South Korea, Italy and Saudi Arabia have done particularly well, whereas Sierra Leone, Haiti, Sudan and Bangladesh have, for various reasons, done conspicuously badly. Despite these discrepancies, systemic interdependence displays strong elements of what R. J. Barry Jones calls *common fate* (Jones and Willetts, 1984, pp. 50–60). Just as states share a common fate in relation to their collective dependence on maintenance of the planetary ecosphere, and avoidance of nuclear war between the superpowers, so also are their fates linked in the complex global pattern of the international economy. Global booms and recessions are a type of common fate interdependence.

From this systemic perspective, interdependence can be seen as a major intervening variable affecting the patterns of political organisation and interaction in the international system. Here again, Waltz's distinction between *hierarchic* (centralised government) and *anarchic* (decentralised government) international political structures is useful. As outlined above, Waltz argues that hierarchic structures generate (and are generated by) units that are dissimilar because they have adopted specialised roles within a division of labour. Anarchic structures generate (and are generated by) units that are similar because the imperatives of survival in a self-help system require them to undertake the broad range of similar tasks associated with sovereign self-government. Hierarchic structures, such as states, are thus designed both to reflect and to sustain interdependence within themselves, whereas anarchic structures are designed to resist it.

Given that the present international system is unquestionably anarchic in structure, and likely to remain so for the foreseeable future, arguments about the rise of systemic interdependence seem to pose a mounting contradiction. Interdependence may not yet raise questions about the viability of independent sovereign states. But at the very least, it requires serious thinking about the definition of what constitutes 'good government' in such states, and about the character of international relations (and therefore of foreign policy) in a system that is both anarchic and inter-dependent. Only a very extreme definition of anarchy would require units to be not only self-governing (sovereign) but also self-contained in economic and societal terms (*autarkic*). In such a system, the requirements for good government and sound foreign policy can be defined in terms of fairly clear self-centred national interests.

But those requirements are quite different in a system in which not only the imperatives of density, but also the desire of states for prosperity, have compromised and eroded the condition of autarky. How is the national interest to be defined under conditions of interdependence? Inasmuch as national welfare depends on the maintenance of mutual dependencies, and inasmuch as domestic political stability depends on the maintenance of at least existing levels of welfare, then interdependence gives governments a much greater interest in, and responsibility for, international relations, than does autarky. Whatever else it may mean, interdependence is certainly about defining the context within which state policy has to be formulated. Where interdependence is strong, it redefines the interests and responsi-bilities of governments by raising the importance of external relations in the conduct of internal ones. In this sense, interdependence is a way of expressing the contradiction between the fragmentation of a robust system of sovereign states on the one hand, and the integrative force of a dynamic, international capitalist economy on the other.

The combination of sovereignty and interdependence creates odd con-ditions for both domestic rule and external relations. Under such con-ditions, governments can neither ignore each other, nor insulate their domestic priorities from systemic effects. Their policy options are con-strained by entanglement in a web of mutual dependencies that are costly and difficult to break. In compensation, they may well have access to a much wider range of resources for the purposes of government than would be the case for autarkic states, which by definition are restricted in their range of access to outside contacts and supplies. Many Third World governments, from Angola to Kampuchea, actually depend on external sources for the resources that enable them to function as governments.

This line of enquiry leads to the normative aspect of interdependence: is it to be seen as a desirable condition, and therefore as a political objective, or as an undesirable one, and therefore as a political problem? The positive view stems from the liberal tradition in which free trade is seen as a way both of increasing welfare all round, and of reducing the incentives for war.

Welfare is increased by the improved economic efficiency and opportunity offered both by economies of scale and a specialised division of labour. Security is improved, because the open market divorces the creation of wealth from the control of territory, thereby making traditional military imperialism seem a risky, costly and inefficient way for powerful states to pursue their national interests.

The negative view has roots ranging from conservative nationalism and ideological puritanism, to the purely rational calculation that the contradiction between anarchy and interdependence is unsustainable and dangerous. Waltz (1970, p. 205), for example, argues that too much close contact generates disputes, and that a lessening of interdependence would therefore be the best approach to peace. This view points back to the debate outlined above about the difficulty of providing sufficient management to sustain the large-scale security and economic orders required by global interdependence. Breakdowns of the system, like that during the 1930s, can themselves cause periodic bouts of intense disorder and conflict. The current debate about how the liberal international economic order is to be sustained in the face of declining American power is perhaps the major contemporary manifestation of this concern (Buzan, 1984; Keohane, 1984).

The normative aspect of interdependence is in some ways as important as its more purely empirical content. The term has come to represent the view that more weight needs to be given to the emerging realities not only of a globally structured economy, but also of global security and environmental interdependence. It is thus in part a call to change ways of perceiving not only the international system, but also the function of government. The ideological content of interdependence is, in effect, that the art of good government needs to include a substantially higher element of responsible external behaviour than has hitherto been the norm. This call carries an implicit threat to both governments and electorates that if their perceptions do not change, then the central problems in the international system will be misunderstood, and policy will consequently by misguided to the detriment of all.

In this sense, the idea of interdependence is a propaganda weapon against the parochial attitudes that still dominate most of the world's public and elite awareness. It is a call to widen political visions, and to reorient political priorities away from self-centred local issues and towards broader collective concerns. The logic is that the broader concerns of interdependence are now crucial to the survival of most local values. The fear is that unless attitudes shift to a wider awareness, the contradiction between anarchy and interdependence will become unmanageable, and the decay of

American hegemony will eventually lead to a major crisis of international order.

One way of trying to understand the impact of interdependence on a state such as Britain is to consider the following two questions: (i) 'is it possible to define the type(s) of interdependence to which Britain is subject?'; and (ii) 'if interdependence is perceived as having a significant impact on Britain, what are the empirical questions that would have to be tackled to provide evidence of its nature and extent?' These apparently straight-forward questions are not as simple to answer as they might at first appear to be. Understanding why they are not is a good way to get some insight into both why the concept is important for Britain, and why it is difficult to translate directly into policy prescriptions.

Defining types of interdependence

As noted above, interdependence applies to sets of two or more states. In relation to a single state one can enquire only about *dependencies*: on what, or whom, is Britain dependent, and who, or what is dependent on Britian? Sometimes, these two questions will line up to produce a neat, clear and self-contained issue. Britain and France, for example, are mutually dependent on each other in relation to the authorisation, financing and construction of the Channel Tunnel. More often, however, the patterns of interdependence are neither simple nor directly reciprocal. If one seeks to uncover the chains of dependency that affect the value of Britain's currency, one enters a vast labyrinth of connections ranging from the behaviour of oil-producing states, through the mood of international money markets, to the policies and performances of other countries possessing major international currencies. The resultant picture will not only be extremely complex, but also lacks any clear, reciprocal, counter-dependency. Britain's policies and performance will have some impact on the values of others' currencies, but in the nature of systemic inter-dependence, the effect is likely to be widely diffused rather than focused on some single other state.

If the scope of interdependence varies from specific to diffuse, and from local to global, it is also inappropriate to look for some single type of dependence that will neatly wrap up this issue in relation to Britain. As the idea of density suggests, patterns of interdependence are also extremely varied in terms of the range of issues that generate them. There is, for example, a pattern of interdependence involving Britain concerning North Sea herring stocks. The life-cycle of the herring involves the coastal waters of several states. Unless conservation measures are made effective in several places, overfishing in one area can have drastic effects on the availability of stocks in the others. This is a narrow issue, with relatively minor economic consequences that affect a small, but politically concentrated, segment of the British population. Dealing with it requires regular negotiations with several other states, enforcement measures in British waters against both British and foreign fishermen, and the pursuit of scientific information about the herring themselves in order to transform a self-destructive, open-ended 'hunter-gatherer' industry into a stable, steady-state 'farming' one. On issues at this level, one key question is whether the benefits of managing interdependence justify the costs. It is by no means inconceivable that on purely economic grounds the argument would fall in favour of fishing the herring, and the fishing industry, into commercial extinction. Moral, environmental and political considerations might, however, tip the balance against such a purely economic calculation.

At the other end of the spectrum lies the pattern of interdependence that relates to the avoidance of nuclear war. Each nuclear weapon state, and many non-nuclear weapon states, depend for their survival on the exercise of military restraint by other nuclear powers. The nuclear powers in particular are locked into a close pattern of interdependence known as deterrence, based on the interaction of threat and restraint. Britain is part of this system of strategic interdependence both as a possible user of nuclear weapons itself, and as a likely part of the target area should nuclear war break out between the superpowers. This is an issue that is global in scope. In some senses it is quite simple (the basic logic of deterrence), but in others very technical and complex (weapons policy and alliance deterrence strategy). It has the curious feature of affecting relatively few people most of the time, but potentially posing a catastrophe for the entire population. The possibility of catastrophe makes the issue highly significant, but the perceived unlikelihood of its eventuality means that it does not dominate the political agenda. Economic considerations play a much lesser part in the dynamics of this type of interdependence, and the government has to face much more extreme policy choices, with much less certain knowledge about the linkage of cause and effect.

The examples of herring and nuclear deterrence illustrate the range and diversity of interdependence issues, and make clear the difficulty of either aggregating interdependencies into a single type, or pursuing a single set of principles for defining policy responses. Regional approaches can sometimes help here, in that a given geopolitical arena, such as Western Europe or the OECD, might encapsulate a given issue or set of issues. In relation to Britain, for example, the European Community includes a legal component of interdependence that is quite distinctive. In general, however, issues overlap arenas with such frequency that any attempt to divide the subject up in this way would create more problems than it solved. Trade issues, for example, extend well beyond both the Western and European and the OECD arenas.

Given the difficulty of establishing general rules or categories, a more fruitful approach might be to tackle the subject in terms of both distinct issue areas or *sectors*, and distinct levels of analysis, or *arenas*. At a rather general level, sectors can be demarcated in terms of military security, international political economy (IPE), scientific knowledge and environment. Although the boundaries between these issue areas are by no means impermeable, they do identify the major areas where interdependence is a matter of concern, and where many issues will be distinct enough to fall within the categories. For purposes of more detailed analysis, one might wish to subdivide these general sectors into more specific items like trade and finance, or even to focus on a single issue like oil.

Arenas can be identified partly in geographical terms, and partly in terms of sets of states where the pattern of dependencies relating to Britain is particularly strong. One could start with bilateral relations, where Britain shares a reciprocal dependency with another country. France and the Channel Tunnel have already been mentioned, and one could add Ireland on terrorism, and Argentina on military commitments to the Falklands. On the regional level, Western Europe is the obvious focus, though there may at times be advantages to dealing in subcategories defined by the various Western European organisations of which Britain is a member, most notably the European Community, but also including the Western European Union. On the sub-global level, the OECD, perhaps better thought of as the West, is particularly important for IPE issues. The Commonwealth might also be a candidate here, but one suspects that its importance has been allowed to fade so much that little of its interconnectedness is of sufficient importance to weigh seriously in the scales of interdependence (though again, my personal indifference to the significance of sport – in this case cricket – may not be shared by all). On the global level, the focus is on systemic interdependence, where all, or nearly all, states find themselves dependent on complex global patterns of mutual dependence. Economic and security interdependence both operate powerfully at this level. Security interdependence can be viewed at sub-global levels, such as in the collective security structures of an alliance like NATO, or the regional security dynamics of a sub-system like 'South Asia or the Gulf. But since

Table 2.1. *An analytical framework for interdependence as a policy issue*

	SECTORS			
	Military security	IPE	Scientific knowledge	Environment
ARENAS				
Bilateral				
Regional				
Sub-global				
Global				

security interdependence operates competitively, the macro level of great power rivalry has a pervasive global effect. The securities of all the major power centres – the United States, Western Europe, the Soviet Union, China and Japan – are linked together in a global pattern of mutual dependence.

By arranging sectors and arenas into a matrix, as in table 2.1, one can generate a rough framework for enquiry. This crude apparatus is on the very bottom rung of the ladder leading to systematic theory, but it does offer a way to select, focus and compare, within what would otherwise be an unmanageably complex whole.

This exercise points towards the conclusion that although inter-dependence may be difficult to pin down in any concise overall formula-tion, the main reason for this difficulty is the extremely long and varied agenda of interdependence issues in which Britain is enmeshed. The significance of interdependence is therefore that on many issues British governments cannot pursue policy without taking into account, or involv-ing, external actors. Across a large and expanding array of issues, many of which might at first glance seem purely domestic, British policy options are constrained by interdependence. On some, such as pollution, the con-straint will be that Britain does not control all of the factors necessary to implement policy. On others, such as tariffs, it will be that unilateral implementation will affect the interests of others, whose responses need to be anticipated in calculating whether the policy is workable. The effect of interdependence is thus to blur what used to be fairly clear boundaries between domestic and foreign policy (Hanrieder, 1978). Foreign policy becomes much more complex because it has to deal with a much wider agenda. Conversely, domestic policy becomes much less insular because of its external consequences. Interdependence is therefore important not only because of its impact on particular issues, but also because it fundamentally changes the nature of the governing process. As suggested above, interdependence redefines the performance criteria for 'good government.'

Problems of formulating national policy responses to interdependence

If one accepts the conclusion that interdependence has a basic and wide-ranging impact on how Britain is governed, this still leaves open the issue of what sort of policy response interdependence requires. The apparently obvious next question is: 'if interdependence is seen as having a significant impact on Britain, what are the empirical questions that would have to be tackled to provide evidence of its nature and extent?' This seems, at first glance, a reasonable way to proceed. Is there a possibility that interdependence can be tackled scientifically, using positivist, inductive methodology?

This sort of question, however, presupposes that positivist methodology is a workable and appropriate approach to the study of interdependence. One way to illustrate the shortcomings of such an assumption is to substitute the word 'love' for 'interdependence', and the word 'me' for 'Britain'. The essential logic of the statement remains the same, but the unwiseness of the approach is perhaps more obvious. Love might unquestionably be seen as having a significant impact on oneself, but one would not expect to master the subject by seeking empirical evidence of its nature and extent. Among other things, relevant empirical questions adequate to cover the full scope of the enquiry would be extremely difficult to formulate, and even harder to answer. As argued above, interdependence is like many concepts in the social sciences in that it has no concise agreed meaning, is difficult to measure in any comprehensive sense and contains fundamental ideological elements that distinguish it profoundly from the more concrete concepts of the physical world like mass, velocity and charge (Little, 1981). Despite their scientific shortcomings, such concepts, including justice, freedom, security and power, none the less occupy central ground in most of the world's political debates. If one is debating about justice, one knows what the debate is about, and one can make arguments about its importance, even though one is unable to measure it or pin down its exact meaning.

The range of meaning, and the inherent ambiguities of interpretation, affecting a concept such as interdependence pose three difficulties for those trying to understand how a general idea links to the particular policy environment of a single country. The first difficulty is to do with limitations on measurement, the second concerns unavoidable normative (and therefore political) judgements in the evaluation of evidence, and the third involves differentials between the scope of theory as compared to that of policy. It is worth examining each of these problems in some detail.

Limitations on measurement

It would not be valid to argue that there is no room at all for empirical and inductive approaches to the analysis of interdependence. Economists, for example, will rightly argue that in their domain interdependence can be measured in terms of the ratio of trade to total national product. But such approaches can make only limited inroads into the subject. Any overall approach that is confined to the relative certainties of the observable and measurable will not only miss much of what is important about interdependence, but will also generate a data collection and analysis task of truly mountainous proportions. The sheer size of the task sets perhaps the most obvious limits to the systematic, empirical study of interdependence. As table 2.1 suggests, the total ground to be covered in any attempt at a comprehensive assessment of Britain and interdependence is immense. Even a preliminary filling in of the matrix between sectors and arenas would quickly reveal the huge number and variety of things to be covered. The subdivision of items under IPE multiplies rapidly as one asks more and more specific questions. To treat interdependence on the single issue level suggested by the illustration about herring given above, would not be unreasonable in terms of creating a basis for policy. But it would require literally hundreds, if not thousands, of in-depth studies to cover the economy as a whole. Such studies would date quickly, and would therefore require permanent revision if they were to provide an accurate basis for policy.

Aside from the cost of such an enterprise, one has to consider whether it would be the most fruitful approach even if it could be done. The issue here concerns the merits of an inductive, 'bottom-up', approach to interdependence. It seems far from certain that the amassing of data about numerous specific patterns of dependence would yield a coherent overall picture of the phenomenon. The sheer mass of data would represent a problem in its own right, posing the danger that one could not see the wood for the trees. The 'whole' of interdependence is, as with all significant systems, more than the sum of its parts. It is not obvious what rules one would use to assemble data about the parts into a meaningful picture of the whole. How does interdependence on issues like fish and tunnels relate to that on issues like nuclear deterrence and world trade? How does interdependence on the bilateral level relate to that on the regional and global levels? We have no way of answering these questions, and an inductive approach does not seem likely to alter this situation for the better.

Questions about whether extensive empirical approaches are worthwhile must also be set into the context of the extent to which they are possible. In some areas, it may well be feasible to construct empirical referents to measure the patterns of dependence. Trade flows, for example, are well monitored in terms of both discrete items such as oil and motor vehicles, and aggregate values to and from various destinations. As a general rule, such measurement will be easier for economic than for other issues. On many issues, however, reliable data will be impossible to acquire. This can be the case either because no ways have been devised to measure some things, or because the relationship between causes and effects is not sufficiently well understood to identify what the relevant data are.

Difficulties of measurement can simply reflect a combination of natural difficulties and the limits of scientific resources and capabilities. Assessing the true size of fish stocks, or the full extent of atmospheric pollution, are examples of this type of problem. They can also reflect the trickier difficulties of finding appropriate terms of measurement. Even such a basic task as translating national currency values into a common scale has proved exceedingly difficult where currencies are not traded in the market-place. Despite much effort, there is still no agreement on how to convert Soviet and Chinese expenditures on defence into equivalent amounts of Western currency. Measuring relative military capabilities is even more difficult. Numbers of troops, tanks and aircraft may well be known, as in the Middle East. But non-quantifiable variables ranging from morale and training, through degrees of technological sophistication and equipment maintenance, to particular conditions of battle like surprise and intelligence, make all the difference to the outcome. Convincing oneself that a knowledge of raw numbers equals a comparative understanding of military capability is an exercise in self-delusion which may be more harmful than helpful to decision-making about policy. All of these problems are compounded by the fact that most states engage in secrecy and disinformation on issues they consider sensitive.

An even greater restraint on the empirical approach than problems of data, is inadequate understanding of many of the fundamental cause–effect relations that bear on interdependence. There is, for example, no comprehensive theory that covers fluctuations in the annual size and the long-run sustainability of fish stocks. The level of fishing is obviously one factor, and it is known that some stocks are more sensitive to this type of pressure than others because of the particular characteristics of their reproductive cycles. But knowledge of how other factors – pollution, changes in ocean currents and temperatures, and interactions with other species (as predators and prey) – impact on particular species is notably imperfect. In the absence of such knowledge, it is impossible to devise scientific management policies to sustain a predictable relationship between fishing effort and stock levels. Does a stock collapse like that of anchovies off the west coast of Latin America represent a consequence of overfishing, or some little-understood shift in the movement of ocean currents from the Antarctic?

Similar problems of theory arise on the whole range of interdependence issues. On pollution, for example, the relationship between causes such as emissions of sulphur dioxide and nitrogen oxide, and effects such as acidification of lakes and diseased trees is a matter of controversy. The problem is of sufficient scale and range to fit within the policy framework of interdependence, but without firm understanding of its dynamics there is no clear scientific basis for trying to negotiate common policies. Uncertainties of information thus exacerbate the already formidable barriers to joint policies posed by an uneven distribution of interests in relation to causes and effects. On this issue, for example, Britain's interest is in maintaining cheap waste disposal, while countries further to the east (i.e. downwind) suffer disproportionately in terms of effects.

Even on something as fundamental to security interdependence as nuclear deterrence, there is no firm understanding of the logic of cause and effect. The theory states clearly that aggressive behaviour is deterred by credible threats to inflict large-scale losses, whether on the attacking forces themselves, or on other assets of value to the would-be aggressor. The presence of such threats has correlated with the absence of war in Europe for four decades. But no matter how indicative this evidence might be, it does not constitute proof. An equally plausible explanation for the absence of Soviet attack is that their motivation to do so is, or has become, low. Perhaps the Soviets see the limits to their ability to control an empire in the turbulent history of Eastern Europe. Perhaps the Russians have no desire to compete for dominance with 80 million Germans *inside* their empire. In either case, deterrence logic would not be the correct or complete explanation for the observed behaviour.

All sorts of questions vital to a full understanding of interdependence cannot be answered because, as a rule, we do not command reliable knowledge of how complex, large-scale human systems work. We cannot measure security, so we do not know whether our situation in that sector is improving or deteriorating. We do not know what causes war, and whether the probability of it is rising or falling. And we cannot assess the stability of international economic arrangements, and therefore do not know whether contemporary arrangements are fragile, and close to collapse, or robust, and likely to endure all foreseeable crises with relative ease. We cannot yet reliably tell the difference between the impact of our collective activities on the planetary ecosphere, and the natural changes in it that result from the subtle dynamics of celestial mechanics. These deficiencies in our knowledge will not disappear soon, and they define one major limit to any short-term assault on interdependence using empirical, inductive, methodology.

Unavoidable normative judgements
The fact that policy-makers have to operate with imperfect information and incomplete knowledge forces them to deal with many interdependence issues on a normative basis, that is, on the basis of preferred political values. Even if these constraints on the empirical approach no longer existed, however, there are two reasons why it would still be impossible to devise a value-free policy approach to interdependence.

   Firstly, in relation to the interests of any particular country the concept of dependence is itself inherently political in character. Although there is a sense in which dependence is an objective condition (human beings are dependent on access to supplies of air and water in order to live), the concept has no political interest unless the condition of dependence makes one's well-being appear precarious. Deciding what is, or is not, an acceptable level of dependence is thus a matter of political judgement. The equation by which such judgements must be calculated will usually be a complex one containing a variety of sometimes contradictory factors. What is the probability that one's dependence will be either exploited or terminated to one's disadvantage by the actions of others? Is one vulnerable to intentional manipulation by others, or does the threat come from structural forces larger than the behaviour of any single actor? Are the costs attendant on the disruption of the dependency so great as to constitute a threat to the stability of society? How do the costs, risks and benefits of the dependency compare with those of either alternative arrangements to cover the same issue, or forgoing altogether the interaction that produces the dependency? Dependency will not be an issue if no negative consequences arise from it. More adaptive and secure individuals and cultures will take a degree of dependency risk in their stride, without considering it to be a basic problem. The less adaptive and less secure will be more sensitive, and feel the need to define dependency as a problem even at relatively low levels. Objectively similar levels of dependence and interdependence will thus generate quite different degrees of political response across a range of actors.

The unavoidability of normative judgements also arises even when there is no dispute about the existence and significance of interdependence, because highly contradictory policy options frequently emerge in response to the same objective condition. This can be illustrated by reference to a variety of system-level issues, where the reality and importance of interdependence are not in question. Regardless of the limits of empiricism discussed above, there is, for example, widespread agreement that the states within the international system are locked into complex patterns of interdependence that profoundly affect both their military security and their economic well-being. In the security sector, two world wars within living memory have underlined the point that major breakdowns of international order quickly spread to engulf almost the entire community of states. World war was a life or death matter for many of the states engaged in it even earlier in this century. Under modern technological conditions, it is not controversial to assert that a Third World War would threaten the tenure of human life on the planet. Similarly, in the IPE sector, the reality of interdependence is clearly demonstrated by the system-wide effects of booms, recessions, depressions and inflations. This reality was illustrated by the impact of the 1930s depression. Given the rapid growth of international trade, investment and production since 1945, there is no reason to think that the degree of interdependence has lessened for most states, and considerable reason to think that it has become more intense. On these broad questions, the existence and importance of interdependence are not in question, and therefore the need for a policy response is not, in itself, controversial. Awareness and understanding of the issue does not, alas, point to a single, obvious, and uncontroversial policy response.

On the question of European (and therefore British) security, for example, there is no doubt that the peace and survival of Europe is intimately bound up in the complex pattern of security interdependence centred on the rivalry between the superpowers. As a result of two world wars, the European states not only lost control of a global system centred on their power, but also became the central object of contention in a new bipolar power system dominated by the United States and the Soviet Union. The wrecked balance of power system in Europe was overlaid by the forward defence policies adopted by both superpowers. The consequence of these developments was that the security of Europe became dependent on peace between the superpowers, and the security of the superpowers became dependent on peace in Europe. The existence of this complex pattern of security interdependence is not in dispute, but the question of how best to respond to it raises deep controversy.

From a Western European perspective, several options are under debate. Some think that the best response is to maintain for as long as possible the existing NATO arrangements in which the United States plays a major direct role in offsetting Soviet military strength in Europe. Others think that Western Europe should take on more responsibility for its own defence, either within a 'two-pillar' NATO, or in the context of a phased move away from dependence on the United States towards a more independent position between the superpowers. The option of more independence could lean towards the assertion of Western Europe as a great power in its own right, or towards a more neutralist stance in which Western Europe sought to define itself as a robust defensive buffer. Others would prefer national defence policies based on individual European states, avoiding both alignment with the superpowers and enganglement in a Western European entity of some sort. And still others would prefer some sort of accommodation with the Soviet Union, in which the Western European states accepted a degree of 'Finlandisation' in order to escape from the permanent insecurities of being the highly militarised front line between two opposing systems.

The policy choice amongst these alternatives cannot be made as an objective response to the condition of security interdependence. The condition itself is durable, and would not be removed by adoption of any of these responses. The choices reflect different evaluations of how Western European states should deal with their irremovable entanglement in the security priorities of the superpowers. Being squeezed in the nutcracker of superpower forward defence strategies, the Western Europeans face complicated choices about how to balance between the risk of aggression on the one hand, and the risk of war on the other. Some feel that the risk of war is paramount, and that political sacrifices should be made to reduce it. Others feel that the risk of aggression should be given priority, and that enduring a risk of war is an unavoidable cost. These choices are affected by the degree of threat seen to come from the Soviet Union; the degree of risk seen to lie in maintaining a highly armed military balance; the degree of trust in, and common feeling with, the United States; and the balance of feelings between nationalism and attachment to a larger European identity. None of these factors is objectively measurable. All of them reflect values that impinge heavily on how the condition of security interdependence is understood. The study of interdependence cannot therefore lead directly to policy prescriptions. At best it can help to clarify choices.

Exactly the same conclusion can be reached by looking again at systemic interdependence in the economic sector. There is not much disagreement with the view that the economic welfare of the Western states, and also of most of the states in the Third World, has come to depend heavily on the byzantine networks of complex interdependence that bind them together. Prosperity, security, and in some cases survival and political stability, depend on the maintenance of extensive flows of trade, information, finance and people. This is true notwithstanding Waltz's argument that interdependence in the whole system has declined because of the polarisation based on two large superpowers between which there is relatively little economic or social traffic (Waltz, 1970).

Economic interdependence can, and has, become a political issue for two types of reasons: firstly, assessments of the balance between costs and benefits even when the system is working smoothly; and secondly, estimates of how stable the system is, and what the consequences will be if the networks begin to collapse. When the complex interdependence of a liberal international economic order is running smoothly, it offers the advantages of expanded markets and sources of supply, improved opportunities for growth, access to finance, downward pressure on consumer prices, maximum opportunity to specialise according to the logic of comparative advantage, and high incentives for technological innovation. But it also means restrictions on the freedom to pursue certain domestic political objectives (for example, where these would conflict with reciprocal rules on trade); exposure to a highly competitive international economy whose operation may severely damage local industries; competitive disadvantages for late industrialisers trying to enter low-technology markets already suffering from surplus capacity; vulnerability to boom and bust cycles in the international economy; penetration by a cosmopolitan consumer culture that may threaten local social structures; and loss of control by governments over many commanding aspects of their national economies. The costs and benefits of interdependence can be weighed both in terms of the particular balance experienced by any given actor, or in terms of ideologically determined priorities about what constitutes good government. Conclusions drawn on this basis then need to be considered against the overall stability and durability of the system. According to how this is assessed, the decision could be that interdependence is worth pursuing even for limited periods; or it could be that the system is durable, and that the danger of collapse is therefore insignificant; or it could be that the dangers of systemic collapse are too great to justify such benefits as the system generates while it is working.

Judgements on this forbidding array of empirical and normative questions can lead down either of two policy paths: that leading towards protectionism, and that leading towards free trade. Both of these positions are themselves highly politicised, as indicated in the discussion about the origins of interdependence above. Protectionism defines economic interdependence as a problem, and seeks solutions (or rather a different mixture of costs and benefits) by restructuring the economy away from the network of dependencies. The liberal approach sees economic interdependence as an opportunity. It seeks to stabilise the system by encouraging adaptive behaviour at home, and responsible behaviour in the international system. In general, policy choices will tend in one direction or the other. It may be possible to fudge, by going one way on some issues and the other way on others. Occasionally, it may be possible to have it both ways by pursuing a regional customs union like that encapsulated by the European Community in which greater liberalism within a restricted group is balanced by greater protectionism against the rest of the world. Whatever choices are eventually made, they will reflect major value judgements.

The issue of openness versus closedness as a response to interdependence can also be found in the scientific knowledge sector. Advances in scientific knowledge unquestionably occur more efficiently and more rapidly in an environment of open exchange of information that in an environment where the exchange of views is restricted. The mechanism here is the simple one that exchanges of views and experiences frequently generate the insights necessary to overcome problems at the frontiers of knowledge. The benefits of free exchange, have, however, to be weighed against the national security issues involved in allowing open access to work bearing on advanced military technologies. This problem is particularly acute for a country like the United States, where freedom is highly valued, and where military policy emphasises the advantages of keeping technologically ahead of one's opponent. If the Americans adopt an open policy in response to the interdependence of knowledge, then they cannot stop the Soviet Union from benefiting militarily through its access to American research. In an open system, the US government therefore has to gamble that the great openness of American society will enable its scientific research continuously to outpace the more sclerotic Soviet system. US security would then be based on the greater ability of the American system to adapt to, and benefit from, an open information environment. If the Americans choose to close their research, in order to reduce Soviet free-riding, then they risk slowing down the pace of innovation on which they ultimately depend. There is no known empirical approach that could provide data accurate enough, and penetrating enough, to enable objective choices to be made about which policy is the best response to interdependence in the knowledge sector.

Differences between the logics of theory and policy

A third set of difficulties in formulating national policy responses to an abstract concept like interdependence stems from the quite different objectives and constraints that shape the logic leading to policy on the one hand, and that leading to academic theory on the other. An academic theory such as interdependence does not necessarily, or even probably, provide much specific policy guidance. There are several reasons for this mismatch.

For example, the system level of analysis used in the previous section, which is often central to theorists, is, almost by definition, beyond both the mandate and the power of policy-makers who are based in, and responsible towards, a single state. The logic of policy is to define behaviours that both serve and reflect the national interests of a state. Policy is often responsive to, and focused on, quite narrow issues. Decisions about policy are subject to influence from a wide variety of pressure groups within the state, and may also be affected by domestic political factors such as electoral dynamics or incipient rebellions. Policy decisions have to be cost-conscious, and need to reflect the limited range of resources available to the state. Given that policy-making capability is always in short supply relative to the number of issues competing for attention, the logic of policy is also subject to the vigorous filtering process by which state policy priorities are determined. The art of policy logic is to juggle all of these considerations in such a way as to produce behaviour that is acceptable to a variety of constituencies, affordable, effective, timely, and in keeping with the general image and posture of both the government and the state.

The logic driving theory, by contrast, is simply to try to understand what is going on. Finding such understanding is much easier on the macro level, than it is on the micro one. On the macro level, the confusions of day-to-day events can be aggregated into broader categories, and these in turn can be used to search for general patterns, or structures, that offer some hope of grasping the overall character and direction of events. On the micro level, the diversity, speed and confusion of activity do not provide fruitful ground for the theorist. When events are observed on a day-to-day basis, what stands out are the particular circumstances, personalities, histories and interactions that make each one unique. Trying to construct theory on this level is rather like physicists trying to determine the precise orbits of individual electrons around a nucleus. The task is too difficult to be worthwhile, and much of interest can anyway be learned by treating the electrons in terms of an aggregated model. The confusion and individuality of specific events thus tend naturally to push theorists towards analysis at the macro level. By contrast, the natural imperative driving policy tends towards the micro level, where specific events like invasion, or inflation, or trade problems, or illegal immigration need to be dealt with. Because of these quite different imperatives governing their logical dynamics, there is no reason to assume that the logic of academic theory can be connected to that of policy in any directly useful way.

In this respect, interdependence theory is a typical example of a general problem. The main logical thrust of the theory is towards the system level. Although the phenomenon can be found at lower levels, its most important manifestation is amongst large aggregates of states. Theoretical interest focuses on *complex interdependence* (Keohane and Nye, 1977, ch. 2), which is an attempt to define the overall character of international relations, either within the system as a whole (the international economy) or within some major sub-system (the European Community, the OECD). On this level, the theorist can try to use a structural condition (complex networks of mutual dependency) to predict, or simply to explain, system- (or sub-system-) wide changes in the way states relate to each other. Inter-dependence has been used, *inter alia*, to make arguments about the declining utility of force, about changes in the character of issues on the international agenda away from security matters and towards economic ones, about the spread of common norms among states, and about the problems of collective management of the international economy.

Unfortunately, none of this is of much direct help to the policy-maker. At best it may provide policy-makers with insight into the general context of their activities, but it cannot guide them on the inherently political questions about how to respond either to particular events or to the situation as a whole. In addition to the problems raised in the previous two sections, there is the additional difficulty that the scope of theoretical insight is often beyond the range, capability and responsibility of the policy-maker. For example, it could be argued that the most important policy-relevant insight of interdependence theory is that a system of complex interdependence needs to be managed if it is to remain stable. Historically, this management function has been provided by one exceptionally powerful 'hegemonic' state (first Britain, then the United States). The system is currently moving into a management crisis, because American capability and willingness to play the hegemonic role is irreversibly declining.

What does this insight do for the policy-maker in a state like Britain? In the first instance the policy-maker has to find time to understand it, which given the pressure of other responsibilities may terminate the process immediately. If the theory passes this hurdle, the policy-maker must then make some judgement as to the accuracy of the theory as a basis for policy.

There is no guarantee in the social sciences that a theory either is, or will long remain, an accurate representation of all or part of reality. Theorists in the social sciences not only face the hazard common to all science that one's theory may be displaced by someone else's. They have also to face a problem not of concern to natural scientists, which is the erratic behaviour of their subject-matter: human beings do not behave with anything like the predictability of atoms. If a theory of human behaviour became known, that knowledge would itself destroy the conditions that made the theory valid in the first place.

Even if the hegemonic theory is judged to be correct, there is little that Britain can do about it. There is no obvious hegemonic successor to the United States, certainly not Britain. The insight might be used to add Britain's weight to calls for the creation of collective management. In the other direction, it might serve as a rationale for more enthusiastic engagement with the European Community as a way of creating a larger bastion should the international economy collapse. This latter response, however, raises the danger of transforming a theoretical prediction into a self-fulfilling prophecy. Either way, the theory is unlikely to become a major focus for policy. The problem it defines is simply too big in scope, too uncertain in manifestation and too distant in time to justify large allocations of either scarce policy-making time, or limited policy-implementing resources. Any attempt to make the issue a central focus would invite attack from domestic opponents, and would be unlikely to reap electoral rewards within what is generally a highly parochial and short-sighted domestic political environment. It would also encounter resistance in the international environment on grounds of indifference, disagreement, vested interest, and the feeling that the problem is simply too big for anyone to be able to do anything except muddle through.

The problem for theories about the international system is that there is no appropriate political constituency for them to address. Nobody speaks for the system as a whole, nobody is responsible for it, and almost nobody has sufficient power or authority to do anything about it. International system theorists thus occupy a position similar in some respects to astronomers and weather forecasters. All three professions can observe some large-scale patterns in the systems that they study, and have some understanding of how the systems operate. All three have a degree of predictive capability, the astronomers here being the most advanced. But none of them can employ its understanding to change the structures that they observe. The forces in play are simply too large for human agencies yet to have devised significant instruments of leverage.

CONCLUSIONS

What then is the signficance of the abstract academic concept of interdependence for the concrete policy needs of a country like Britain? The two
conclusions that emerge from this study seem at first to be depressingly at
odds with each other. On the one hand, interdependence is said to be
transforming the conditions of existence in the international system, and
influencing the policy environment of Britain in myriad important ways.
But on the other, it is argued that the concept is difficult to operationalise,
inherently political, and often beyond the reach of existing policy-making
machinery.

For reasons that I hope are now clear, the solution to this dilemma cannot
be an objective, scientific one. The very nature of interdependence requires
that it be addressed politically. On this basis the conclusion reached in the
general discussion of the term (p. 165) serves equally well for Britain:

[Interdependence] is thus in part a call to change ways of perceiving not only the
international system, but also the function of government. The ideological content
of interdependence is, in effect, that the art of good government needs to include a
substantially higher element of responsible external behaviour than has hitherto
been the norm. This call carries an implicit threat to both governments and
electorates that if their perceptions do not change, then the central problems in the
international system will be misunderstood, and policy will consequently be
misguided to the detriment of all. In this sense, the idea of interdependence is a
propaganda weapon against the parochial attitudes that still dominate most of the
world's public and elite awareness. It is a call to widen political visions, and to
reorient political priorities away from self-centred local issues and towards broader
collective concerns. The logic is that the broader concerns of interdependence are
now crucial to the survival of most local values.

Since Britain is only a medium-sized country, and is embedded in a region of
exceptionally high density, this argument bears on it with particular force. The
challenge of interdependence is not just to external relations, but to the structure
and outlook of government as a whole. Domestic and foreign relations are
increasingly difficult to make distinct, which forces both governments and their
electorates to adjust to a radically altered policy environment. If interdependence
was just a matter of choosing between liberal and mercantilist modes of economic
organisation, then real alternatives would exist. A country like Britain could choose
to isolate itself rather than participate in a larger economic game. But because
interdependence is also, and more deeply, driven by density, this choice does not
really exist. Britain can no longer be governed as an isolated entity.

The question is therefore not whether the political life of the country will adjust
to interdependence, but whether its adjustment will be timely and efficient, or
turbulent, slow and unnecessarily costly. In this perspective, the overall attitude of
the country towards the relentless rise in importance of its external environment in
relation to its domestic one, is more crucial than attitudes towards the many
particular issues of interdependence raised singly. It is the overall attitude,
amorphous though it may be, that sets the tone for detailed British responses to
interdependence across the whole agenda.

3 ~ Foreign policy analysis and the study of British foreign policy

Steve Smith

This paper is concerned with the issue of what foreign policy analysis (FPA) has to offer the study of British foreign policy. My aim is to review the progress within the sub-field of FPA so as to indicate both those approaches that appear to be dead-ends and those approaches that seem to be promising avenues for the study of foreign policy. The paper will then address the definitional question concerning the nature of foreign policy in the contemporary world. Finally the paper will examine in some depth the interrelationship between the theoretical and empirical aspects of foreign policy as they apply to Britain: this will lead to a series of critical issues in British foreign policy that the theories available are unable to explain. My concern is not so much to provide a listing of the available theory as it is to point to areas where no theories are suitable, as well as highlighting the 'islands of theory' that do look promising. Such a survey is, of course, bound to be partial, and I write as someone committed to an FPA view of things; specifically, my judgement is that middle-range theories offer the most fruitful way forward for the study of British foreign policy. Having said which, I will not spend pages justifying this position: but I should make explicit early on both my optimism regarding the role (as well as the track record) of middle-range theory.

Before turning to provide a brief overview of the stage that FPA has reached, it will be useful to summarise the ways in which British foreign policy has been studied up to this point. FPA, the approach that will be used in this paper, is not simply a mixture or amalgam of the other ways that have been used to study British foreign policy, although it does draw upon them. Rather, it is an alternative to each of them, and is differentiated from them by a more explicit concern with theory. FPA, then, is a distinctive approach, and therefore we need to distinguish it from the other main ways of explaining British foreign policy.

Broadly speaking there are four ways in which British foreign policy has been studied. First of all there is what can be called the historical approach, by which is meant the analysis of British foreign policy from a historical perspective, stressing the centrality of providing a narrative that makes sense of events. Such a narrative concentrates on the thoughts of those who made the decisions, and eschews any explicit concern with theory; accordingly, the account is judged against rival accounts in terms of the extent of evidence cited and the coherence of the explanation of decision-makers' perceptions offered. Particularly good examples of this type of approach can be found in Gilbert (1971–86), Medlicott (1968) and Young (1984). Above all, this work moves from the evidence to an explanation, seeing such explanations as logically entailed by the evidence offered: it does not construct pre-theories or hypotheses to be tests, nor does it start with a theory which is then applied to the specific cases to be explained. This kind of approach is inductive, constructing explanations from evidence, and using as evidence the explanations of behaviour offered by those who made the decisions.

A second approach is a subset of the first: it, too, is historical, but is written with a sympathy to social science generally and to either international relations theory or foreign policy analysis specifically. Such accounts, of which outstanding examples are Steiner (1969), Watt (1965), Thorne (1972, 1978) and Kennedy (1981), analyse British foreign policy by examining the historical evidence, but do so with an explicit consideration of theories developed within social science. Thus, such accounts will look at the impact of psychological processes, or bureaucratic politics or the domestic inputs to British foreign policy, and will use these approaches to structure their treatment of the historical evidence. As such, they seek to explain specific historical events as examples of more widely applicable psychological or political phenomena. For these writers, there is an explicit concern with patterns and regularities, and this is well illustrated by their citation of, and reliance upon, theories of decision-making and psychology.

A third approach is that which treats British foreign policy from an international relations perspective. This is to say that it locates explanations of British foreign policy within explanations of international relations. Thus accounts such as Wallace (1975), Kaiser and Morgan (1971), Jones (1974), Northedge (1974), Barber (1976), Frankel (1975), Boardman and Groom (1973), Wallace (1984) and Tugendhat and Wallace (1988) stress the role of British foreign policy as a way of balancing the requirements of the British state and society with the changing nature of the international system. These accounts, although focused on explaining the foreign policy of Britain, do so by discussing the ways in which Britain makes foreign policy according to the dual imperatives of domestic and international constraints and demands. For these writers, Britain is above all a state existing within the international society of states, and this location imposes demands and limitations on British foreign policy that are reflected both in the ways in which that foreign policy is made and in its content.

Finally, there are those approaches that explain British foreign policy from a domestic institutional perspective. These accounts, for example Richards (1967), Vital (1968), Coker (1986) and Shlaim, Jones and Sainsbury (1977), develop their explanations of British foreign policy by stressing the institutional setting in which it is made. Accordingly, they stress the role of constitutional and political factors within Britain as accounting for the content of, and machinery for making, British foreign policy.

The approach that is being discussed in this paper, though, is rather different: it is the approach known as FPA, which has few adherents in the international relations community in Britain although it has had considerably more in the US international relations community. Indeed, one of the first points that can be made about FPA is that it has been very much a US subject, with virtually all the major approaches being developed in that country. Not only does this raise the question of whether this leads to ethnocentrism in the subject, but it also causes us to ask why FPA has not been so visible in the study of British foreign policy. Having said which, there is an identifiable group of FPA scholars in Britain and, having produced a couple of general theoretical books (Clarke and White, 1981, 1989; Smith and Clarke, 1985), they have recently turned their attention to the study of British foreign policy (Smith et al., 1988). The basic assumption of FPA can be stated simply: it is that foreign policy is a subject that can be studied fruitfully by looking at the regularities and patterns that exist for all states. That is to say, the foreign policy of a state can best be explained by treating that state as an example of a class of actors undertaking a set of behavioural activities. Despite the differences between states and between their foreign policy agendas, they make their foreign policy as the result of a similar set of influences. Accordingly, there are patterns and regularities that can be observed in both the processes by which foreign policy is made and in its substance.

FPA, therefore, is primarily concerned with foreign policy as an activity; the unique factors of the state and issue concerned are of secondary analytical importance. This means that FPA stands firmly within a social science methodology, being opposed to the assumptions of a view of history which sees the task as one of reconstructing the actor's thoughts. To adhere to an FPA approach therefore involves downplaying factors such as the views of those who took the decisions *per se* (although they might well be explained as examples of psychological patterns of perception and misperception) since FPA axiomatically involves a more structuralist version of the structure–agent relationship than is commonly found in the discipline of history. All that is meant by this is that FPA treats the perceptions of leaders as the result of causal factors such as the position they occupy in the bureaucracy or as the result of group pressures in the decision-making process. In history these perceptions are more likely to be treated as the starting-point for analysis. Think of the Westland affair; for many historians the task of explaining that event consisted of portraying it as a battle between two powerful individuals. It was a personality clash, or a clash between two men who hoped to become leader of the country. Whereas, for FPA scholars, the event is to be seen primarily as a clash of bureaucratic interests. This is not to say that the personalities of the individuals were unimportant, only to maintain that the central dispute concerned bureaucratic interests. The implication of this line of argument is that if the individuals swapped roles, they would swap policy preferences.

Within FPA there have been a variety of approaches, and it is fair to say that many of these have proved to be intellectual dead-ends. The most obvious example of a failed approach is that known as Comparative Foreign Policy (CFP), which is a data-based search for a general theory of foreign policy. Although it still has many adherents in the United States (see, for example, their recent manifesto for the future development of the approach, Hermann et al., 1987), its inability to move beyond description and its continued acceptance of a rather naïve form of positivism results in its remaining bogged down in arcane disputes over how best to manipulate data. At the risk of oversimplification, the search for general theory looks like a fruitless quest. Similarly the reliance on general accounts of foreign policy provided by theories of international relations also have proved to be dead-ends. One has in mind here Morgenthau's 'realism', with its central explanatory concept of the 'national interest', as well as the systems theories of Kaplan, Rosecrance and Waltz. Although these have utility in explaining the interactions between states, none of them has proved very useful for explaining the complications of foreign policy: after all, each assumes that the domestic environment is essentially unimportant in the determination of foreign policy. Whilst this might be of theoretical importance in analysing global patterns of conflict, it captures only a very small part of the agenda of foreign policy that applies to most states.

If FPA therefore rejects reconstructionist history on the one hand and has a poor track record in its search for general theory on the other, what is the state of play in the subject in the late 1980s? To many outside the subject the failure of Rosenauian general theory is the failure of FPA (see Berridge, 1980, 1981; Smith, 1982). This is too simple and convenient an assessment: FPA has developed in the last two decades so that it is now a collection of what we can call middle-range theories each of which appears to be of considerable utility for the explanation of certain aspects of the

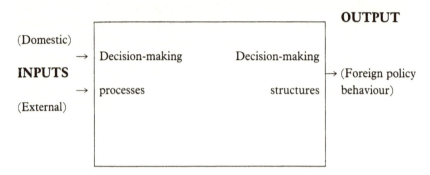

Figure 3.1. The foreign policy system in Clarke and White, 1981

foreign policies of certain types of states. Of course, these middle-range theories have not been, and are unlikely to be, combined into an overall general theory, and that is a common criticism of the sub-field. Yet these middle-range theories do offer potentially massive insights into foreign policy as they have clearly identified a number of regularities in the making of foreign policy. There is, in each case, a sizeable literature of studies that utilise middle-range theories to study a foreign policy activity of a country, so that within FPA there is little doubt that these approaches offer a promising road forward for the study of foreign policy. What middle-range theories do is to concentrate on either one relationship within the analytical foreign policy system or on a substantive area of foreign policy behaviour. Each attempts to explain the behaviour of the dependent variable (foreign policy) by reference to one of a number of independent variables (such as bureaucratic politics, groupthink, implementation, misperceptions, operational codes). Note that whilst the task of combining these to form *a* theory of foreign policy is simply not possible, because each account has a distinct set of assumptions as to the impact of the varying structures and processes on the output, the great advantage of middle-range theory is that it allows (even encourages) comparisons between states and across time. To give just one example, if leaders in any state tend to follow certain patterns of misperception in a given situation (for example, a crisis) then it seems that we have discovered a regularity that, on the rule of parsimony, is more powerful an explanation than those that concentrate on the actors' perceptions and treat these as the independent variable. Similar arguments apply to the other middle-range theories.

So, if FPA has developed to the stage whereby we can for all intents and purposes ignore the general theory approach to foreign policy theory (as well, of course, as the general theories developed by systems theorists), and if we wish to move beyond a reliance on history, which either results in an essentially descriptive enterprise or has to invoke implicit psychological theories of perception and motivation, what middle-range theories are currently popular within the FPA literature? These middle-range theories each attempt to explain part of foreign policy behaviour. Accordingly, they can best be understood by seeing them as attempting to explain the relationship between different parts of the causal process by which foreign policy is made. The most convenient way of representing this is to use the analytical construct of a foreign policy system. This seems to be the underlying structure of the middle-range theory approach, with the plethora of theories making sense because of the notion that each is dealing with only part of the system of structures and processes that result in foreign policy behaviour. The concept of a foreign policy system owes its origins to work in political science in the 1950s, but was developed in the foreign policy field by Clarke (1981): see figure 3.1. Each middle-range theory explains the output (foreign policy) by reference to a specific independent variable within the system. For example, bureaucratic politics sees foreign policy behaviour as the result of the decision-making structures, whereas groupthink, misperceptions and belief systems all see it as the result of different parts of the decision-making processes. Finally, implementation sees foreign policy behaviour as the result of the way it is implemented, that is to say the output results from the ways that the output is undertaken. We can now look at the main middle-range theories.

THE FOREIGN POLICY SYSTEM: MIDDLE-RANGE THEORIES

Bureaucratic politics

The basic claim of this approach is that foreign policy is to be explained by bargaining between those who make the decisions. Following Allison (1971), there are two main features of bureaucratic position, and the foreign policy that results is not necessarily consistent with the preferences of any individual: it may, in short, represent a compromise. This approach has been widely used in the explanation of United States foreign policy (for an example see Smith, 1985a), although it has been strongly criticised on a number of levels (see Smith, 1980), amongst which is the claim that it does not apply to Britain (Wallace, 1975, p. 9). Nevertheless, there is no doubt that the alternative account of foreign policy provided by this approach has been of considerable importance in challenging the orthodoxy of rational choice analysis, and bureaucratic politics, for all its theoretical shortcomings and methodological problems, is a central component of the FPA approach.

Groupthink

This approach, based on the work of Irving Janis (1972, 1982; Janis and Mann, 1977), explains foreign policy by reference to the processes at work within decision-making groups. It, too, has been subject to criticism (see Longley and Pruitt, 1980; Flowers, 1977; Tetlock, 1979), but it has led to considerable insights into certain foreign policy decisions (see Janis, 1972, 1982; Smith, 1985b). Crucially, it helps explain why decision-makers held the views they hold, and, as such, as with bureaucratic politics, represents a more parsimonious account than that offered by reconstructionist historians.

Belief systems

There has been an explosion of work examining the impact of the relatively sophisticated psychological processes of cognitive consistency and value/ evidence mechanisms on perception, with many sub-fields within this general heading which follows from Boulding (1956) and Holsti (1969). For a collection of essays discussing the approach see Little and Smith (1988). Common to all these approaches is an attempt to explain foreign policy preferences by reference to the coherent views of the world held by actors: specifically, what is central is the actor's attempt to maintain consistency in his or her world view. There are major research findings surrounding the variants of this general approach, such as Axelrod's work on cognitive maps (Axelrod, 1976), Jervis's and Burgess's work on images (Jervis, 1970; Burgess, 1966), Leites's work on the operational code (Leites, 1951; George, 1969) and May's use of the concept of 'lessons of the past' (May, 1973; Neustadt and May, 1986). For applications of belief systems to a British case, see Dillon (1988) and White (1988).

Misperceptions

A slightly separate approach is to be found in the work of Robert Jervis (1976) on the causes of misperception. Again this has led to a sizeable amount of research, with the major focus being on the patterns of misperception in foreign policy decision-making.

Implementation

A more radical account has been that pioneered by Clarke (1979) which uses the processes of implementing decisions to explain not only the behaviour itself but also the ways in which the foreign policy system operates. This approach derives from Allison's other alternative account of foreign policy, the organisational process (which he later merged with bureaucratic politics, see Allison and Halperin, 1972), and has led to one set of studies of foreign policy from this perspective (Smith and Clarke, 1985).

Brecher research design

A very different middle-range approach is that developed by Michael Brecher (Brecher et al., 1969; Brecher, 1979), in which a conception of the foreign policy system based on the distinction between operational and psychological environments is used as a framework for researching specific decisions: the intention is to use a set of these studies to build up inductive findings on foreign policy causation. In many respects this has been the most successful research enterprise with a set of the studies already published and more on the way (for an excellent example, see Shlaim, 1983). It is important to note that the theoretical pay-off remains to be seen, since all that has currently emerged are the individual studies, but, even then, these have evidently resulted in a considerable advance in our understanding of the foreign policy decisions under analysis.

These six middle-range approaches all concentrate on specific aspects of the foreign policy system and are concerned to use a theoretical framework to guide research and, crucially, to generate findings that apply across time and space. There are other approaches that are under way (for a recent example, see Walker, 1987), but if FPA proponents were asked to set out their stall, the six approaches discussed above would be in a prime location. Each has led to follow-on research and there are strong indications of research communities being established around them. In marked contrast to the general theory quest of the mid-1960s to mid-1970s, cumulative research is taking place. Having said which, it must be noted that much of this is based in North America. FPA, as of today, then, comprises a set of promising middle-range theories, each with a small set of followers. That these cannot lead to the development of a general theory leads many 'true believers' to continue that particular search. That they are explicit in their use of, and reliance on, theory puts off many historians. Depending on how you look at it they are either neither one thing nor the other, or they are successful attempts to integrate historical analysis with explicit theory. For those who adhere to FPA, middle-range theory has utility precisely because it attempts to use theory to guide analysis without resorting to the number-crunching of the general theorists, whilst avoiding the focus on the unique and on the actor's own view that characterises much historical analysis. The findings therefore inform both the explanation of the specific case being analysed and the development of the approach being used.

THE DECLINE OF REALISM

If that is the state of the subject at the present, what is the current state of thinking about the activity we are attempting to explain, namely foreign policy? Of course, to many international relations scholars in the period up to the mid-1970s, this was not a particularly complex issue. Foreign policy could be relatively easily defined, as could the nature of the actor undertaking it. As behaviour, it was mainly, although not exclusively, military in character, concerned with issues of war and peace: as a process, it was essentially a bipartisan activity carried out only at the highest reaches of government with only rare instances of public involvement (or interest). Such characteristics derived from the structure of international society and the lack of democratic participation in government. International society is structured in a manner that makes it convenient to think of states as closed units, interacting one with another, with little of the content of these interactions being of concern to the populations involved. The balance of power in the international system that existed from the formation of the states-system in the seventeenth century until the Second World War meant that governments of states were involved in complex patterns of alliance construction, in which ideology was relatively unimportant. The structure of international society, then, made it easy for states' decision-makers and populations to think that each state had a set of interests that were in a crucial sense unaffected by ideology or values. The lack of a government above the states meant that each state was judge in its own cause, and thus foreign policy was seen as a professional activity focused on using diplomacy and force to advance the interests of the state. This is not to say that leaders did not advance economic goals, only that foreign policy, because of the anarchical structure of international society, could be portrayed as something above politics and concerned essentially with the 'high' politics of the management of alliances.

Such a view was enhanced by both the small number of states comprising international society – and these were geographically concentrated in Europe – and by the lack of democratic processes in societies. This may seem a stark view, but it is worth remembering that historically the dominant theory of international relations – realism (Morgenthau, 1948) – is based on just such a view of the world. For realists, the broad nature of the foreign policies of states was basically determined by the structure of international society (lubricated by a dash of selfish human nature). Rationality was assumed in decision-makers, so that the realist, by knowing that all leaders were trying to maximise power, could explain not only what states were doing but also what they should be doing. As International Relations developed as a subject, these state-centric assumptions pervaded the literature, so that even during the so-called 'behaviouralist revolution' the assumptions underlying analysis were nearly always those that saw foreign policy as the action of a unit within the system; ideology and values were less important in understanding the foreign policy of a given state than was an understanding of its location in the international power structure and therefore of its interests.

The point, then, is that much of international relations analysis sees foreign policy as the behaviour of a unit within a system of power relations. Specifically, as John Vasquez has argued (Vasquez, 1979, p. 211), realists accepted three assumptions: (a) that nation states are the dominant actors in international relations; (b) that there is a sharp distinction between domestic and international politics; and (c) international relations is the struggle for power and peace. These assumptions define what has been called the 'state-centric' approach to international relations. What has occurred in the last two decades is that analysts of foreign policy have questioned the utility of these assumptions. In essence, it has been powerfully argued that the nature of foreign policy has been changing. The two main aspects of this change are that states no longer seem to be the only, or even the dominant, actors, and that foreign policy has come increasingly to concern economic matters. In the terms used in the literature, foreign policy has changed because of the rise of transnational (non-state) actors and because of the effects of increasing economic interdependence.

These changes became a focus for study in the early 1970s, and led to a very different conception of what foreign policy was: it was no longer concerned mainly with the military activity of discrete units in international society. Rather it became a matter of governments trying to control and manage a whole range of economic issues in an environment in which not only were states not the sole actors but also the boundaries between international and domestic politics became blurred. The simplicity of the view of states having objective interests was replaced by a notion that foreign policy now included a wide range of issues, the management of which involved dealing with actors other than states; more importantly, states could not therefore be seen as hermetically sealed units, with the process of making foreign policy being essentially a truncated version of the domestic political process; instead interdependence and transnationalism meant that groups in societies did not necessarily see their government as the primary focus for their activity. Rather, they saw non-state actors such as companies in other countries as the target for their attention. All of this, of course, altered the perception of the ways in which foreign policy was made: interdependence and transnationalism, then, challenged the ortho-doxy of what foreign policy behaviour and the foreign policy processes were. By the mid-1970s, many analysts were claiming that foreign policy could not be studied by seeing the state as a unit of international society: theories which were developed to explain how states behaved and how policies were made seemed too simplistic in the face of a situation in which that behaviour now encompassed issues which did not fit into the tradi-tional foreign policy agenda; and conceptions of the foreign policy process that stressed bipartisanship and saw a small elite as determining policy seemed inadequate in a world in which the dominance of economic issues brought foreign policy into the domestic political realm. The vast increase in the number of states in international society and the increased democrat-isation of many states exacerbated this trend.

To summarise this discussion, then, what is meant by foreign policy is not a matter for neutral definition. Both the content of foreign policy and the ways in which it is made have changed in the last two decades: these changes have resulted in a situation in which British foreign policy has changed in its content, as Britain adapts not only to a changing inter-national political situation but also to a rising salience of economic factors, and in the way it is made. One of the recurrent themes in the literature concerns exactly this point: how much has the content of British foreign policy altered in the era of interdependence, and what changes has this caused in the ways in which that foreign policy is made? Having said this, though, it is important to note that in the last few years the debate on 'what foreign policy is' has changed again. A decade ago the literature of International Relations contained a powerful argument that the changes in the content and processes of foreign policy induced by the rise of interdependence and transnationalism represented a once-and-for-all transformation in the nature of foreign policy. This is certainly how many analysts in the United States saw the situation (Mansbach et al., 1976; Mansbach and Vasquez, 1981). Not only did they believe that the changes that had occurred in world politics represented a linear shift in the content of foreign policy, but they also argued that such a shift rendered obsolete the existing theory of foreign policy. Indeed, it is clear that just this concern was pivotal in the decline of comparative foreign policy analysis as a sub-field in the United States in the mid-to-late 1970s; after all, if the state was no longer the dominant actor, if the boundaries between international and domestic politics were becoming blurred, and if the most pressing issues were economic and not military, then theories of how the unit called the state behaved in the international system seemed rather at odds with these events. However, the events of the late 1970s and early 1980s altered this picture considerably: on the one hand, the renewed hostility between the United States and the Soviet Union after the Soviet intervention in Afghanistan brought the state back on to centre-stage in world politics; on the other, the revival of military and political tensions pushed economic issues out of the limelight a little. By the late 1980s the picture has again shifted with the warming of US-Soviet relations and the changing constitutions of Eastern Europe. Nevertheless, it is evident that the state is still a critically important actor and that military factors are continuing to dominate aspects of international relations.

The present situation, then, is one in which the claims of transnationalist and interdependence scholars that the state had been transcended as the dominant actor seem overstated. The 1970s did not witness a once-and-for-all transformation in the nature of international society. In the literature on international relations this has been reflected in the rise of neo-realist thought (see Waltz, 1979; Keohane, 1986). But it is central to the argument of this paper that it is clear that whilst the notion of the replacement of state-centric theory that gained prominence in the 1970s may have been overstated, this does not mean that one must return to pre-1970s conceptions of international relations. The current situation is not one in which the assumptions of state-centrism are acceptable, nor one in which the assumptions of transnationalism and interdependence apply; rather, the late 1980s see a world in which *both* military and economic issues dominate the political agenda, and in which both states and non-state actors are important actors. These issues and actors are working within a structure that is more interdependent than before. Thus, accounts of foreign policy have to start from a position of complexity: it is a mixed actor world with issues that are of differential salience to the actors involved. Foreign policy is both economic and military and involves influencing a wide variety of types of actors, within an interdependent international society. As such the content of foreign policy is neither as solely concerned with 'high' politics as some theorists claimed up until the 1970s, nor as was portrayed by the interdependence and transnationalist theories in the 1970s; it is both. Accordingly, the processes by which foreign policy is made are inordinately complex: just as the traditional view of an elite bipartisan process is inaccurate, so is the 1970s view of a complete merging of international and domestic politics. In the late 1980s, the ways in which foreign policy is made are critically dependent on the issue involved: in military areas there is still little democratic participation, in economic areas the processes involve wide sections of domestic political activity. So, in both the content and the process dimensions of foreign policy the situation is more complex than scholars thought it was in either the 1960s or the 1970s. What this means is that the term foreign policy is in an important sense rather misleading, in that it implies an identifiable area of policy, presumably one that is distinct in terms of its content and the ways in which it is made. Foreign policy is, rather, a cover-all, generic term for actions taken by governments to influence or manage the actions of actors located outside the state's boundaries. As such, it involves so many different types of issues, involves dealing with such a diverse set of actors and is made by a constantly shifting set of processes that we should think of it as being multidimensional. All of these are particularly relevant in the British case.

Foreign policy, therefore, is now a hybrid; its empirical content varies from state to state and from issue to issue. It takes on different forms, involves very different types of implementation and, crucially, makes a nonsense of simple distinctions between domestic and international society. Not only this, but also we should note that the actor usually seen as undertaking foreign policy, the state, has itself undergone change both domestically and internationally. In Britain's case, interdependence and the alteration in the domestic role of the state in the last decade have resulted in a much more fragmented state in terms of its dealings with the external environment. The state that acts in the European Community (EC) is different according to the issue being discussed; it involves a constantly shifting coalition of groups within government, with policy being very tightly co-ordinated by a complex set of networks. Nevertheless, it is not clear that the same 'Britain' is involved in any two instances of external behaviour, but nor is it at all obvious that the terms 'foreign' and 'policy' are anything other than a convenient shorthand. It is, of course, exactly this fact that makes the search for general theory all the more fruitless, since there is no such thing as a 'foreign policy' that means the same in any two policy arenas or across different types of states. Finally, one should point out that even the domestic environment has altered considerably in the last twenty years: interdependence and transnationalism have resulted in a much more diffuse pattern of policy-making, with previously 'foreign' issues and actors increasingly becoming part of the domestic environment. The hierarchy of issues for the domestic audience has changed so much that the old simple (simplistic?) notions of the domestic environment's role, and interest, in foreign policy are no longer relevant.

One upshot of this analysis is that concepts of sovereignty are increasingly problematic (see Wallace, 1986); although it is very much part of the political debate about Britain's role in the EC, its assumptions seem to bear little relevance to the behavioural dimension of British foreign policy. Similarly, whilst it was once claimed that foreign policy could be distinguished from domestic policy by the processes involved, the preceding analysis indicates that this view is no longer tenable. For, if the domestic and external environments of the state are increasingly being merged, if similar coalitions of actors are involved in issues of 'domestic' and 'foreign' policy, and if the processes for making those policies result from such policy communities, then there seems little possibility of distinguishing domestic from foreign policy in terms of the processes involved. Furthermore, even attempts to distinguish foreign from domestic politics according to the substance involved seem problematic, since a very large proportion of 'foreign' policy has 'domestic' consequences, and vice versa. Virtually all EC activity straddles the domestic/foreign divide, as, increasingly, do questions of defence. Foreign policy in the late 1980s cannot, therefore, be easily distinguished from domestic policy in terms of either substance or the processes involved.

The problem for FPA, then, is to accommodate the theories of interdependence into the middle-range theories. This is particularly the case in explaining the foreign policy of a country such as Britain, where the effects of interdependence have altered the nature of the foreign policy process, as well as its content, more than is the case with many other countries. It is important to note that interdependence means something rather less radical in the United States, where, after all, the middle-range theories have been developed.

Before turning to look at the central frontier issues that define the current state of FPA it is necessary to say something about the empirical context of these debates when it comes to looking at British foreign policy. What features of British foreign policy illustrate these general problems? If we want to look at the frontier questions facing FPA in any study of British foreign policy, we need to be clear as to the main features of that foreign policy.

The setting of British foreign policy in the late 1980s is one of interdependence. The developments that have occurred since the mid-1960s in the financial, technological, manufacturing, defence and communications fields have resulted in a transformation in British foreign policy.

As William Wallace succinctly notes, Britain is in a predicament, 'as a result of rapid and continuing changes in technology, communications and industrial and financial integration which have eroded national boundaries and the powers of government but left the structure – and the rhetoric – of national politics in place' (Wallace, 1986, p. 367). Wallace paints the picture of successive British governments as having a confused attitude towards the interdependent world in which Britain finds itself.

On the one hand, British governments continue to attach much importance to symbols of national independence, such as the independent nuclear deterrent. They also claim to be protecting British sovereignty, an example of which would be the Falklands conflict. Yet, this is matched by a realisation that Britain is part of an interdependent international economy, most especially in Europe, which involves some loss of sovereignty. The results of this mixed set of reactions is that British governments have become enormously confused when issues arise that juxtapose the competing demands of interdependence and sovereignty. One recent example would be the British attitude to the European Exchange Rate Mechanism, where the government has steadfastly refused to join it, while acting as if it was a member. Another would be the bitter and acrimonious battle over the sale of Westland Helicopters, where the debate soon came down to arguments about sovereignty. A similar set of arguments was involved in the issue of the proposed sale of British Leyland to a 'foreign' company. Further examples would include the row over the Nimrod versus AWACS radar system, and the future main British battle tank. In all these cases, those who argue that certain aspects of the economy have to be kept in British hands in order to maintain sovereignty are opposed to those who see the primary requirement as being one of getting the best value for money.

Of course, the arguments are much more involved than this summary implies, but the critical point is that Britain is part of an interdependent world economy, the involvement with which necessitates the acceptance of a certain loss of autonomy. Yet, at the same time, British governments pay a lot of lip-service to notions of national interest and sovereignty, which imply that the government has much more control over events than is the case.

Nowhere is this contradictory stance more clearly indicated than in the British attitude to the European Community. On the one hand, the British government has evolved a complex and efficient network to oversee the co-ordination of British policy towards the community. Britain is an active member of the community, and operationally accepts the constraints on autonomy as well as the limits on the exercise of sovereignty that this implies. On the other hand, successive British leaders have maintained a public stance of stemming the tide of encroachment on British sovereignty, the most explicit recent statement of which can be found in Mrs Thatcher's 1988 speech in Bruges. Operationally Britain accepts, and works constructively within, the interdependencies of the European Community, yet when it comes to declaratory policy, British leaders express a commitment to limit incursions into British sovereignty. This, of course, was one of the main issues in the debates over British membership of the European Community in the 1950s, 1960s and 1970s, but the issue remains in the political domain even after getting on for twenty years' membership of the EC.

A similar contradiction occurs in defence policy. British acceptance of the common defence, as reflected in the commitment to NATO, is matched by a perception of a wider defence role (the Gulf, and the Falklands, for example). The British attitude to South Africa brings out this ambivalence in the context of the Commonwealth, where an acceptance of a common involvement in events is tempered by a requirement that Britain is sovereign and can hold out against the majority. Finally, one can point to the tensions between sovereignty and the fact of interdependence in the British–American relationship. Two examples will suffice: first, Britain maintains that its nuclear deterrent is both independent and is a contribution to the common defence. Yet, how independent is it? It depends on US technology for its delivery systems, and of US information systems for its targeting (which will be increasingly problematic for notions of independence with the purchase of the Trident system). A second example is the British decision to allow the United States to use British bases to bomb Libya in April 1986. The official explanation given by the British Prime Minister was that the aircraft, F-111s, flown from British bases were needed to ensure accuracy in the bombing mission. But, it soon emerged that this was not so: not only did the aircraft carriers in the Mediterranean have aircraft with the same targeting equipment, but it was also the case that the USAF only wanted to be involved because there was a feeling that the US Navy was getting 'too much of the action'. The crucial reason for the request to use British bases was in order to get political support for the raid from at least one European government. Now, the point is that the British Prime Minister, for all her statements about sovereignty, felt that she could not turn down the American request, especially in view of the support given to Britain by the US administration during the Falklands conflict. This decision reflected the realities of interdependence, yet the rhetoric remained that of national sovereignty.

None the less, the main policy arena within which the greatest change has occurred in the last twenty years, the one that has had to adapt most to the conditions of interdependence, is that of Britain's relations with the other countries within the Organisation of Economic Co-operation and Development (OECD), predominantly the other EC members. William Wallace has noted eight empirical aspects of the rise in interdependence (1986, pp. 375–9): *first*, the integration of international production, whereby national companies have increasingly been replaced by multi-national corporations. These corporations use components manufactured in a variety of countries, and undertake design centrally. As he points out, this is most obvious in the case of the car industry. He cites the surprising statistic that one-quarter of British trade consists of trade between affiliates of the same company (1986, p. 376). The picture is the same in many industries, so that the situation is one in which 'there are fewer and fewer industrial sectors in which the British market is the appropriate frame of reference' (1986, p. 376).

His *second* area is military procurement, where the situation has changed rapidly in the last two decades. There are now few national weapons procurement programmes, and the trend is for more international procure-ment initiatives. The *third* area is the integration of international business, where British companies have increasingly been taken over by foreign companies. This process is currently increasing in pace as multinational firms ensure that they have a base within the community before the integration of the market in 1992. The *fourth* area is the integration of military intelligence, command and control; here the situation is one of British dependence on US satellites for targeting and strategic intelligence. *Fifth*, is the area of financial integration, where the picture is one of the creation of a single financial market. Currencies and stocks are traded in several key markets around the clock, the most important markets being London, New York and Tokyo. As Wallace points out, this makes the British financial community much more oriented towards the international economy than the national economy. This process has speeded up since the 'Big Bang', and, as the big crash of autumn 1987 showed, the result is a much more tightly integrated international financial market than before.

The *sixth* area Wallace discusses concerns the integration of international communications. This has been an evident area of increasing integration for the last two decades, with the development of international telephone and data transmission networks that together make it possible for infor-mation to travel without hindrance between countries. But the recent advent of direct satellite broadcasting and the proposed deregulation of the television industry mean that it will be even more difficult in the future for British governments to control the flow of information across national borders. The *seventh* area results from the last two, and is simply that international monetary and financial markets are now much more unstable. Increased communications and financial integration mean that it is more difficult to control the commodity and financial markets, as the attempts by the US government to control the dollar exchange rate attest. The *final* area is that of intergovernmental collaboration. The result of the decline of US hegemony over the international economy has been that Western leaders are more concerned than ever to try and collaborate to manage the international economy. Wallace notes that from 1982 to 1985 Mrs Thatcher attended eight to ten heads of government meetings a year, compared to only about one to two a year for Edward Heath when he was Prime Minister from 1970 to 1974 (1986, p. 378). A similar picture applies to virtually all senior ministers. More importantly, these meetings require preparatory meetings and lead to lengthy processes of continuing intergovernmental collaboration. Both of these mean that civil servants are regularly involved in extensive international contacts.

The picture that Wallace paints in this important article is that Britain is caught up in a network of international interdependence that will not go away. In fact, he believes that the situation will get worse over the next decade. The contrast is between a national policy debate focusing on sovereignty and national control, and an operational policy that recognises and works within interdependence. He offers a set of well-considered propositions as to the nature of the framework that policy must emerge from, the most important of which are that the pace of integration is unlikely to slow down in the next ten to fifteen years; that there is a contradiction between economic integration and national accountability; that international markets do not manage themselves, they are structured to the advantage of those who exercise the most influence over them; and that the international and domestic economies are interrelated (1986, p. 388).

If this is the picture with regard to the changing setting of British foreign policy, then a similar picture can be painted with regard to the processes by which that policy is made. As Clarke (1988) has pointed out in his study of the foreign policy-making process in Britain: 'The international environment, then, presents Britain with a web of commitments, difficult to visualize with any precision, probably greater than at any other time and showing every sign of a constant increase' (p. 81). In this context, the difficulty is one of co-ordinating and managing this situation – the problem is one of overload.

Whereas it was easy in the past to define foreign policy, in the sense that it referred to Britain's diplomatic relations, it is now much more difficult. Foreign policy now involves a massively increased range of factors, and these, the sum total of external relations, involve a very different (and much wider) set of individuals and groups in the making of foreign policy. Therefore, it is not simply that the content of foreign policy has changed in the last two decades, but also so has the process by which it is made. In turn, this change in process does not just mean that different people and different procedures are involved, but rather that the domestic/international divide is now impossible to draw. Where does British foreign policy stop and British domestic politics begin? As Clarke concludes: 'It is not just that the foreign policy process is *affected* by the forces of transnationalism and interdependence; rather that it is *part* of a transnational and interdependent structure which exists throughout the OECD world' (1988, p. 95).

Given this rather complex and confusing empirical picture, it is not surprising that general and historical accounts have found it difficult to explain British foreign policy, nor that any attempt to develop theory in this area has proven very problematic. This is so because the study of British foreign policy has to deal with four sets of changes: the changing nature of our theoretical work on foreign policy; the impact of interdependence and transnationalism on the content of foreign and domestic policy (especially the intersection between them); the changing international and domestic environments that result; and the effects of these factors on the ways in which policy is made and implemented.

Having earlier outlined the state of FPA and then having spent some time looking at the observable state of Britain's external relations, we can now turn to look at how FPA can get to grips with explaining British foreign policy. We will do this by looking at nine frontier questions that focus on the difficult issues for an account of British foreign policy. Recollect that we have already claimed that general theories and historical approaches suffer from very serious problems in explaining the complexities of contemporary foreign policy, and that the assumption behind this paper is that an FPA approach is the most fruitful way forward; what, then, are the problems that face an FPA account of British foreign policy?

FPA AND BRITISH FOREIGN POLICY

What is foreign policy?

This is a rather obvious question to start with and we have already said a lot about it, but it is absolutely crucial that we admit that the definition of foreign policy is particularly problematic. The complexities of interdependence have created a situation in which the standard definitions of what is British foreign policy simply do not hold. Which organs of state does one look at if one is to study British foreign policy (think of the range of departments involved in external relations)? Which government departments have a foreign policy role? How can we decide on what to study if we do not define the range of behaviour and actors that are to be included in our analysis? Not only is this a problem of coverage, it is also a question of depth, since, if one takes away crises and the declaratory aspects of foreign policy, what is left? FPA is very good at dealing with crises (since there is usually a great deal of information, and the actors are normally easy to define) but most, virtually all, British foreign policy does not fit into that category: the norm is interdepartmental co-ordination with each departmental representative working according to standard operating procedures. Together the problems of coverage and depth of analysis combine to pose a real dilemma for FPA; such an approach is social scientific, and thereby requires some explicit means of identifying evidence, yet the problems of defining what is evidence relevant to the study of British foreign policy is far more problematic in the contemporary era than ever before. Whatever the theoretical deficiencies of realism, its definition of foreign policy was uncomplicated. The complexities introduced by rising interdependence leave the FPA theorist with a real headache in trying to arrive at a way of defining that behaviour which is to be studied; note that this will be particularly awkward when the objective is to produce cumulative findings, since the FPA theorist cannot resort to allowing either the political system or the salience of issues to define the evidence for the study. An additional difficulty is simply that so much policy is made in an ad hoc, informal way.

There has to be some device to produce a demarcation of what is foreign policy from what is not. How do we do this – by content, process, agency involved, target, impact, policy community, legal definition, or analytical technique (virtually, how it is reported in the foreign press)? Accordingly, much of the frontier work in FPA is concerned with how to define foreign policy (Callaghan et al., 1982; Hermann et al., 1987; Wilkenfeld et al., 1980; East et al., 1978). The problem with nearly all of this work is, however, that it soon degenerates into debates about data manipulation. Quite frankly, *any* study of foreign policy is going to have a problem defining what content and processes are to be included: most studies will not make explicit the ways in which this definitional activity is carried out. From my perspective, as someone writing from within an FPA tradition, I think it might be better for us to face this problem head on and accept that our definition of what foreign policy is will have massive effects on our study. As a contrast note the vagueness of most official statements about

British foreign policy. From an FPA viewpoint the question of what constitutes foreign policy is actually the central problem facing the subject.

What do we study when we study foreign policy?

Whereas the previous problem relates to the demarcation between what is and what is not foreign policy, the second problem issue concerns the equally basic question of what it is we are studying. Not only is the empirical content of foreign policy an unresolved question in FPA, but there is also a serious dispute over what we, as analysts, focus on in order to explain whatever content we have defined as relevant. To put this at its most straightforward, the dominant method within FPA is to analyse decisions; accordingly, analysts build up evidence over how the decisions were taken, by whom, and with what outcomes. Yet such a focus carries the crucial implication that foreign policy *behaviour* is related to the decisions taken by bureaucrats and politicians. Of course, there is a well-established literature to deal with the problems caused by non-decisions, and the bulk of the FPA literature moves away from a mere reconstruction of the chronology of decision towards an analysis of the processes at work: these may involve notions of bureaucratic politics, misperception, group dynamics, etc. Nevertheless, we should note that, even then, there follows the implication that foreign policy is best understood from the decision-making process. The alternative argument is that such a focus distorts our understanding of foreign policy, since, in many cases, it does not consist of identifiable decisions by key actors. The complexities of the foreign policy setting and agenda facing Britain in the late 1980s mean that there may simply be no discrete 'decisions' over separated issues; rather, foreign policy may well best be understood by viewing it from another direction altogether, namely the implementation perspective. Such a perspective starts with what the output actually was and then traces back how it came to be. Doing so often results in a vast gap emerging between what decision-makers intended and what happened. A very clear example of this is British foreign policy within the EC, where skilful implementation often masks the absence of a clear policy. Thus, FPA faces two related difficulties in deciding what to study: first, the dominant models are models of decision-making, yet there may not be identifiable decisions over each issue; second, the gap between decision and behaviour may be so great that a better understanding of the behaviour can be gained by utilising an implementation perspective than can be obtained from a decision-making viewpoint. The dilemma that this creates for FPA is the obvious one that both accounts illuminate foreign policy, yet they cannot be easily combined. One is a model of choice and preference; the other is a model of organisational process, in which behaviour is governed by standard operating procedures.

What is the actor undertaking foreign policy?

Again, we have commented on this already, but it is nevertheless a critical problem for any FPA study of British foreign policy. There are two aspects to this issue and both concern the utility of continuing to base our explanations of foreign policy on an actor called the state. This viewpoint dominated the study of international relations for the first fifty years of the discipline's existence, and one should make it very clear that much of the explanatory power of theories of international relations comes from having a monolithic unit that exists within a system. It is precisely in this way that international relations theories explain international politics. If the state as unit of analysis is removed from theories, then much of the theoretical power of the discipline is also removed: after all, the dominant theory in the subject's history – realism – had explanatory power primarily because it could point to the impact of structure on the behaviour of the constituent units (states) of that system. Within foreign policy studies, the first works to break out of the realist mould of explanation nevertheless based their accounts on the decision-makers who acted on behalf of the state. Thus for all major theories of international relations, and the main works early on in the history of FPA, the state was assumed to be the actor and its behaviour was virtually taken for granted as being defined by the output of foreign and defence ministries.

Yet the events of the last decade or so have really upset this picture of the state as actor. The two aspects referred to above refer to different sides of this problem: first, how does FPA deal with the state if the state is not a monolith and if the parts of state-as-actor result in the subject being able to cover only part of the policy agenda and part of the salient behaviour? This leads to a more empirical issue: how does – or should – Britain deal with transnational actors? Does their existence make policy-making and implementation more difficult? Is the state unable to stop their activities and is it responsive to their needs and demands? Furthermore, to what extent does the existence of transnational actors in Britain limit the British government's autonomy (as distinct from sovereignty)?

Political economy and foreign policy

Not surprisingly, the problems that interdependence and transnationalism cause for the study of foreign policy extend to the empirical dimension in another form, and this concerns the difficulty of dealing with the dominance of political economy issues within a foreign policy framework. Admittedly, this is really a frontier question that faces the whole subject of international relations, especially given the important role in the subject for those theories that are based on system–unit relationships. Basically, realism utilised a notion of power politics that never really translated well to the economic dimension of state behaviour, and it was for this reason that international political economy developed almost as an alternative to the dominant (whether traditionalist or realist) power politics model. In FPA this antagonism was clear in the approaches that were at the forefront of the subject in the 1950s and 1960s. And, it was the changing perception of the role of political economy, following the events of the early 1970s (the Nixon 'shocks' and the 1973 oil crises), that were partly responsible for the incredible loss of direction (and faith) in FPA in the United States. Put simply, the subject-matter seemed to concern a variety of types of actors in behaviour that was mainly economic; FPA's founding theories and approaches were much better able to deal with military/political behaviour, in which states were the targets of discussions and decisions. Some leading theorists even claimed that FPA could not progress in such a changed international climate, and the subject lost its way around the mid-1970s (there were, of course, many other factors at work, not least amongst which was the problem of moving from evidence to explanation). Yet, just as the scholars started to move towards a more 'issue politics' approach (see Mansbach and Vasquez, 1981), the resurgence of a second Cold War caused attention to be refocused on the state and on the military dimension of international relations.

What this has led to is a situation in which, frankly, FPA and political economy theories each attempt to explain part of foreign policy (albeit with very different notions of what that involves and who acts), but there is little attempt to combine the two (for an exception within FPA, see Moon, 1987). Susan Strange (1988) deals with exactly this problem from an international political economy perspective. This does not mean that each approach includes in its analysis evidence only related to its own perspective, and it would be absurd to claim that the two approaches exist in isolation to one another, but from a theoretical point of view one has to state that FPA has not been able successfully to apply its models and theories to the kinds of issues that are the concern of political economists. On the one hand this is not surprising because the political economists tend not to see the same actors acting as do the foreign policy scholars, nor is the most salient behaviour the same for both theoretical perspectives. On the other, it is still rare to find the application of FPA theories to political economy issues. A glance through any of the recent texts or collections of essays will substantiate this claim.

Is this inherent in FPA's definition of foreign policy and the actors involved? My own view is that it is not, and that middle-range theories do offer a set of tools that can be used to examine political economy issues. But one problem remains for FPA and that is simply that its preoccupation with 'big' issues and with focusing explanation on discrete decisions by identifiable decision-makers results in a view of the subject that does not include much of the political economy activity. Now, whilst the evidence is rather more difficult to obtain on these issues, and despite the fact that the actors involved may not commonly be the small group of leaders meeting during a crisis so loved by FPA theorists, tools such as implementation and bureaucratic politics seem ideal for capturing the governmental side of political economy issues. What this does not really solve, of course, is the difficulty of studying behaviour that is not undertaken by the state, but this is merely to repeat a problem that bedevils international relations as a subject. For the British case, there are many examples, of which some of the most obvious are in the areas of energy, transport and civil aviation. There are ways forward on this problem, but FPA has tended to go on looking at governmental decisions, and this may be wholly inappropriate to the case of Britain in a situation of complex interdependence. To study Britain in the contemporary world will require an explicit examination of the way in which the rising importance of economic issues affects decision-making processes within government and will almost certainly require a discussion of the utility of the assumptions of most theories of foreign policy. Perhaps the problem is actually more to do with the dominance of power politics models (even if in behaviouralist guise) on the training of the academics in the field. Having said which, it is evident that political economy accounts are themselves very limited in the behaviour they include, and they are certainly open to the criticism that they underestimate the impact of the states-system on the freedom of manoeuvre of the state. The problem remains, however, that it is difficult within FPA to conceptualise and characterise the nature of international political economy issues, and for that reason alone the study of British foreign policy, because of the country's role in the international economy, is particularly intriguing and offers a potentially fascinating case study of this linkage.

Britain's place in the world

The location of Britain in the international political system offers another challenge to foreign policy theory, since Britain appears to be at a crucial intersection in the political, military and economic cleavages in the world. In one light, Britain is very much a part of Europe and therefore offers a paradigmatic example of how a country makes foreign policy within a complex institutional setting. Additionally, Britain plays a central role in the international financial and economic system, and this results in evident intersections between government and economic institutions that point up the inadequacies of simple models of international relations. Yet Britain also (at least at the moment) enjoys a 'special relationship' with the United States, at the same time as it possesses an independent (at least in name) nuclear deterrent. Taken together these pose a formidable agenda for any theory of foreign policy (or of international relations, for that matter). There is simply no convenient classification within which Britain fits: it is not a superpower, nor a middle power; it has aspects of a great power, but is caught up in a very complex set of interdependencies; it has to be involved in bargaining within defence and economic alliances and organisations, yet it is not a small power. No other country has quite this profile. Yet, exactly because Britain slips between the conceptual categories, it offers a very real challenge to international relations theory. Indeed, the British case brings up most of the major theoretical questions in the subject of international relations generally, and in FPA specifically. More saliently, for an FPA analyst, there is no reason why Britain's 'place' in the world should undermine the utility of using FPA theories. The strength of FPA is that it can deal with every state, because it is neutral on the nature of the policy and on the nature of the environment. The utility of a focus on the foreign policy system remains.

The nature of the domestic environment

Theories of foreign policy commonly utilise a number of models of the domestic political environment; similarly, domestic politics theories make assumptions about the impact of democratic structure on decision-making in foreign and defence policies. Yet, the changes that seem to have been occurring in Britain's domestic environment seem to challenge these assumptions. How viable are the standard views of public opinion's role in foreign policy-making? What is the size of the attentive public? This has been recognised by some British politics specialists, but many still make pre-interdependence assumptions about the foreign policy-making process. Specifically, events in the last decade or so have challenged the assumptions of foreign policy theory regarding the domestic setting in two (admittedly rather contradictory) ways.

First, the impact of complex interdependence has made nonsense of the distinction between a domestic and a foreign policy process. Because the foreign policy/domestic policy divide is now much harder to draw, the old assumption that foreign policy involved a much narrower public, with little interest group activity, is clearly inadequate. Interdependence has politicised the foreign policy arena. A similar process is at work in the defence arena, where the rise of a second Cold War, especially when this coincided with INF deployment and the modernisation of the British independent nuclear deterrent, opened up the defence policy arena to an unprecedented degree. Because these developments result in a merging of the domestic and the foreign policy arenas and agendas, the theoretically most powerful models of foreign policy appear to be very outmoded. In this light, the politicisation of foreign and defence issues resulting from interdependence and the changed defence climate has not been assimilated into foreign policy theory.

Yet, this must be set against a second factor, one that pulls in the opposite direction. For, if these areas are increasingly politicised, it remains the case that domestic politics theories of policy-making do *not* readily apply to foreign and defence policy-making. Not only this, but foreign policy theories that focus on the decision as the starting-point for explanation do not appear well suited to the task of explaining technical areas of decision-making. We thus have a curious contrast between a politicised domestic environment on the one hand, and a policy-making process that remains firmly shielded from the hurly-burly of domestic politics on the other. Think for a moment about the way in which policy was made over the issue of the modernisation of the British nuclear deterrent (both Chevaline and Trident), or of the public outburst, but lack of impact, over Cruise missiles. In the former case, decisions were made by small groups within the government, with Parliament having no say at all until the official accouncement of the decisions (or, in the case of Chevaline, no role at all, as the Labour government hid its costs in the defence estimates). In the latter case, the fact that elections are not fought on single issues massively reduced CND's impact on the 1983 and 1987 general elections. Public protest did not affect government policy.

Together these two aspects raise the question of how we comprehend the domestic environment; is it the case that foreign and defence policies are influenced by domestic pressures or are they still carried out far away from the public gaze? How do we conceptualise the linkage between the domestic political process and that of foreign policy? Can foreign policy ever be seen as a political issue in terms of the cleavages involved? Maybe the problem is that foreign and defence policy need to be understood within a class of types of policy arenas, namely those that are essentially technical, have little short-term political effect and are, at the end of the day, relatively unimportant in determining voting patterns. Naturally, there are several different processes at work here, and several of the above points run counter to one another, but the point is that interdependence has shattered the assumptions about the domestic environment's role in foreign policy-making (since it has shattered our very notion of what foreign policy is!) at the same time as activities in the defence policy arena seem to indicate the lack of domestic political impact. This contrast created a serious problem for any attempt to construct theory: what it does, of course, support is middle-range as opposed to general theory.

The impact of bureaucratic politics

We now turn to look at the final three frontier questions, and these are all to do with the major theoretical issues facing the middle-range theories listed previously. The three areas are concerned with the extent to which specific middle-range theories apply to the British case. In other words, what follows is my list of the theoretical questions that I would hope a study of British foreign policy would enable me to answer. Since each refers to a body of literature that has already been discussed, they can be summarised briefly.

The first is the contentious issue of whether, and to what extent, bureaucratic politics or organisational process (implementation) models apply in the British case. Studies of US decision-making can rely on masses of data, and participants who are usually willing to talk about how decisions were made. This is not anything like as common in the British case, and the tradition of secrecy makes it almost impossible to undertake the kind of in-depth study that is necessary for investigating bureaucratic politics types of accounts. But to accept this does not mean that bureaucratic politics or organisational processes are not at work, and in many ways the single most important task that a study of British foreign policy could perform for FPA would be to investigate the phenomena of bureaucratic and organisational politics at a variety of levels within government and over a variety of policy issue-areas. As it stands, we simply do not know the extent to which they operate in the British case. We know the arguments for and against in the case of the United States (and even in the Soviet one!) but we, as FPA theorists, do not know the caveats that must be applied to the findings that come from over the Atlantic.

Although Whitehall is not Washington, does this mean that the dominant alternative foreign policy approach in the US literature is of little or no use in explaining British foreign policy? Not only could such an approach be usefully tested in a series of case studies involving central British 'decisions', or processes of implementation, but the approaches would seem to offer a particularly interesting way of examining the wider notion of foreign policy for a country such as Britain: after all, because British foreign policy is now carried out in a situation of complex interdependence, both parts of the bureaucratic politics paradigm would seem to have considerable explanatory power. One example would be the impact of bureaucratic position within EC negotiations (both for individual ministers and departmental representatives, and for the British Foreign Secretary in his or her role as rotating chair of the Council of Ministers). Do British representatives to EC bodies represent 'Britain' or their departments? Are their allies other British officials from other ministries or the members of corresponding ministries from other countries? Similarly, the implementation perspective, because of its focus on standard operating procedures, seems ideally suited to an examination of the processes of intergovernmental and international decision-making. So, the alternative bureaucratic politics paradigm seems on the surface to be crying out for testing against the British example, precisely because it seems the most appropriate theory for dealing with the kind of foreign policy behaviour found in situations of complex interdependence.

The utility of psychological approaches

There is a wide variety of work to be found in the psychologically based literature of FPA, and much of this could be readily applied to the British case. The frontier questions relate to issues such as whether or not misperception applies to British foreign policy-making (for example, in the case of the Falklands War): whether groupthink explains crisis behaviour in British foreign policy; and what is the impact of 'lessons of the past' on British foreign policy-makers? However, the one aspect of the psychological literature that seems particularly appropriate to the British case is the work on operational codes and belief systems (see, for example, Burgess and Edwards, 1988). Taking the content of this work as given, the fascinating question is to what extent do British foreign policy-makers share an operational code or belief system? Do these apply across generations and across political parties? This is particularly opportune because of the widespread view of the Thatcher administration as being radical in its political outlook: do we, in fact, find that despite differences in ideology, foreign policy operational codes and belief systems tend to be similiar for Conservative and Labour leaders? This, of course, opens up the critical theoretical question of the impact of role on perception and links immediately to work in the area of structural theory. It is also, naturally, important in explaining areas of bipartisanship.

Within FPA there is general agreement that belief systems are important, but there is no real attempt to evaluate when they are important, or the extent to which they are more important than other explanations. An examination of British foreign policy would face these questions in a harsh light since Britain has parts of its foreign policy behaviour that seem to fit psychological theories rather well (military issues, conflict, alliance politics, etc.), yet it also has numerous instances of much more routine foreign policy (economic issues within the EC, aid, trade, etc.). The really difficult question for psychological theories is not so much whether or not they are important, but in what circumstances and in what kinds of issues. Furthermore, what is the relationship between political ideology and operational code? Because of Britain's unique place at the intersection of a set of structural influences, any examination of the impact of psychological accounts in the British case would seem to force an examination of these frontier issues.

Do American theories apply?

Finally, we can point out that one of the most difficult questions for FPA to answer at present is whether or not theories developed in the United States apply to other countries. As has already been noted, virtually all the theories in FPA are American theories, developed within a very specific political system and not necessarily applying to any other. FPA scholars in the United States tend to think that their theories apply universally, but certainly in the FPA community in Britain there is a strong feeling that they do not fit the British political system at all well. If theories do not travel well across the Atlantic this will have enormous consequences for any attempt to build up FPA theory. The reasons why US theories might not apply in Britain are obvious: differences in political system, very different levels of access to information, and different power position and policy agendas. Does this mean that even the research framework of Brecher cannot be used to structure research into British foreign policy? Does the lack of information prohibit the use of theories such as groupthink? Does the policy agenda facing British decision-makers differ so much from that confronting their counterparts in the United States that the same theories cannot explain both? Are the differences between political systems simply too great to allow cumulative theorising?

As someone working within FPA my answer is (naturally) that the transfer is by no means impossible: but this is largely an act of faith on my part since although the US literature is widely used in the teaching of foreign policy (and British foreign policy) courses in Britain, it does not tend to guide research. Rare is the study of British foreign policy that tests an American theory (or, to be more precise, any theory). Of course, testing others' theories is rather boring, and American theories do tend to be framed in a very distinctive methodology, one that is alien to most British international relations academics. The intellectual climates in the two countries are different in important ways. Yet, testing of theories does not exactly dominate the US literature on foreign policy!

Thus, one absolutely frontier question for FPA is exactly whether or not American theories apply to the British case. The other issue this raises is whether middle-range theories explain distinct aspects of foreign policy behaviour; in other words, does the application of the extant theories to the British case reveal a pattern of explanation, with one theory explaining a certain type of foreign policy, another being appropriate to other aspects of foreign policy? As was stated earlier there is no prospect of simply combining middle-range theories to form some overall general theory, but the most fundamental question for an FPA theorist remains that of which theories explain which types of foreign policy behaviour for what kinds of states.

CONCLUSION

This paper started out by reviewing the development of FPA as an approach to studying foreign policy behaviour. It then discussed recent challenges to the traditional notions of what foreign policy consists of. These two sections formed the basis for a discussion of the major problems facing the subject-area of FPA, and nine of these were outlined. My assessment of the difficulties FPA would face in analysing British foreign policy would not be accepted by many in the field and certainly would be seen as unduly pessimistic by many of the leading practitioners of the subject in the United States. Similarly, many more historically inclined scholars in Britain would take such a list of the problems of FPA to be an extremely good example of why the subject is of limited utility in explaining foreign policy behaviour.

However, I want to make it very clear that my concern has been to try to highlight the difficulties FPA faces in explaining the foreign policy of a country such as Britain. I have done this for three reasons: first, although many FPA true-believers would try to play down the problems, preferring instead to concentrate on the achievements and thereby imply that the best way to study British foreign policy is via the FPA route, my inclination is that academic enquiry proceeds more fruitfully if academics are explicit about the shortcomings of their subject. Secondly, it is crucial to the purpose of this paper that I make explicit my belief that other approaches to studying foreign policy suffer from an essentially similar set of difficulties to those I have discussed above. The only difference is that those difficulties are virtually always hidden, either by statistical overload or by historical detail.

Put simply, it is my view that the study of foreign policy in an era of complex interdependence is fundamentally problematic. The range of activities included, the levels of governmental behaviour involved and the structural influences on the perceptions of those making the decisions are considerable. Neither the general systems theorist nor the historian can avoid these problems even if they pretend that they do not exist, that their account is focused on factors that are 'simpler' to study. The final reason for presenting the areas of foreign policy that FPA finds difficult to explain is that it is my belief that middle-range theories offer the most fruitful way of studying the foreign policy of a country such as Britain. This is because general theories cannot capture the complexities of Britain's foreign policy and because historical accounts cannot build up cumulative findings unless they rely on implicit theoretical structures. Precisely because the list of problems facing the study of British foreign policy indicates the vast number of factors that need to be taken into account and the very different types of behaviour subsumed under the term foreign policy, middle-range theories seem the most fruitful way of generating explanations of that behaviour. These middle-range theories do not take one definition of the content of foreign policy, they relate to different aspects of the decision-making system, and can thereby capture the variety of actors and behaviour involved in the foreign policy of a power caught up in a web of complex interdependence.

Therefore, from a theoretical perspective the study of British foreign policy should enable us to answer two questions: first, are there regularities in British foreign policy behaviour, and if so how do we explain them? Second, how useful are the theories developed within the FPA literature? Each of these leads off to several other secondary lines of enquiry, but for an FPA scholar they are the critical questions. Britain is actually a particularly interesting state for a foreign policy scholar since it occupies a unique situation in the international system (a former great power, highly interdependent, especially with the EC, having a special relationship with the United States and possessing an independent nuclear deterrent).

The most important task facing FPA given the relative lack of cumulative work generally, and virtual absence of it in the case of Britain, is the use of case studies to test the extant theories. These case studies would allow us to assess the adequacy of foreign policy theory, but they should also provide some answers to the enduring question of whether or not there are regularities in British foreign policy. Is British foreign policy really made on a pragmatic basis or does the sum total of discrete decisions result in a pattern of behaviour, with identifiable causal relationships operating outside the perceptions of those involved?

This paper has outlined where FPA is, and has indicated the areas that FPA finds it difficult to explain. These difficulties will pervade all attempts to offer explanations of British foreign policy even if (especially if?) they are dismissed as irrelevant. Within foreign policy studies, general theory is dead and historical case studies stressing the unique cannot lead to an explanation of the patterns that FPA theorists believe are inherent in foreign policy. Outside foreign policy studies, general theories of international relations and theories of domestic politics each have difficulties in explaining both the detail of foreign policy and its formation within a powerful set of structural constraints. Foreign policy, after all, puts us firmly within the agent–structure debate, and adds to this issues concerning the impact of system structure on unit behaviour, the link between economics and politics, and the blurring of the boundaries between domestic and international politics. For these reasons, middle-range theories seem to be the most promising route forward for the study of foreign policy, and the study of British foreign policy is no exception.

4 ～ *Defence and security in Britain's external relations*

Michael Clarke

Britain finds itself at the forefront of a series of dramatic security and defence arguments in the 1990s. All states in the West are facing some dramatic reappraisals of their security environment, but in Britain's case, its strategic position in the Atlantic Alliance, both geographically and politically, puts it in a more acute position than most. At any given time in the last forty years, of course, Britain could be said to have been facing major defence choices: the future is uncertain and security policy is notoriously full of new issues. Nevertheless, in the 1990s the Western world is clearly facing a series of issues which are 'new' in a deeper and more conceptual sense. The security environment is in process of major change in both empirical and perceptual senses and this will have to be addressed not only by policy-makers concerned to implement national policy, but also by theoreticians of security relations, if they are to understand the nature of the security environment into which we are moving.

This chapter, therefore, seeks to locate questions about Britain's security not just within a changing international environment but also in a changing intellectual framework within which the nature of military security issues are normally addressed. The first section attempts to define the ways in which this framework appears to be changing. The second section looks at the changing nature of the international security environment that is most relevant to Britain. The final section considers the conceptual and empirical implications of such changes for the choices that British policy-makers face.

THE INTELLECTUAL FRAMEWORK OF SECURITY STUDIES IN THE 1990S

Strategic Studies has become the conceptual home for most aspects of the study of the defence of nations and their security problems, and it has invested them with its own premises and assumptions. Like many sub-disciplines within the field of Politics, Strategic Studies has developed a separate identity over the last forty years that has created for it both a degree of specialism and also a certain isolation from other areas of the discipline. In this, it is hardly unique, and shares with sub-disciplines such as Political Economy and Comparative Politics all the virtues and vices of a well-developed specialism. Like them, it is now under pressure to become more interdisciplinary as it tries to accommodate the scope and depth of the major empirical changes that are taking place, particularly in the politics of the East and West developed worlds. It is, therefore, a commonplace observation that Strategic Studies is in something of a transition, though many writers are not very precise about the nature of such a movement. It involves more than merely an awareness that the Cold War and the nuclear stalemate appear to be steeply declining forces in world politics. In essence, Strategic Studies is changing, not because the prevailing paradigm that has shaped the sub-discipline is being replaced, but rather because it is being more completely explored, and now shares the perceptual stage with other paradigmatic frameworks.

The prevailing paradigm of Strategic Studies is a realist one: world politics are determined essentially by relations between states, and the security arrangements between states are fundamental to global, and individual, safety. The structure of interstate relations, the hierarchy of powers, and in particular, the way in which they dispose of their physical capacities, therefore, are the keys to a realist explanation of the nature of international security. The realist does not take a necessarily crude view of the complexities of International Relations: there is immense scope in the realist paradigm to account for domestic pressures, the forces of inter-dependence, the increasing role of international organisations or the imperatives of global management. What gives realism its distinguishing characteristic is the belief that forces such as these only exist because the structure of relations between the most physically powerful and salient states allow it (Waltz, 1979; Bull, 1977). Such an assumption is common to realist writings that span several academic generations. A good recent attempt, for example, to encompass the nature of 'changing issue-areas' as they apply to 'international security policies' is instructive, for in it the authors (Hopple and Gathright, 1987) are keen to be interdisciplinary but still try to explain themselves by reference to the policies of the major powers in so far as they affect the security of lesser states. In this view, therefore, the international hierarchy is, at the very least, a permissive condition for the existence of other political phenomena. Since so much of the post-war theorising in International Relations has originated in the United States, where foreign policy has been dominated by the Cold War, the characteristics of realism and the attachment of the majority of writers to it are perhaps not surprising (Smith, 1985c).

Strategic Studies has been a rather precise application of realism: a development of the paradigm which created a framework that was both elegant and significant. It was elegant because it established key concepts such as deterrence, disarmament, arms control, arms racing, defence and proliferation (Buzan, 1987) and elaborated them in relation to each other as part of a central scheme – the achievement of armed stability in a world of inherent instability. Indeed, nuclear deterrence provides one of the best examples of a concept that has lent itself to the development of an elegant formal theory of international interactions derived from mathematically based game theories (Nicholson, 1989, pp. 88–93). It was significant because it has provided a political rationale for nuclear defence policies that has proved consistently persuasive. Strategic Studies is concerned with much more than the role of nuclear weapons. But its political significance and its undoubted relevance to modern society has nevertheless been based to a very large extent on the way in which the study has shaped the public perception of the utility of nuclear technologies (Freedman, 1985, p. 30).

The problem for Strategic Studies, and the grounds chiefly upon which it is now being roundly criticised, is that having established a series of key political concepts – most prominent among them that of deterrence – it has elaborated them in a mechanistic way (Tunander, 1989; Booth, 1990). It has become a baroque form of military studies rather than a creative form of political thinking (Prins, 1983; Dando and Rogers, 1984). There is much substance in this criticism. During the 1960s Strategic Studies – certainly in the field of nuclear deterrence – was driven by predominantly American thinking which gave little or no credence to the cultural or historical context in which deterrence was perceived to exist. The concept of nuclear deterrence upon which the West relied, was developed by academics who knew very little about the Soviet Union, and used, without qualification, to justify defence policies by leaders who seemed to care even less (McNamara, 1987). During the 1970s, however, the bipolar structure of the Cold War began to change and the tasks that deterrence was called upon to perform came to seem infinitely more complicated, while new and elaborate weapons systems became available for the delivery of nuclear devices (Freedman, 1981). During these years the concept of deterrence was invoked to justify increasingly tortured defence policy arguments that were often simply contradictory, mere assertions, or both (Finnis et al., 1987; Halperin, 1987).

Many developments have occurred in the last decade to challenge the conceptual blandness into which Strategic Studies had fallen. The domestic politicisation of defence policies that broke the prevailing consensus over nuclear weapons in Western societies stimulated many radical critiques of

Strategic Studies: during the last decade the United States has been repeatedly reminded of the limits to the political utility of military force and has begun to take a more particular view of the applicability of nuclear deterrence doctrines; above all, the nature of the Cold War has changed fundamentally since the advent of economic and political reform in the socialist bloc and the collapse of the authority of communist parties throughout the socialist world. The perception of 'the threat' itself, so central to the justification of deterrent logic, and so seldom specified, has been reappraised since the late 1980s so that it is now regarded in more specific, and limited, terms. In the face of such challenges the more glib expressions of the logic of nuclear deterrence have proved to be simply unsustainable, even in the domestic political arena (Roberts, 1987).

The result of all this has not been that Strategic Studies has ceased to be realist. Rather, it has begun to extend its scope within the realist paradigm: to explore the broader political implications of its attempts to engender security in a fundamentally state-centric and insecure world. For more than thirty years perceptive strategists have understood the importance of integrating the political context properly into the study of strategy's key concepts, but in practice the subject became stultified under the weight of the increasing amount of empirical data which confronted it (Howard, 1989). It became a private and exciting – not to mention well-funded – language which lost touch with the wiser realist perceptions of some of its founders.

The so-called new approaches of recent years, therefore, are, in effect, a return to some older insights (Nye, 1989). The ethnocentrism of Strategic Studies has been well addressed (Booth, 1979; Segal, 1984). No good realist, for instance, should continue to assume that strategic decision-making in the Soviet Union is simply a mirror image of the United States, even if the theoretical elaborations of deterrence require that this be regarded as the case. The process of arms control should not be interpreted in as 'mechanistic' and 'incremental' a way as it has been (Sheehan, 1988, p. 163). Arms control is not simply a process which tries to put a brake on the arms race. It is a thoroughly political phenomenon which reflects the nature of the security order at any given moment (Freedman, 1986, p. 70). And since the conclusion of the Intermediate Nuclear Forces Treaty in December 1987 the political scope of arms control has increased dramatically to encompass conventional forces, confidence-building measures, the discussion of strategic plans, and has served as the focal point for some unprecedentedly flexible thinking about the nature of future security arrangements in Europe. Similarly, the good realist will want to review all the possible circumstances that make for security in a particular context and accord nuclear (and non-nuclear) deterrence its appropriate place. Only the unreconstituted strategist, or the politician, would claim that 'nuclear deterrence has kept the peace in Europe since 1945' (Clarke and Mowlam, 1982, p. 22). There are many probable reasons for the peace in Europe: the good strategist is keen to investigate the relationships between them. Even if deterrence is a necessary condition of East–West stability, it is certainly not a sufficient one. None of these issues would seem strange to an older generation of post-war realists who took up strategy in the 1950s, though they are apparently being addressed as new issues by many of a younger generation of strategists who took up realism in the 1980s.

The second major change in the security paradigm is that while realism is being explored more honestly, it coexists with other paradigms that bear on security issues in a situation of much greater conceptual pluralism. This should not be characterised merely as a competition between paradigms, as between, say, a liberal and a marxist view of the world. The discipline of International Relations is no longer a battleground between paradigms; it has become a rather more mature arena in which several exist together.

For Strategic Studies this has encouraged a particular sort of reappraisal. Strategists have been faced with a number of different perspectives which have not replaced the realist paradigm but rather have indicated the limitations in its explanatory power. The most obvious reappraisal is that the state-centric model of security structures does not seem to be as universally applicable as it was even twenty years ago. A realist, state-centric, paradigm may still provide an adequate explanation for the nature of international security as it exists in Southern Africa, or in South American or the Indian sub-continent. It provides a much less satisfactory explanation for the nature of contemporary security in Europe. Realism may explain why NATO, for example, has remained an alliance of sovereign nations with all that implies, and it accounts for a good many of NATO's operational inefficiencies. States enter alliances of their own free will and may leave them in the same way. The realist paradigm can certainly explain the existence of a highly complex alliance such as NATO. It does not, however, explain very well how European defence industries come to be on the verge of wholesale international mergers: or how governments have found their procurement budgets to be the single biggest item of government support to key domestic industries. Western governments take what may be wholly rational defence decisions given the international, economic and social pressures that they are under. Such decisions, however, embody a mixture of motives in which the short-term pressures will tend to dominate. Sensible political decisions, therefore, though good responses to a range of different pressures, may make little strategic or military sense in themselves and certainly cannot be wholly explained as if they were realist strategic responses to the challenges posed by the international environment.

Similarly, both domestic and global threats to security raise further doubts about the explanatory power of state-centric realism. It cannot easily account for the threats to security posed by terrorism, organised international crime or civil violence, still less the threats to physical and perceptual well-being posed by global environmental problems. The late 1980s witnessed a belated recognition of the power of essentially non-military threats to global and individual security. Ecological breakdown is regarded by some writers as a potent cause of immediate physical insecurity on a global scale (McKibben, 1989; Timberlake, 1988; Newsome, 1989). Other writers see ecological and environmental problems becoming the source of more particular instabilities, straining the fabric of existing domestic and international political institutions. Only about 0.5 per cent of the earth's water is available for human needs, for example: demand for it is in the process of doubling over a twenty-year period, and the fact remains that rivers such as the Danube flow through twelve states, the Niger through ten, the Zambezi and the Rhine through eight each, and so on (Walker, n.d.; Myers, 1989). Other studies have examined international crime and domestic disorder as potent sources of threats to the physical and psychological well-being of modern societies (Dziedzic, 1989; Safer World Project, 1990; Renner, 1989).

If Strategic Studies is defined broadly as a sub-discipline that is concerned with the physical and psychological security of political communities – the well-being of citizens – then it must also try to take account of the essentially non-military and non-state threats to such security that are being recognised in the 1990s. If, on the other hand, the strategist would argue that the subject is only and properly concerned with specifically military relations between states, then we must accept that the focus of Strategic Studies is on only one type of physical security, the universal applicability of which must now be in doubt. As Buzan (1983, p. 245) has pointed out, 'The concept of security binds together individuals, states and the international system so closely that it demands to be treated in a holistic perspective.'

Another limitation on the applicability of realism has been exposed by the paradigms that support the study of Political Economy. Few would deny that economic well-being is a fundamental component of physical, and perhaps even more of psychological, security. Indeed, economic security was identified by Morgenthau in his archetypical realist work (1948) as an essential part of a state's national interest. But if this was a commonplace observation, the implications of it were not properly recognised. Realism drew all the intellectual sustenance it needed from the politico-military aspects of the Cold War, and International Political Economy went its own, somewhat neglected, way for more than twenty years. It was not until the economic crises of the 1970s that International Political Economy became fashionable again with the recognition that it was as much a part of 'security' as was Strategic Studies. Yet International Political Economy is inherently less state-centric than Strategic Studies. In the inventive conception of Susan Strange (1988), the world economy is characterised by 'primary structures' – security, finance, production and knowledge – and 'secondary structures' – transport, trade, energy and welfare – all of which have to be approached from an essentially holistic perspective. Thus if one of the purposes of 'security' is to engender favourable conditions in this matrix of structures, then Strategic Studies must be prepared to encompass the methods by which some of these matrices are maintained. It is not sufficient for the strategist merely to uphold a realist position that interstate security relations provide the overarching, permissive framework for the evolution of other structures. As Strange demonstrates, the security structure is no more 'primary' than any of the others to which it is intimately connected. Buzan (1983) points out that whatever paradigm is adopted by the Political Economist (and he contrasts mercantilist with liberal economic paradigms) will create 'quite different international environments for national security' (p. 149). And Kennedy (1989) makes a powerful case for a somewhat determinist view that security structures are a function of the international political economy. Different economic paradigms, in other words, make varying assumptions about the role of the state in national and international economic behaviour, and about the political methods that characterise the management of economic systems that are perceived to be Marxist, Liberal, Mercantilist, Structuralist, or whatever. Very few Political Economists would regard the realist paradigm – even in the sophisticated formulations of Manning (1962), Bull (1977) or Wight (1986) – as a satisfactory device to explain the nature of *contemporary* international political economy. And even the wise strategic realist cannot escape the necessity of choosing an economic paradigm with which to interpret this vital component of peace and security.

None of this means that Strategic Studies is likely to go out of business. As Freedman (1981, p. 399) commented some time ago in reviewing arguments about nuclear deterrence, 'The Emperor Deterrence may have no clothes, but he is still Emperor.' More specifically, the existential nature of deterrence in the East–West context – the nature of 'general deterrence'

– may, like the music of Tchaikovsky, be better than it sounds. The central concepts of Strategy are still valid, even where their applicability is disputed. Our purpose here is to point to a growing recognition in the field of Strategic Studies that good strategists have to be good realists within their own paradigm *and* conceptual pluralists in their contemplation of the basic concerns of the subject. As Britain faces the world of the 1990s it is, of course, easier to recognise the need for more inventive political thinking than to do it.

THE NATURE OF BRITAIN'S SECURITY ENVIRONMENT

Though the arguments outlined above may seem somewhat arcane, they are a vital component in any understanding of Britain's future security. The shifts we have noted are responses both to changing academic mores and to rapid and frankly astonishing developments in the empirical world in which policy-makers have to exist. Though it is tempting for policy-makers to claim that their focus is strictly pragmatic, or for some strategists to claim that they merely adopt a positivist approach, the fact remains, in the words of Nye (1989), that 'In the long term sound security policy must rest upon sound theoretical work.'

In this respect it is important to try to interpret Britain's current security environment at domestic, national and international levels, and in a way that is able to range across a number of sub-disciplines in the study of politics. For in looking at 'environmental' forces we are interested not so much in the current issues that defence policies have to face, which are normally a mixture of old and new problems, but rather at those developments which affect the processes by which security arrangements are arrived at.

On the face of it there is much in Britain's security environment for which the pragmatist, and the positivist, should be grateful. There is a great deal in the picture of the 1990s that the analyst can recognise from the 1960s, or even the 1940s, and the familiarity of it is a force for genuine political stability. In the superpower and European contexts, the Western world, and in particular the Atlantic Alliance, continue to succeed in safeguarding the security of the Liberal Democracies (and some not-so-liberal democracies). Indeed, the longevity and casual vitality of the Anglo-Saxon world order that was established in 1945 have been remarkable and still retain a deep-seated place in British political culture (Wallace, 1986, p. 373). If the Western world is now troubled by domestic dissent over security issues, this is a symptom of its essential success. Indeed, there is nothing new about political dissent in Europe over security questions.

Whether or not it can be successfully accommodated it is at least not difficult to understand: it poses few conceptual problems. Outside the superpower and European contexts there is no shortage of threats to international or collective security: wars in the Middle East, civil violence in Asia, undeclared wars in Africa, and so on. Again, such threats may or may not be regarded as serious in Britain's security environment, but they do not pose great conceptual challenges either. A wise realist will understand the mixture of domestic, economic and international pressures that produce such threats.

It is, however, possible to define at least three major trends that seem to run counter to the elements of continuity in Britain's security environment. All of these trends pose conceptual – in some cases, paradigmatic – challenges.

The first is that the purpose for which NATO was established is now in question. This is not to say that the Soviet threat has disappeared. On the other hand, few would deny that its nature appears to be changing perhaps in a quite fundamental way. There is a great deal of empirical writing on this emergent phenomenon, though rather less consideration of its implications for the application of Strategy (Herspring, 1989). In traditional realist thinking NATO's objective was to act as a deterrent to war. It did this in both a conventional and a nuclear sense. The existence of a deterrent presupposes a threat (MccGwire, 1986). In this case it was based on a clear perception that to deter war the West had to deter Soviet aggression. Without the deterrent that NATO constituted, the Soviet Union was thought to be considerably more likely to launch an aggressive war against the West. The conviction that there was something to deter was based on two mutually reinforcing realist assumptions: that the Soviet Union was a threat because it was communist; and that it was a threat because it was a great power next to smaller ones. Gorbachev has not altered either of these facts, of course, but he has changed the West's perception of their implications. It is difficult now to sustain the view that the Soviet Union has aggressive intentions towards Western Europe. On the other hand, there is a realistic fear that the Soviet Union could still behave aggressively through mismanagement, irrationality, domestic instability, or a catastrophic breakdown in the norms of the security system that have evolved in Europe over the last forty years.

In this respect, the nature of the threat may be changing more than it appears. As Michael Howard, among many others, has commented (1986), the threat is not the Soviet Union as such, whose intentions indicate a long-standing acceptance of the status quo in relation to Western Europe, but rather any scenario in Europe that would seriously disturb such acceptance. The threat is systemic rather than specific: the danger is war through political breakdown rather than through Soviet aggression. If this is the case, then the question arises as to whether deterrence – nuclear or conventional – is likely to ameliorate or exacerbate the systemic threat. There is already some discussion on what this might imply for the concept of deterrence. It is possible to argue, for instance, that 'general deterrence' can help to uphold systemic stability – the mere knowledge that great care is required in all dealings within the system – whereas 'immediate deterrence', by definition, is invoked in an attempt to affect a state's behaviour over a single issue. It is thus likely to create tension and possibly instability (Freedman, 1989a; Downs, 1989).

But if this is a valuable insight there is little discussion about the broader political implications of such reappraisals. How should NATO continue to pursue its objective of deterring war? If 'general' and 'immediate' deterrence work in opposite directions then NATO ought to concentrate on policies and deployments that increase the former and eliminate the latter. This conceptual distinction, however, is very difficult to apply in practice, and if it can be applied, then almost certainly has to be done co-operatively by all the major members of the security system in question.

In other words, NATO has to do rather more than absorb the empirical developments taking place in the communist bloc, or look for more of the security we have previously had, but now at lower levels of armaments. It has to consider the most primary strategic question: what does the West regard as 'security', and what now are the major threats to it? As the Cold War has declined there is no longer a clear perception of what NATO's deterrence is supposed to deter. If we continue to believe in the primacy of a state-centric, Soviet threat for the forseeable future, then it is easy to grasp and relatively easy to deter. If, however, we are moving towards the proposition that the threat is a more systemic one, then we have to consider the intellectual framework through which we define the system (Booth, 1990). If a framework based on a systemic concept of security is significantly less state-centric than the existing one, then even the notion of general deterrence may seem inappropriate to the maintenance of security in such a situation.

This leads to the second conceptual question. To what extent *does* the Atlantic Alliance, and in particular its existence as a component of East and West European politics, constitute a security system that is no longer satisfactorily explainable through the realist paradigm? In particular, have the actors and the political processes by which European security has traditionally been secured begun to change? After a decade in which the momentum of political change in both East and West Europe appears to have accelerated dramatically, it is appropriate to wonder whether a qualitative threshold may have been crossed which may have changed the nature of European 'security politics' in general. It would be foolhardy to try to offer definitive answers to such questions, but there are a number of intriguing developments which add credence to claims that a significantly less state-centric and military approach is required to explain the evolving political processes of the present security system.

In fact, we are faced with an interesting hybrid, full of contradictory forces. We can define the 'European security system' as consisting of three political arenas: the intra-West arena; the intra-East arena, and that between East and West. There is also a fourth arena in the sense that Europe – particularly the Western nations – have security interests outside the continent. Though out-of-area considerations may not be regarded as intrinsic to the nature of the security system itself, it is at least arguable that they will loom much larger in the security environment of the West than they have done for a number of years and certainly have the potential to affect security within the various European arenas.

In the intra-East arena the realist paradigm seems to explain quite a lot and may, indeed, be coming more into its own as the ties loosen between the members of the socialist commonwealth. Almost half a century of domination and attempts to impose integration from Moscow have brought the socialist commonwealth in general to the verge of disintegration. The new expressions of nationalism – never in any case far from the surface – have become the demarcation lines between the security of one part of the commonwealth and another, whether they be East European nations or regions within the Soviet Union itself. Indeed, even before the communist revolutions of 1989 it was clear that Moscow's attempts to impose integration on Eastern Europe had the opposite effect: in having no choice but to accept the hierarchy of coercive power controlled by the Soviet Union, Eastern European governments were generally quite clear about the threats to their state's security. They were caught between internal subversion and Soviet intervention. As the Polish declaration of martial law in 1981 so clearly demonstrated, the prospects of a Soviet invasion of the country were regarded as the ultimate threat to Polish security, however bad the crisis of the Communist Party had become. There can be little doubt that East European politics, notwithstanding forty years of marxist ideology, conform ever more closely to realism as Eastern bloc states reassess their futures in more genuinely independent ways.

The intra-West arena, by contrast, where the sovereignty of states has not been subject to coercion, is characterised by the most powerful forms of interdependence which question the validity of the realist paradigm. There can be little doubt that economic and social relations between the West European states are primarily concerned with the management of complex interdependence. This phenomenon is increasing and affects domestic society in Western Europe in major ways: in matters of employment, inward investment, in the agenda of domestic political debate, and so on. Such developments cannot help but have an effect on security politics within the West (Tugendhat and Wallace, 1988; Wallace, 1986). For in the first place, a system of complex interdependence increases the vulnerability of all the units within it; states, companies, international organisations, or private groups. Many of the ultimate objectives for which states have traditionally pursued physical security, therefore – the supply of materials, markets, closer political or cultural contact, independence of national decision-making, even greater degrees of political freedom or social justice – are not now usually facilitated by military security, even at a multinational level. Even greater fulfilment of such objectives often *can* be obtained, however, through co-operative management policies undertaken by state and non-state actors in the system. Secondly, in conditions of complex interdependence national policy-makers have less control over the domestic infrastructure which underpins their defence policies, and other non-state actors may be more influential in shaping defence priorities in a situation where all have a primary interest in maintaining the complex structure (Moravesik, 1990). Certain trends are irresistible. By the mid-1990s, for example, it is likely that there will be only two or three major electronics companies in Western Europe. The Anglo-German GEC/Siemens conglomerate will probably be one of them: Ferranti, Marconi or Racal may well not be. High-tech defence industries have to collaborate, or merge, to survive. Any one set of national priorities on what or how they should produce can, therefore, only be one among a number of other national, transnational, international and domestic priorities.

Defence and security is not a nonsense in these conditions: indeed NATO members have clung tenaciously to the sovereign parts of their defence policies, namely, the command of their own armed forces in their own way. They have maintained control over the 'teeth' of their defences. But they have lost direct control over the infrastructure that supports the sovereign parts. It may nevertheless continue to support them, but if it does it will do so because it is being managed by more than one state and more than one type of actor, probably operating in more than one security arena at once.

In the East–West arena, that most crucial layer of the European security system, it is clear that there are elements of both state-centric realist behaviour and of interdependent system-maintenance behaviour. What is remarkable is the degree to which the latter has developed in so short a time. The interdependence of the West has spawned a great edifice of overlapping international and transnational Western institutions as part of its attempts to manage the structure. Until recently, there has been a reasonably clear functional division between those institutions concerned with security issues and those concerned with economic, social and domestic matters. Two developments, however, have changed the picture. The functional division between types of institutions has begun to melt away as the West tries to manage the ever-more interdependent infra- structure of defence: a European pillar in NATO is necessary partly to meet the high-tech challenge from the United States; European weapons collabo- ration is vital to keep key industries alive; the European Community cannot go much further until it confronts foreign and security issues more squarely; and so on. Secondly, both the European neutrals and the Eastern European states cannot afford to be left out of the evolving structures that seek to manage European interdependence, and some of them are looking to move more deeply into the network.

This threatens to have profound effects on the way in which East–West relations in Europe are conducted. If Austria joins the European Commu- nity after 1992, and if Sweden, Hungary, Czechoslovakia, Yugoslavia and the GDR establish closer institutional relations with it; if Switzerland and Norway continue to shadow many EC policies; if some sort of European pillar emerges within a more loosely structured NATO; above all, if German reunification becomes a reality during the 1990s, then both the style and substance of East–West relations in Europe would be rather different from anything presently envisaged. Both East and West Europe have different, but powerful, economic motives to establish better com- mercial and financial relations. If détente in the 1990s involves economic as much as arms negotiation, then it is inconceivable that economic exchanges could take place on the essentially bilateral basis of the 1970s. Western Europe is now a multilateral economic entity and meaningful discussions about anything more than the small change of international trade would have to be both multilateral and multilevel – in a word, systemic. Western governments would have to integrate security and economic decision- making to a far greater extent than at any time since 1945, and it would be difficult to restrict the process to a predominantly state-to-state nego- tiation.

There is some prospect, in other words, that East–West relations in Europe may be characterised by an extended attempt to manage inter- dependence on a wider scale. If the realists reflect that all this is conceivable only because Gorbachev wills it, they might note that Gorbachev seems to be of the opinion that the Soviet Union has no other manageable choices. If the pragmatists are sceptical at this scenario, they might recall how complex is the present structure of interdependence within the West and how rapidly it developed after 1974. There is, in short, every possibility that a significant degree of interdependence could develop between East and West in Europe, alongside more traditional patterns of interstate relations. Western politicians would have to try to adapt the lessons they have learned over the last two decades about the management of inter-dependence to a situation in which few could ever have thought it would apply. And strategists will have to reappraise what they mean by 'security' in the European context and how it might be maintained.

A third major conceptual question concerns the institutional structures of Western security. Again, the picture is a hybrid one which requires explanation by reference to more than one paradigm. Western world politics, and especially Western European politics, are noted for their extensive institutional architecture. They present a highly multilateralist structure of international relations, characterised by institutions and institutional behaviour which consults, influences, co-ordinates and, in some cases, integrates the policies of Western states. But this unique institutional architecture has also stimulated more intensive bilateral relations between states. Wallace (1984, pp. 12–14) has pointed out how West European multilateral relations feed into the substance of bilateral relations, and vice versa, so that there are, in fact, very few purely bilateral or multilateral issues on the political agenda. Most are a mixture of the two.

The intensity of political interaction between members – particularly European members – of the Western Alliance has increased at all levels. This confounds alike the expectations of both utopian integrationists, who assumed that state-centric politics would inevitably be transcended, and old-fashioned realists, who assumed that none of the fundamentals had changed. In fact, it seems that as the force of superpower bipolarity in East–West politics has diminished, so it has been replaced by a structure of political interactions that is both old and new and far more intense. Issues that were hardly the concern of national government thirty years ago, such as the harmonisation of legal frameworks, the technical detail of industrial collaboration, or the administration of immigration and emigration, are as much a part of the political agenda as the major issues of East–West diplomacy. And issues that were not politicised even fifteen years ago, such as environmental, health or narcotics issues, are vehicles of collaboration across national and ideological boundaries.

For the analyst who is concerned to examine the nature of Britain's security environment in Europe this sort of hybrid poses difficult definitional questions. One of the major features of the political landscape of the Western Alliance, for example, is the growing importance of Franco-German relations in security and economic matters, and to a lesser extent, of Franco-British and German-British relations (Wallace, 1989). Patterns of bilateral and trilateral relations between the most significant European members of NATO have assumed increased significance as the attitude of the United States to European defence has begun to change. It is not wrong, therefore, to define Western Europe as an interstate security arrangement. Similarly, in terms of Soviet bloc relations, there is an argument which maintains that as bipolarity diminishes in Europe it will reveal, like 'receding flood-waters', the pattern of an older political landscape; 'Mitteleuropa is beginning to be discerned' (Powell, 1987). The pattern of bilateral relations that will affect 'Mitteleuropa', if indeed it does emerge from receding bipolarity and the growing influence of neutral states, would also validate a traditional definition of interstate security.

On the other hand, the unique institutional architecture of Europe cannot be ignored. Nor should we ignore its effects on the way in which the political agenda is arranged, or on the way in which the institutional architecture elevates non-state actors such as financial companies, multi-nationals, regulatory bodies or international secretariats to positions of power over the agenda. If the diplomatic channels represented by a 'Paris–Bonn Axis' or a 'Mitteleuropa' look familiar, it is nevertheless the case that the contents of such diplomatic channels are very new and extraordinarily intense; and they are overlaid by international institutions of a depth and scope that is historically unprecedented.

Taken together, these three general trends, contradictory as they are, constitute potentially major changes in the purposes, the processes and the political structures of the East–West security system that is the centrepiece of Britain's security environment. If they seem evolutionary, even tentative, they nevertheless embody a requirement that we be prepared to think both inside and outside the realist paradigm if we are to appreciate the way in which they might influence Britain's security future.

BRITISH SECURITY IN THE 1990S

When attempting to consider some of the more obvious implications of changes in what we have described as the 'security paradigm' and Britain's 'security environment', we should be clear that we are not trying to offer a 'policy agenda for the 1990s' to the defence establishment. Instead, this is a more speculative exercise which attempts, rather, to offer a conceptual agenda for the 1990s to the academic observer. Four particular implications are of interest, all of which are a combination of empirical and conceptual issues and which draw from different paradigms.

The first implication is that there are major political choices, as opposed to management choices, to be made for anyone who is responsible for the security of Britain in the 1990s: choices that are wider, even, than questions of guns or butter. 'For years', says Coker (1987, p. 7), 'we have deluded ourselves that the defence debate was non-political when it was merely non-partisan.' This is undoubtedly true. The bipartisan consensus did not disagree about the threat, the need for Western unity, or the means by which it should be secured. And it was all shored up by a doctrine of nuclear deterrence that passed itself off as an expression of logic rather than a political judgement. All of these old certainties have been challenged in the last decade as the perceptual and empirical context of Britain's security situation has been reappraised.

Students of British defence policy have not been slow to appreciate the fact that defence policy is coming under strain from several directions, and as a result some of the major compromises that have underlain the policy for two generations are back on the top of the agenda as important choices. As Baylis observes (1989), in a period of economic stringency and rapid political change, the government has again to face important choices between maintaining a 'continental commitment' as against a 'maritime strategy', an 'Atlantic' as opposed to a more 'European' orientation, and it has to reappraise the strength of the 'special relationship' with the United States in terms of other bilateral and trilateral arrangements between the allies. Such issues do, indeed, appear to go to the heart of current British defence policy. But all of these issues derive from a framework of security thinking that we have defined as being under major challenge. Indeed, the developments of 1989 in Eastern Europe, developments in arms control since 1987, and reappraisals of United States defence policy, already suggest that such questions may no longer be fundamental enough.

It is not too much to say that Britain is confronted with a choice of alternative visions of its security that transcend some of the more basic security questions that have hitherto been asked. One vision of Britain's future security is a continuation of the existing order; a united West in a divided and still essentially bipolar Europe, continuing to deter a threat in some way, though hoping to do so at the lowest possible levels of armaments. A second, alternative vision is that bipolar Europe is super-seded by a more reunited, and independent Europe, where antagonistic barriers between East and West have disappeared, even if economic barriers remain, and in which both superpowers have an essentially non-military involvement: something rather akin to Gorbachev's vision of a 'common European home' (Malcolm, 1989). A more elaborate alternative would be a Europe that has superseded the bipolar structure entirely to develop a high degree of functional unity as it manages the forces of interdependence, which involves each superpower in its various management structures and is, in turn, involved in other such networks in which the superpowers are involved around the world. These three visions of future security are in themselves very diverse, yet take no account of security arrangements outside the developed world, still less do they address overtly idealistic alternative security formulations such as attempts to generate peace and stability through the promotion of economic development and social justice on a global scale.

Nevertheless, even this range of three alternatives demands a degree of conscious political choice – that is, at least a clear preference for one as opposed to another – on a scale that is anathema to most Western politicians. It is simply not possible to keep all the major options open and approach them with an old-style prudent incrementalism. To adopt the first alternative – an essential continuation of the status quo – may well militate against the achievement of the other two. It may be logically impossible to slide from a bipolar Europe predicated on military power, in particular on a mutual nuclear deterrent, towards a more united continent that is not characterised by military force or the perception of a need to deter. For mutual deterrents are presumably based on prior conceptions of threat. And yet they also create a mutual threat in themselves: there is an element of self-fulfilling prophecy about them. Unless the credibility of both deterrents simply collapsed quickly and spontaneously, or unless they can be negotiated away in one grand package, it is difficult to see how nuclear deterrence in Europe could fade away in a process of gentle transition. At best, European deterrence could perhaps become ritualised until it is perceived to be superfluous, but even then, a deterrent structure is not likely to be dismantled incrementally (Windass, 1985).

To judge by the trend of recent offficial British government statements, of course, there is no desire in the defence establishment to move towards radical alternatives to the bipolar status quo (HMSO, 1989, p. 1). The defence establishment is rather comfortable with the prospects of an essential continuation of the present situation, since, for Britain at least, it has worked rather well (Croft, 1989, p. 23). In particular, there is no serious questioning in official circles that Britain should remain an independent nuclear power if at all possible. Given that the peak expenditures on the Trident replacement for the Polaris system have already, in 1990, begun to be incurred, there is a sense in which Britain has already made a clear and irrevocable choice to remain a nuclear power. But this decision is based upon the implicit assumption that the major determining factor is whether or not a state can afford the expense of an independent deterrent. If it chooses to spend its money in this way then it has purchased a further range of options against the uncertainties of the future. But our discussion of the major trends in Britain's security environment suggests that the continuation of an independent nuclear deterrent may be more notable in foreclosing major political options rather than in opening relatively marginal military ones. There may be more to lose than to gain in attempts to maintain the present deterrent relationship within a bipolar security structure. Certainly, there are considerable political costs in any attempt to keep national nuclear forces out of the arms control reckoning as the superpowers and most of their allies reconsider the security structures of Europe. Something of Gorbachev's 'common European home' is already under construction (though possibly not at the foundations) as non-NATO European states involve themselves more deeply in the traditional institutions of Europe, and as the division between security and economic issues continues to evaporate. Above all, the United States has reappraised its reactions to the developments of the last two or three years in European security politics and intends to reduce its tangible military commitment to Western Europe, whilst participating in the evolution of European defence institutions towards more overtly 'political roles' (USIS, 1989). The implication is that even if bipolarity remains the essential security structure in the Europe of the 1990s, it will almost certainly be a less military version of it and will, in any case, involve a rather different pattern of commitments from the major allied nations.

Some traditional analyses have attempted to outflank this argument by invoking the renewed relevance of out-of-area problems in British defence policy. In this argument, major intellectual reassessments should be avoided since the realist premises of current defence thinking are abundantly confirmed by the conditions of instability that apply to areas outside the Atlantic sphere in which Britain has a legitimate interest (Bentinck, 1986). And in a world where international policing and the containment of regional conflicts may be regarded as a common good to the international community, an 'area of operations' outside the NATO sphere may be an increasingly important political device to safeguard British national interests (Cable, 1985). In its most assertive form, the argument holds that if 'the threat' is no longer obviously coming from the East, then a series of other threats from previously peripheral states will tend to replace it and require the same general type and magnitude of defence commitment.

Such arguments, however, cannot escape the sheer depth of the change in Britain's security environment over recent years. At the most superficial level, there is little doubt that British out-of-area interests are obviously subordinate to its Atlantic and European security concerns (Baylis, 1989, p. 137). The out-of-area capability is residual and already would be incapable of sustaining another Falklands operation. More significantly, any out-of-area operations are far more likely to require joint forces, rather than independent ones, and as such would be part of a multilateral political and military initiative in relation to some particular threat to their common interests. It is certainly not fanciful to believe that a future joint force in a situation analogous to the naval operation in the Gulf during the Iraq–Iran War might well involve East European or Soviet contingents as well as NATO forces. In other words, it may be that the military forces of the developed world are in future to play a series of particular roles on behalf of a concert of major world powers. But even if this is a realistic expectation it remains the case that the political context in which European powers would commit their forces to such operations will be quite new. More significantly, the nature of the interests to be defended in this way is likely to be very different. Cold war manoeuvring in the Third World may be intrinsically less meaningful: a genuine concert of major world powers may prove itself extremely effective by non-military means, as it has already done in relation to ending the Gulf War, encouraging settlements in Southern Africa, encouraging a Middle East peace process, or in forcing reform and political change in South-East Asia: and in the absence of the Cold War it may well be that the attendant risks of military operations will be regarded as greater than the intrinsic value of the interests themselves. In short, the 'out-of-area' argument for a traditional approach to the future of defence policy cannot get around the fact that the European context has changed dramatically because the Cold War has changed dramatically. If the central context of Western security is thereby transformed, then residual interests and rationales cannot help but be affected; perhaps even recast completely.

The political processes of the last forty years are changing, therefore, in all of the security arenas that are intrinsic to contemporary British defence policy. Holding on to the old realities before we are certain about the new ones will not necessarily maintain the old bipolar world, still less produce desirable alternatives. Against the official grain, therefore, the 1990s may be the decade in which some long-term collective visions of a desirable security future, far from being meaningless and obstructive, would be a positive advantage. Under enormous pressure, the West was not short of visionary thinking during most of the 1940s. There is no logical reason why this should not happen in the 1990s, since the coming decade shows every sign of being a period of equally great, if less violent, transition.

The second major implication for Britain that arises from this study is that we have to reconsider the relationship between the government and the domestic economy in so far as it affects defence and security policies. For it seems that a gap is opening up between the sovereign responsibility of British governments to devise appropriate defence policies and their ability to implement them, both in the international and domestic spheres.

The problems of defence budgeting and the intimate relationship between national economic performance and defence expenditure occupy a great deal of a government's time and are one of the main observation points for external commentators on defence matters. The fact that defence budgeting is so prevalent an issue, however, is an expression that the government is carrying out its sovereign responsibility. For this *is* a guns-or-butter choice: to balance expenditure against necessary commitments, and whatever choice is made is a political judgement that is properly the responsibility of the government.

The conceptual problem arises when a government tries to give effect to its choices. For governmental controls over the national economy are becoming increasingly tenuous. Though Thatcher governments have generally believed in putting themselves in the market-place, the fact is that Western governments have found themselves there anyway. Conservative defence policies have become absorbed in getting better value for money from their defence expenditure and have clearly achieved some success (Levene, 1987). But this does not address the most important long-term issues, which involve the relationship between government and the defence industrial base. This relationship is important, firstly, because it affects a government's ability to exercise its sovereign responsibility for defence of the community. If a defence industrial base does not exist, as for instance in the case of Libya, the government can fulfil its sovereign responsibility simply by buying from someone else. If, however, a defence base does exist, particularly if it exists in an international context, then a government's ability to get what it requires from it is important, as is the question of which other governments the defence industrial base may also be serving. Secondly, the structure of the defence industrial base of Western countries is one of the more important factors that determine the range of political choices available to decision-makers as they consider future security options.

In the case of British defence policy, despite the size of the equipment procurement budget, it is clear that the government has increasingly tenuous links with the defence industrial base (Walker and Gummett, 1989; Taylor and Hayward, 1989). For one thing, it is extremely diverse in its nature and not susceptible to government direction (or even close monitoring) in the way that the armed forces are (Cooper, 1990). Defence industries are more than ever in an international market-place. In the case of European defence industries, this trend will be given a considerable boost by the European Community's 1992 programme, making the British defence industrial base even more diverse and international. There have been periodic attempts to counteract this trend where particular firms, such as Westland or Short Brothers, have been subject to various forms of foreign intervention, but national indignation and appeals to strategic independence do nothing to buck the trend. As the defence industrial base becomes more involved with the rest of Europe and other OECD states, so it will deal increasingly with countries outside the NATO framework, and as it is subject to international competition and pressures to merge, so its capacities will conform increasingly to what the market demands and not necessarily to what British governments may want. This is especially true where government spending represents a relatively small, and static, part of the total business of some of the conglomerate companies. Such trends may constitute one of the more persuasive arguments that national defence policies in the future will have to be set in a wider (European/international) systemic context rather than only a (West European/national) NATO Alliance context. As Trevor Taylor points out (1990), there is an interesting paradox in the spectre of governments upholding their sovereignty by pursuing defence procurement policies that rely on the complex inter-actions of the forces that shape International Political Economy: 'if nothing else, developments on the defence industrial front seem to undermine the contribution of Power Politics thinking to our understanding of defence policy, a broad area where such thinking has been traditionally dominant'.

A third implication of this study is that trends suggest that an attitude change is necessary in British, and Western, security thinking over the place of negotiation – particularly arms control negotiation – in defence planning. Western governments have always been prepared to negotiate on arms where they have felt that this was possible and have welcomed the chance under the right conditions to do so. It is also the case, however, that, negotiations between East and West have generally been regarded as a luxury to be enjoyed during periods of relaxation in the Cold War. They were a second priority to the maintenance of a strong and collective defence policy. Negotiations were seen as a component of international security more than of defence policy proper.

The new context of defence policy over recent years has given Britain a more powerful stake in negotiated outcomes of all kinds. There are several reasons for this. NATO's operational strategy has been moving away from a previously heavy reliance on nuclear weapons towards more conventional options. The 'conventionalisation of NATO strategy' appears to be a long-term trend that will tip the balance away from nuclear forces in NATO's order of battle. 'Conventionalisation' has also become one of the newer symbols of unity within NATO as the United States seems prepared to pressure the Europeans much harder than in the past to take on more of the defence burden. Then again, the prospects of any further nuclear deployments in Europe are a political time-bomb that few NATO politicians are prepared to deal with.

Whether Europe likes it or not, conventional forces will have to play a significantly greater role in Western defence. Yet a greater reliance on conventional forces makes negotiation and co-operation essential. Unlike nuclear weapons, the military impact of which is predictable above a certain level, conventional force structures are replete with unquantifiable elements. It is extremely difficult to achieve stability between conventional forces merely through reciprocal action and tacit communication. Negotiations are unavoidable. In the European context they are even more unavoidable since the financial burden of a greater reliance on conventional forces gives Western governments a very strong incentive to try to meet their military commitments with fewer units. Conventionalisation also implies that more negotiations will be conducted between the European allies since much greater co-ordination and efficiency between national Western forces will be required, and conventional forces are far more dependent on the high-technology international defence industrial base.

Similarly, the British and French independent nuclear forces now loom considerably larger in the East–West strategic equation. This is partly because their modernisation increases their capacity so much; partly because absolute numbers of nuclear warheads are likely to decline during the 1990s and British and French stockpiles will, for the first time, constitute a significant portion of the total; and partly because arms control negotiations in all areas have picked up momentum and it is ultimately impossible to exclude independent nuclear forces from any nuclear arms control package in Europe. Last, but not least, Western governments still need to demonstrate to their often cynical publics that they are serious about arms control. Public pressure to negotiate, particularly at the speed now suggested by Soviet and American leaders, is unlikely to decrease.

The implication of all this is not just that British negotiators will be even busier in the 1990s. It is that making ends meet, both financially and politically, will depend on the success of a number of intra-allied and East–West negotiations. Strategists and observers have, as a matter of principle, long since called for a greater integration between arms control policies and national defence policies: they are too easily isolated from one another in separate bureaucratic and perceptual boxes. In the security environment that seems to be evolving for the 1990s, however, it will be difficult to keep them apart (Freedman, 1986b).

Finally, and closely related to this question, there is the implication that what Baylis (1989) refers to as the problem of 'incrementalism versus a radical review' of British defence policy, may have reached a critical point. There is no shortage of criticism of Britain's characteristically incremental style in defence policy-making and as Baylis shows, there are good reasons to defend it. In the past, the issue of incrementalism has usually revolved around defence budgeting – 'present defence policy is bankrupt' (Coker, 1987, p. 7; Baylis, 1986) or the problem of defence priorities between land and naval power – 'NATO is no longer an alliance, it is a way of life . . . an end in itself' (Cable, 1987, p. 126). Some of the criticism, too, is simply an argument about bureaucratic style.

The problem here, however, is that 'incrementalism' and 'radical review' begin to take on new meaning when we consider the choices of the 1990s. In the way the argument has usually been put it is about the method by which the government decides how to match commitments and available resources. But it all takes place within the realist paradigm, applied specifically to the Cold War. If the trends we have identified in the security environment are broadly accurate, however, neither incrementalism nor radicalism in these terms will mean very much. For the commitments/ resources equation may be determined by changes in the nature of our conception of what we are trying to defend rather than in the adjustment up or down of an essentially static threat assessment. Given the defence choices that seem to be looming in the 1990s, incrementalism will be a decision to try to preserve the status quo; a radical review, once it tries to get back to fundamentals, may well find itself adopting a different paradigm of security, defence and alliance management as it applies to the European context.

What seems certain is that British defence policy cannot be usefully debated, as it has been, essentially as a *national* policy in an alliance context. It may make sense as a component of an alliance policy in a *systemic* security context. But even here, we have to be aware that defence is a multilevel activity in Europe that is likely to become ever more diverse, and defence policy-making at the national level may have a good deal less to do with the security of the community than we would like to think.

5 ∾ The political economy of Britain's external relations

Ron Smith

INTRODUCTION

A central conceptual problem for the political economy of British external relations is the appropriate political response to increased economic interdependence. The world economy is being increasingly integrated by improvements in transport and communications and by the increasing flow of goods and services, money and people across national borders. Such integration causes economic processes, such as competition, accumulation and production, to operate at a global rather than merely international or national level. These global economic processes are mediated by Multi-National Companies (MNCs) and international financial and commodity markets. Although this trend is most evident among the advanced capitalist countries, it extends to the socialist and less developed worlds as well.

From the point of view of governments this growing economic integration has a number of implications. Interdependence increases as issues that were once matters of domestic policy decisions now have international ramifications. Autonomy is lost as the traditional instruments of economic policy become less effective, undermined by integration. Foreign policy formation is fragmented as the traditional decision-making centres become overloaded by the quantity and complexity of the economic issues that require international negotiation. The accepted separation of domestic politics from foreign policy breaks down. The fact that the exact prices for individual European agricultural products can only be settled at head of government level is symptomatic.

The expansion of trade, the decision processes of the MNCs and the flows of capital through the financial markets create transnational markets independent of nation states. The world economy becomes much more closely coupled so that shocks are rapidly transmitted through the system. However, new shock absorbers have also appeared, with the result that although the system has shaken on its springs in response to the buffeting of the last decade, it has not yet collapsed as it did in the 1930s. The Crash of October 1987 is illustrative in this respect. One day, stock markets across the world suddenly, simultaneously, and for reasons that still remain obscure, decided that equities were 25 per cent less valuable. Although this prompted fears of financial crisis and recession, the subsequent years saw little sign of any effects on the real economy.

Within national borders, states provide a framework and infrastructure for economic activity. Global economic processes require global frameworks, increased economic interdependence requires increased co-ordination. Mechanisms to provide such functions are necessary but problematical, and the politics of such provision, whether by co-operative regimes, international organisations or hegemonic powers, is a major issue. States have to decide how they will contribute to such mechanisms. British responses to the single market and European Monetary Union are an important case in point.

This then is the framework that will be used to examine the conceptual premises of the political economy of Britain's external relations. Throughout the examination, the dialectical interaction of economics and politics as material processes at a global level will be a major theme in the analysis. However, before confronting the substantive issues, a minor theme must be addressed; the undialectical interaction of economics and politics as academic subjects. This is done in the next section which considers questions of method and then examines how the central phenomenon, economic interdependence, can be characterised.

The second section examines how the system is organised: the sources of order in the international political economy. Some order is provided by sovereign states and markets, but both are also sources of anarchy, and regulation of the system is supplemented by co-ordinating regimes, international organisations and hegemonic powers. Each of these sources of order is examined. The third section discusses the trajectory of the system: the trends towards integration in communications, trade, production and finance. The final section briefly comments on the policy issues.

Within this review there is a tension between the general treatment which is required to identify the broad themes, and the very specific material which is required to illustrate the heterogeneity and complexity of the issues involved in Britain's international economic relations. Where possible I have tried to illustrate the broad themes with concrete examples of current concern.

Politics and economics

Both International Relations, the study of the political interactions between states, and International Economics, the study of the flows of money and commodities between nations, have long histories and highly developed theoretical structures. The two disciplines have evolved separately. Thus they differ in focus, what they regard as the interesting problems; in method, how they analyse their problems; and in assumptions, what they take for granted (Strange, 1988, pp. 14–15). Economics operates with a relatively static undifferentiated view of states and state power, International Politics with a relatively static and undifferentiated view of markets and market forces. For many of the questions that concern each discipline such simplification is a powerful aid to analysis. But as international economic negotiation becomes an increasingly important feature of the interaction between states, a range of questions arise which lie on the border between the disciplines, where such simplifications are inappropriate.

This is not a peaceful border, but the scene of continual battles about the appropriate framework for analysing politico-economic interactions. Although the economists and the political scientists studying International Political Economy have been fighting over the same ground for a considerable time, and the differences in approach have been extensively discussed, this has not produced any simple characterisation, let alone a satisfactory snythesis (Kindleberger, 1970, ch. 1; Rhoads, 1985; Calleo and Strange, in Strange, 1984; Strange, 1988; Hirshleifer, 1985). An important factor in their incompatibility is the clash between their methods of abstraction – mathematical or philosophical – and their methods of empiricism – statistical or institutional.

Clearly neither discipline is autarkic and there is substantial trade between them, yet the difference in approach prompts a considerable degree of antagonism and intolerance which does not aid communication and leads to each group stigmatising the work of the other. Two quotes on the same subject might illustrate the point. 'Henry Aubrey has written a pamphlet to suggest that international monetary questions are essentially political. Too true. The difficulty in resolving them is that economists know no political science, and political scientists know nothing about them at all' (Kindleberger, 1970, p. 227). 'To find the things that interest them, political scientists have to sift through the trash of economic analysis' (Calleo and Strange in Strange, 1984, p. 92).

The accumulated antagonisms and the structural differences, such as the use of mutually contradictory assumptions, make methodological pluralism a difficult option in this area. None the less, being neither an International Economist nor an International Political Economist, I shall make the attempt, trying to avoid the second level of dispute, the heated controversies between the competing schools within each discipline.

I have treated the subject 'International Political Economy' (IPE) as a speciality within political science, in the same way as International Economics is a speciality within economics. This seems justified since the major achievement of IPE has been to reveal the insights obtained from the political analysis of economic problems. However, while it has encouraged paying attention to a broader range of considerations than is common in either discipline it has not provided a distinct theory of the economic-political interaction.

Wiles (1986, p. 295), in the introduction to his Stevenson Memorial Lecture at LSE, puts the position rather bluntly. After saying that it was an honour to be encouraged to practise the new speciality of International Political Economy, he says of it: 'There is little valid theory in this subject – and I am particularly happy to note [such a change from economics] that there is not much invalid theory either. The whole field seems still to be thoroughly "applied", the only question being exactly what to apply.'

The central methodological problem within International Political Economy is the lack of a convincing conceptual framework which can be used to structure the detailed empirical and institutional studies of the various sectors under review: a problem of concepts chasing realities. Various devices are used to provide a framework, but none is completely satisfactory.

One approach is to start from alternative perceptions of the system, and link the political and economic dimensions of these perspectives. Thus one can contrast the realist-mercantilist, the liberal-neoclassical and the marxist; then use these different doctrines to organise alternative pictures of the world system. Gill and Law (1988) and Gilpin (1987) discuss these approaches. Although this can be suggestive, there are asymmetries between the political and economic dimensions of each of these doctrines, which makes conflating them misleading. Whereas realist International Relations is a highly developed explanatory structure, there has been no developed mercantilist economic theory for two centuries, despite the prevalence of mercantilist policies. The economic theories that justify protection either of the 'strategic trade theory' variety (Krugman, 1986) or the macro-economic arguments for import controls made by the Cambridge Economic Policy Group are of a quite different type. Likewise, while neo-classical economics is a highly developed structure, there has been no developed liberal international political theory for a century. This asymmetry is even characteristic of the marxist analysis. The marxists have an advantage, in that their well-developed economic and political theories are constructed within an integrated intellectual framework, explicitly designed to conceptualise economic-political interactions. None the less, the marxist economists and political theorists have reproduced a similar academic division between themselves.

Strange (1988) provides a different type of framework. She organises the analysis by beginning with a matrix, which has the four basic power structures: security, production, finance and knowledge, on one axis; with two types of organisation: authority (state) and market on the other axis. She then examines the state–market balance within each structure mediated through state and market responses impact on the distribution of basic values: security, wealth, justice and freedom.

This matrix is used to provide a structured set of boxes, within which the historical interactions of economic and political factors in particular sectors can be described very effectively. But it does not provide a framework for theorising about the interactions themselves; they happen within the boxes. Nor does the matrix itself arise deductively from theoretical considerations, rather it arises inductively to provide a taxonomy for the interesting empirical phenomena. This causes difficulties over the status of the categories. For instance, states and markets are not the only forms of political and economic organisation. In the case of politics, Strange recognises this and includes sources of authority other than states. In the case of economics, in addition to markets there are economic hierarchies, particularly within multinational firms, and important economic transfers take place through familial, criminal or charitable relationships unmediated by markets, even at an international level. From an economic point of view, emphasising the distinction between production and finance is arbitrary. The neo-classical would not make any fundamental distinction between them; the marxist would wish to distinguish circuits of money, productive and commodity capital; adding exchange as an extra distinction to production and finance.

However, these are quibbles. Strange used this structure very effectively, for the purpose for which it was intended: to suggest new questions, and direct attention at a broader range of considerations, and I have nothing better to offer in the way of an organising theory. None the less, it seems important to recognise the inherent difficulties that we face in analysing politico-economic interactions. One consequence of this lack of analytical ability is that reality may appear incoherent.

A certain incoherence inevitably arises as a result of the fracture of Economics from Politics, both at a material level and at a disciplinary level. Each sphere has a certain internal coherence both in its specific mode of operation and in the specific mode of analysis which is applied to it. However, these modes are not transferable between spheres and both the economics of politics and the politics of economics provide very partial perspectives.

This causes particular difficulties in this review because the focus of attention is the form of interaction between two spheres, for which neither the economic nor political modes are appropriate. In interaction, the economic and political spheres constitute a system which has its own emergent mode of operation which is quite distinct from either the purely economic or purely political. The central conceptual problem is to provide a corresponding mode of analysis which will allow us to theorise about the interactions and the behaviour of the system as a whole, for instance in terms of the constraints that it puts on the operation of economic and political processes.

One general feature of the relationship between economic and political process is that the structure and institutions of the international economy are changing at a remarkable rate, while perceptions, actions and institutions in the political sphere, more subject to inertia, have not kept pace with this transformation. The contradictions between the two spheres are thus a potentially dangerous source of strain. Rather than adjusting gradually, the rigidities cause tensions to accumulate until the system cracks and the tensions are violently released.

The crucial feature of the economic transformation, which will be emphasised in this chapter, is the trend to increasing integration and globalisation of economic processes. The characterisation of integration is discussed in the next section.

Integration

Historical factors, such as the entrepôt tradition, early industrialisation and the empire, have made Britain very open, tightly linked into the world economy. This has resulted in British institutions, such as the City of London, being highly internationalised. On top of this has been superimposed a global trend towards increased integration. There is a common-sense meaning to a view that the world is getting smaller, more integrated, more interdependent. However, making precise the nature of the transformation is not straightforward.

The terms used to describe the linkages to the world economy – openness, interdependence, integration – do not have straightforward meanings (Michaeli, 1984). At the simplest level the openness of an economy is usually measured by the value of trade (exports or imports) as a percentage of GDP, but for many purposes it is the percentage of trade in particular items to particular destinations that matters. Economic interdependence is often used in a very similar way to refer to the monetary value of transactions among regions or countries either in absolute terms or relative to their total transactions, i.e. as an average relationship. Cooper (1986, pp. 289–93) uses it in a more restricted sense to refer to the sensitivity of transactions between countries to economic developments within them, which emphasises the marginal relationship, their responses to change in the other. For instance, we may import a large amount of a commodity from country x, a high average relationship; but be able easily to substitute supplies from country y in the event of disruption in country x. Thus our sensitivity to change in country x is small despite a large amount of trade. Short-run and long-run sensitivity may also differ, depending on the flexibility of the domestic structure; the ease with which markets, policies and society as a whole can adjust.

While interdependence implies a two-way sensitivity, dependence suggests a one-way sensitivity. Associated with both there is concern with a quite distinct problem: vulnerability. Vulnerability arises from the risk of costly disruption of the relationship, cutting off oil supplies for instance, which may be exploited, by one or other partner, to gain influence or leverage. Who is vulnerable to whom in a transaction may be contingent: depending on circumstances, you may be dependent on them for a market or they may be dependent on you for an essential input. Keohane and Nye (1977) distinguish susceptibility (being open to damage from the world system) and vulnerability (susceptibility qualified by the ability to limit the damage).

Defences against external vulnerability can be provided in a number of ways – self-sufficiency, insurance or diversification, for instance – but there are costs involved. Self-sufficiency may reduce vulnerability to external agents, such as the Organisation of Petroleum Exporting Countries (OPEC) in the case of energy, but may increase internal vulnerability to nuclear accidents or miners' strikes, for instance. Insurance, through stragetic stockpiles, the development of substitutes or conservation measures, can only be expensive and appear wasted should the threat not be implemented. Diversification of sources or supply or demand may involve economic costs (higher prices or lower returns from alternative sources) and is effective only against certain sorts of risk. *Ex ante*, it is not straightforward to decide whether the costs of such defences are justified, since the calculation requires identification of possible threats, assessment of their probability and choice of the appropriate degree of risk aversion. Finlayson and Haglund (1987) discuss this problem with respect to the once feared 'resource war'.

Economic or market integration is usually seen as involving equality of prices, which is achieved by some degree of mobility and substitutability between countries of goods, services or factors of production, such as labour and capital. The linkages and connections which tend to equalise prices mean that changes in one part of the system cause changes in other parts. These feedbacks then reverberate making the collective behaviour of the system different from the expectations and priorities of the individual units that comprise it. Integrated markets gain a life of their own, quite distinct from the individual states involved, who can see themselves as vulnerable to alien, impersonal forces.

Paul Krugman (in Padoa-Schioppa, 1987) provides an excellent non-technical summary of the economics of international integration. He summarises the traditional economic view of the effects of integration as follows:

International trade increases world efficiency by allowing countries to specialise in activities in which they are relatively productive, or that use intensively their relatively abundant resources. International factor mobility, whether of capital or labour, similarly raises world efficiency by transferring resources to countries where their marginal product is higher. On the other hand, both trade and factor mobility may have strong effects on income distribution, so that the owners of initially scarce factors – which become less scarce as a result of increased integration – may be left worse off despite gains for the nation as a whole. And the process of adjustment to increased integration may be difficult, involving temporary unemployment of labour or capital. (p. 117)

Economic integration produces transnational institutions (MNCs, financial markets, etc) that not only transcend national boundaries but constrain the autonomy of nation states. Economic agents, such as firms, may sell a currency or switch production if they do not like the economic effects on their profitability of the policies of a particular government. Even when the firm's motivation is purely economic, maximising profits, the actions have political effects, influencing the popularity or scope for action of the government.

The importance of global markets means that international economics cannot be analysed purely in terms of interstate relations nor can the world economy be analysed as merely a complex of national economies. It is closer to a system of 'complex interdependence' (Keohane and Nye, 1977): in which actors other than states participate in world politics; force ceases to be an effective instrument of policy; the traditional hierarchy of issues topped by security no longer prevails; and instead there is a complex issue structure with no unique ranking of states by influence across issues.

Although we talk of trade between states, in fact, most of the economic processes do not involve relations between states, as represented by governments, but between firms and people. Britain as a state does little trade itself, but it provides part of the environment within which trade takes place, and thus it has an implicit responsibility. The growth of trade and other forms of economic integration has two implications for governments. At a national level, they lose autonomy, at an international level they gain a role in the construction of co-ordinating structures. Domestically, their actions are more constrained by international market forces, traditional instruments lose their effectiveness and national economies are more sensitive to policy actions of other governments. Internationally, the success of their policies will depend on the rules of the game which provide the global or regional framework for economic interaction. If the governments join the appropriate clubs, then they can have a role in the construction of those rules. The next section examines the construction of those rules: the sources of order in international economic interactions.

However, before proceeding it should be mentioned that the perspective presented in this chapter, of increased integration and reduced autonomy, while a common one, is not universal. The evidence can be read in quite different ways. The opposite view is put very forcefully by Gordon (1988) who concludes:

> First I would argue that we have *not* witnessed movement towards an increasingly 'open' international economy with productive capital buzzing around the globe, but that we have moved towards an increasingly 'closed' economy for productive investment, with production and investment decisions increasingly dependent upon a range of institutional policies and activities and a pattern of differential and specialization among countries in the LDCs . . .
>
> Second and correspondingly, the role of the State has grown substantially since the early 1970s; State policies have become increasingly decisive on the international front, not more futile. (p. 63)

SOURCES OF ORDER

States

In political theory, nation states are the basic units of analysis and their sovereignty the central organising principle. Thus the nature of the state and of sovereignty and the economic degree of freedom available to nation states become central conceptual issues, lying behind more pragmatic questions about the appropriate policies for individual states. Traditionally, sovereignty is seen as having two aspects (Bull, 1977). Internal sovereignty involves supremacy over all other authorities within a territory and population; while external sovereignty involves independence from outside authorities. There is a final and absolute authority within a nation, but none above the nation. In this sense, the international political system is anarchic, there is no overall authority. Any organisation of the system is the outcome of the interaction, whether violent or peaceful, of the individual states.

The states are usually regarded as acting in their own national interest. Such a unitary state, which can be treated as a rational actor attempting to identify and maximise some well-defined national interest (often summarised by economists as a social welfare function), using instruments over which it has sovereign control, is a convenient fiction. It is a fiction which simplifies the analysis and helps to clarify certain types of issue. However, it is worth briefly restating the objections to it. The state is not unitary, but composed of disparate, often conflicting, bureaucratic and political interests in the administration, civil service, legislature and judiciary. The individuals and groups who administer the state may be following their own good rather than some general good identified with the national interest. Thus the sovereignty of the state apparatus would be quite distinct from national sovereignty. The nation itself is composed of different, perhaps antagonistic, groups, such as classes, and in general there is no way of aggregating their interests into a coherent national objective or social welfare function. The state, then, functions as an arena, in which classes or other groups attempt to promote their own ends and to create an ideology which identifies their own interests with that of the nation. Even were there coherent national objectives, the complexities and uncertainties of the environment may be such as to make it impossible for the administration to define a 'rational' policy to meet them. In particular, short-term advantage may conflict with the long-term interest that would benefit from developing, say, a co-operative regime. Even if some part of the state apparatus could decide on a 'rational' policy, it may not be able to implement the required changes to the policy instruments. The most important international relations may not be those between states, but between other groups. The relationship between as US citizen and a British citizen may be dominated not by their national affiliation but their ethnic affiliation (for example, both seeing themselves as Irish), their profession (for example, scientific or sporting), their employment by the same multinational, or their religion.

Each of these objections has a considerable weight and is the subject of a considerable literature. But these objections will often be ignored, in order to allow us to focus on the economic role of the state, both internal and external. Following post-war reconstruction, the economic role of the state was seen in a positive light. Western governments saw themselves as managing macro-economic performance, intervening to correct market failures and providing the general co-ordination, guidance and infrastructure necessary to maintain the growth trajectory. Within this basically optimistic and interventionist framework, national economic policies were seen as possible, identifiable and desirable; a vision questioned by current conditions. The possibility of national policies has been reduced because the relative autonomy of states has been severely constrained both by the operation of economic processes on a global scale mediated by MNCs and international markets and by the multitude of obligations incurred under international agreements. Power to tax, make laws and provide a money of your own, all seen as inherent attributes of sovereignty, are being undermined by integration. The policies are made less identifiable by the ambiguities associated with national economic interest. They may be less desirable because insistence on the attributes of sovereignty and the right to pursue short-term national interests by individual states may actually reduce autonomy by obstructing attempts to regulate and stabilise the integrated global economy.

It is useful to distinguish sovereignty and autonomy and to recognise that there may be trade-offs between them: 'In fact, nations retain actual as well as legal control over their instruments of policy (sovereignty); the problem arises because these instruments of policy lose their effectiveness, so that countries find themselves able to pursue their objectives but unable to achieve them' (Cooper, 1986, p. 21). Sovereignty may be defined relative to other states or relative to transnational actors, and these may be conflicting. To establish control over financial markets or MNCs may require sharing sovereignty with other governments, and vice versa.

Autonomy and sovereignty are dimensions in a wider space of factors that characterise the degree of freedom available to a nation state. Of course it is difficult in practice to characterise the exact degree of freedom: to determine just how much is possible. It may be that the state's objectives are such that the constraints to which it is subject are not in fact binding in a particular area, leaving it a considerable degree of freedom. But this does not mean that the constraints do not exist. Nor are the constraints, even when binding, absolute. They can be moved by repudiation of agreements and expropriation of foreign assets, for example. But this requires considerable political will, and imposes economic costs. For instance, Strange (1986, p. 50) argues that the 'growth of tax havens and bank-regulation havens could easily have been checked at any early stage' by the United States. While the required regulations might have been imposed (the 1987 actions against Netherlands Antilles are an example), whether they would have stopped the growth is a more open question. The ingenuity shown in avoidance when substantial profits are involved is striking. The consequence might only have been a greater flight of financial institutions from the United States.

Nor should autonomy be identified with power. Rather, power and influence themselves can constrain action, because influential actors have to take account of the repercussions of their actions on the expectations and responses of other states. It may be possible that freedom and purpose are options which are only available to relatively powerless states, for they can ignore the effects of their actions on the system and behave 'irresponsibly'.

The degree of freedom will be context-dependent. Loss of freedom, whether in the means available or the ends achievable, will be perceived quite differently in different areas, although formally the loss may be equivalent. In particular, sovereignty and autonomy are often willingly sacrificed because of the great benefits integration can bring. Britain could be like Albania, almost autarkic with great independence in domestic policy, but the cost would be great. In many areas it is widely perceived that the surrender of sovereignty can enhance national interest, in the sense that national well-being is increased by renouncing control and accepting dependence. This belief is a corner-stone of British defence policy, expressed through the obligations imposed by membership of NATO, the presence of US bases, and dependence on the United States for the provision of strategic nuclear delivery systems. In the nuclear context John Baylis comments: 'Britain might have to become more dependent on the US to maintain her independence, but the capability to act independently remained an essential facet of British policy' (in Edmonds, 1986, p. 24). One might object to the substance of the argument, and the syntax, but the point is clear: surrendering some freedoms can increase other freedoms.

Loss of independence and autonomy can also arise from necessary constraints inherent in the system. Such a case arises from the $N-1$ problem. If there are N countries in a system, at most only $N-1$ of them can act completely independently in their external economic policy. It is impossible for all countries to devalue (someone must appreciate) just as it is impossible for all countries to run a balance of payments surplus. In principle, the surpluses and deficits must cancel out. The fact that the world as a whole ran a deficit of \$114bn in 1982 (the largest recorded) just reflects measurement biases (IMF Survey, 1987, p. 71). The $N-1$ problem is a fairly clear case; there are many other relationships where the issue is less clear, and what many economists take for granted as determinate characteristics of the system, inherent constraints on states, others tend to regard as matters of political choice. Likewise, economists tend to emphasise the benefits from exchange and the gains from trade, thus they are much less risk averse about surrendering autonomy than those in the realist tradition of international relations who emphasise the dangers inherent in incurring dependence.

Economists also tend to regard sovereignty as having purely instrumental value. For instance, Kay and Posner (1989, p. 56), in discussing 1992 and European integration, say 'the notion of "sovereignty" in economic matters has a flavour of government interference which is perhaps a little dated', and that the relevant issue is 'which level of government is appropriate for the exercise of specific economic powers'. Politically, however, sovereignty involves more than formal control over the instruments of policy. In particular it involves attitudes towards symbols of national identity. In all matters of issuance, rights and British government control, there may be no difference between a traditional British passport and a European Community (EC) standardised British passport. But the change in size and colour is seen by many as representing a loss of sovereignty. In these circumstances sovereignty is seen as an end in itself, rather than a means to enhance national interests.

There is a sense in which some would regard national interest as effectively undefinable in the absence of certain aspects of sovereignty; since it is the attributes of sovereignty which define the nation that has the interest. This is central to attitudes towards the EC. For instance, in her Bruges speech to the College of Europe in September 1988, Mrs Thatcher's first guiding principle emphasised the role of the independent sovereign states; the damage that would be done by trying to suppress nationhood; and the pride that lay in being British or Belgian or Dutch or German. The speech welcomed economic integration, the Single European Market, particularly where it was produced by free trade and enterprise, but resisted the extension of the institutions of political integration. More generally, political issues of sovereignty – recognising German financial hegemony by becoming part of the Deutschmark bloc – seemed more important than the economic issues in the British refusal to join the Exchange Rate Mechanism of the European Monetary System.

Markets

In economic theory, markets are seen as the basic organising procedures: the 'invisible hand' which emerges from the individual pursuit of self-interest, the propensity in human nature to truck, barter and exchange. Under certain conditions competitive markets exhibit properties of 'pareto-optimality' (nobody can be better off without making somebody worse off) much emphasised by neo-classical economists. Although markets are the dominant form of economic organisation, not all economic transactions are mediated by exchange relationships; some involve coercive or altruistic relationships. To talk of markets is a metaphor, market-places where buyers and sellers haggle over prices are relatively rare; none the less the power of 'market forces', the operation of the profit motive and the price system is undeniable. They persuade the whole world to conspire to fill the shelves of your local supermarket, and motivate incredible feats of logistics and co-ordination.

One of the most lyrical descriptions of the achievements of this system, which 'has accomplished wonders far surpassing Egyptian pyramids, Roman aqueducts and Gothic cathederals', is by Marx and Engels in the Communist Manifesto. But Marx also emphasised the other side, the anarchy of the market: they are uncontrolled, geared to profit, not social need, producing volatility in prices and quantities, inequality in income and wealth.

Markets are not independent of the state. Political structures are a necessary condition for their existence. In particular they require an effective legal system: why bother to truck, barter and exchange, to use Adam Smith's terms, when you can rob, pillage and loot? But there is also a range of other functions that need to be provided in order for markets to operate effectively. Markets also fail in certain well-known ways, and their failures provoke state intervention. Typically economists characterise such interventions as being for allocative, stabilisation and redistributive reasons. Intervention can improve resource allocation and efficiency when markets generate monopolies or externalities such as pollution; stabilise the system when markets are excessively volatile; and produce a more acceptable distribution of income. Even in the presence of such market failures, intervention need not lead to improvements over the free market outcome. There is a Liberal tradition that argues that 'political failure' is as likely as 'market failure'.

These tensions between state and market, in particular the terms under which the state exerts sovereignty over trade within its territory, represent important material phenomena; but they also correspond to the major ideological divide in economics. To talk of a state's sovereignty over a market is a convenient but somewhat ambiguous metaphor. It may cover the power to allow the market to exist (those for slaves, stolen goods and certain types of drugs or weapons are generally forbidden); it may cover regulation of the terms of the exchange (markets for labour, banking and medical services are widely restricted); it may cover control of the prices and quantities transacted; and it almost invariably includes the power to raise taxes.

The control of prices and quantities may be done by tariffs and quotas in international trade, intervention schemes like the European Common Agricultural Policy (CAP), or direct fiat. In general, given the characteristics of supply and demand it is difficult to obtain independent control of both prices and quantities. The desired control may be first order (establishing a level or mean value for the price or quantity) or second order (minimising fluctuations or the variance around the mean). Second-order controls are thought appropriate for markets such as primary products and foreign exchange where prices are very volatile, though it is often difficult to identify the appropriate mean around which they should be stabilised, and mistakes by intervention authorities, such as the International Tin Council, can be expensive.

If the volatility is exogenous, originating outside the system from variations in the weather, for instance, stabilising prices may increase the volatility of quantities, and vice versa. The CAP has managed to stabilise both prices and quantities in Europe, but at the expense of transferring the instability and the required adjustment to the world market, mainly at the expense of Less Developed Country (LDC) producers (Roarty, 1987). In some circumstances, it may be better not to attempt to stabilise prices or quantities directly but some other related variable, such as producer's income.

The instability may not be exogenous but endogenous, generated by the market itself, through 'bubbles' of self-fulfilling speculative expectations, and fads and fashions among participants. In such cases, state intervention can be stabilising. Whether the large observed fluctuations in exchange rates are primarily responses to exogenous forces, in particular misguided national economic policies, or endogenous, produced by speculative excess, is a central international policy question. Some see the foreign exchange market as a fairly efficient shock absorber, others see it as a dangerous rogue elephant. Even among those who see it as a dangerous rogue elephant, there is scepticism both about the power of the individual national monetary authorities to cage it, given the size of the market relative to national reserves; and the wisdom with which authorities would exercise available power.

The general process of state intervention to control markets is complicated by a wide variety of other factors. There are costs to control in terms of administrative structures to regulate, monitor and enforce the system. These costs will depend in part on the scope for avoidance and evasion and their relative profitability. There are feedbacks through the market. Supply and demand pressures depend on private agents' conjectures about how effective and how resolute government action will be. Depending on the incentives these conjectures may be stabilising or destabilising.

Regulations can become outdated as markets innovate rapidly, and regulators in each country will be competing to attract business by providing convivial locations for sellers and assurances of quality to buyers. This produces what Kane (in Portes and Swoboda, 1987) calls the regulatory dialectic, a process of regulation, avoidance and reregulation, driven by regulatory competition and market arbitrage between alternative regulatory structures as firms relocate their activities to an attractive system. He emphasises the danger that such a system may encourage risk by providing too many implicit or conjectural government guarantees which are not well understood by those providing them. There may also be the problem that during a crisis when the guarantees are needed or expected to be honoured, governments renege on their obligations as they did in the case of tin.

There are alternative forms of regulatory structure each with advantages and disadvantages. In their ideal types the forms include: the 'American' model of highly codified rules arbitrated in courts; the 'British' model of a more informal club atmosphere resting on understandings and agreements between well-established participants; and the 'French' model of giving administrators great discretionary powers to use as they think appropriate. The American system provides a greater degree of certainty and equity but is cumbersome, inflexible, slow to adapt to change and involves heavy litigation costs. The British system is more flexible and operated by those who are best informed, but is vulnerable to exploitation by the self-interested participants and to entry by newcomers unwilling to abide by existing informal agreements. The French system can adjust very quickly, has less risk of exploitation by insiders, but leaves considerable uncertainty and poses the danger of the exercise of arbitrary powers by poorly informed administrators.

Even at a national level relations between state and market raise difficult questions, and the difficulties are magnified when the question is posed at a global level. Markets are driven by profit opportunities and these are not confined within national boundaries. Expansion overseas provides gains from trade, access to a wide resource base, economies of scale, insurance through diversification, and more rapid diffusion of technology. States could prohibit such expansion and some do, but at great cost, since they forgo such large economic rewards. Thus markets internationalise, and a question arises about how sovereignty over international markets is established by an individual nation state, or a group of states acting in conjunction. This is of particular relevance when international markets are seen as competing with states, usurping powers that should be matters of political choice. Monetary and fiscal policies become dominated by the movements in international financial and product markets. Employment, investment, tax revenue and balance of payments of a country become subordinated to the production location decisions of MNCs. Even when these MNCs are national companies, their interest is in global profitability, to which their country of origin may contribute very little.

There is also a more general question about the organisation of the global economic system. In order for economic processes and markets to operate efficiently, certain state functions are required, though some economists would argue that even these could be provided by the market. The list of necessary state functions include such things as a monetary system to facilitiate transactions; a legal system to provide security of property and enforceability of contracts; certain types of standards; and basic infrastructure. These are a domestic function of national governments, but there is no world government to provide these functions at a global level. As economic processes become globalised the need for these functions to be provided at an international level grows.

The domestic analogy is a useful one. It leads one to ask how functions provided by the state at a national level are provided at an international level. It also prompts the reverse question. Before considering regulation of international processes, for example, the control of world money supply, ask: 'how successful have national governments been at controlling the domestic equivalents within their own borders?' However, it should be emphasised that it is an analogy. There is certainly no necessary reason to suppose that these 'quasi-state functions', as I shall call them, actually require some world government to provide them. Parties to a contract can agree to invoice in the money of a particular state and accept arbitration by a specified private body in London. Trade has always taken place on such terms. In addition, the rules of the game may not be imposed by an outside authority but arise spontaneously, as actors establish self-enforcing conventions based on salient features of the environment. In such circumstances, it may not be sensible to ask the natural questions posed by the domestic analogy: who sets the rules and who enforces them? However, it does appear that growing integration has increased the demand for such quasi-state functions while the supply of them has not kept pace and in some cases has been disrupted. Thus it is useful to examine their provision. They can be provided by a co-operative agreement between states to co-ordinate international economic processes, they can be provided by international organisations, or they can be provided by a single state for the system as a whole. Although in practice all three forms overlap they will be examined separately in the next three sections.

Co-ordination

Given a perceived need to provide such quasi-state functions at an international level, states have an incentive to come together to agree a basic co-ordinating framework. Within the Economics literature policy-co-ordination tends to be used in a very specific sense to refer to the co-ordination of macro-economic policy where a range of very specific technical issues appear (Artis and Ostry, 1986). Here it will be used in a much wider sense to refer to any setting of policy which is fitted into a wider framework, whether agreement on international standards (for sharing radio frequencies or electronic transmission), ensuring harmonisation of regulations (for example, for banks), or sharing information (for example, on tax evasion). This co-ordination may be done through the formal international institutions that have proliferated and are discussed further in the next section or through informal meetings; it may be done on a multilateral or on a bilateral basis; it may be confined to governments or include private institutions such as firms and banks; it may produce legally binding agreements or merely mutual understanding, it may even be purely spontaneous based on separate recognition of salient conventions. By such processes 'rules of the game' are developed: self-reinforcing patterns of mutual expectations about the right conduct in defined circumstances, which operate like rules of the road in helping to avoid unwanted collisions (Cohen, 1981).

Co-ordination arises for many reasons. Unconcerted national action is increasingly ineffective, whereas co-ordinated policies may have multiplied impact effects on national economies. There may be 'network' externalities which mean that common standards increase efficiency. Common rules of the game may increase the stability of the system. But the rules of the game are also subject to disintegrative forces. Circumstances change rapidly in the economic arena and new actors emerge. This can introduce new conflicts of interest, undermine conventions for appropriate behaviour, leave vacuums where there are no rules, or make the application of the old rules uncertain. Co-ordination is also difficult where the parties face different information, face problems monitoring compliance with agreements, and have doubts about the credibility or commitment of the other partners.

Within the literature terms such as co-ordination, co-operation, concertation, convergence have multiple, unclear uses. Henry Wallich (cited in Artis and Ostry, 1986, p. 75) provides one taxonomy.

Coordination, harmonization, cooperation, consultation; these in descending order are the terms by which nations recognise – sometimes reluctantly – that they are not alone in the world ... 'Cooperation' falls well short of 'coordination', a concept which implies a significant modification of national policies in recognition of international economic interdependence. It falls short of 'harmonisation', a polite term indicating a somewhat great reluctance to limit one's freedom of action. But 'cooperation' is more than consultation, which may mean little more than that other interested parties will be kept informed.

Meanings also differ in different forums. Lord Cockfield, then vice president of the European Commission responsible for the internal market, chooses to talk of 'approximation' of indirect taxation, rather than 'harmonisation', to calm the fears aroused over the Commission's alleged attempts to abolish zero rates of VAT (*Financial Times*, 22 July 1987).

Whatever we call it, the first reason for coming together is the reduced effectiveness of national policies. Co-ordination internalises the international spill-overs of domestic policy-making. Given the lack of national regulation of economic processes, some international regulation is required, states have to agree rules of the game between them. As a result states choose further to restrict their sovereignty by signing a large variety of treaties. Civil servants have to operate within these constraints, as do British firms. Once (upon a time?), dealing with foreigners was a specialist activity, to be left to the experts: the Foreign Office. Now the quantity and complexity of issues involving international negotiations is such that civil servants in all departments are involved in foreign negotiations and many of them also have foreign postings. Whether it is the Ministry of Agriculture, Fisheries and Food and the CAP; the Ministry of Defence and collaborative weapons ventures; the Home Office and the international aspects of crime; the Law Departments and extradition or extra-territorial application of US laws; the Scottish Office competing with the Austrians to get a Japanese firm to set up in Silicon Glen; nearly every department involves international aspects.

As an example of how one function of a nation state, tax collection, can only be effectively implemented by international collaboration, consider how Inland Revenue can deal with taxpayers' exploitation of the different tests of residence applied by different countries. One US entrepreneur who sought to avoid being classified as a resident in any of the four countries in which he was active, the United States, Canada, Britain and Israel, was caught after the four tax authorities exchanged their files on him (*Financial Times*, 12 June 1987). Most co-operation is at this level of detail, specialised agreements negotiated between experts, and it is at this level that it is probably most effective and successful. But such technical agreement takes place within a wider framework.

One way of thinking about such co-operation is as elements of a particular regime. Regimes are structures, broader than the particular institutions or agreements, which involve principles (stating purposes), norms (general injunctions or definitions of legitimacy), rules (specific rights and obligations) and procedures (formal structures stressing means rather than substance) (Keohane, 1984; Mathews, 1986).

A general feature of such structures is for co-operation, or rule observance, to be jointly optimal but unstable, since there are immediate gains from defection or non-co-operation. This structure can be described in many ways, for instance in terms of international public goods (Kindleberger, 1986) where there are incentives to free-ride; or in terms of prisoners' dilemma and other types of game (Snidal, 1985) where there are incentives to defect. There is now a considerable game-theory literature on creating co-operative regimes. Although the analysis is very dependent on the particular solution chosen and the characterisation of the game, the co-operation problem seems pervasive. The position is somewhat better if the game is regularly repeated or if reputation matters; then, in the long run, 'nicer' strategies are more effective. There are also important differences between security and economic groupings. Whereas in the security sphere co-operating alliances tend to be motivated by the desire to maintain a balance of power (Walt 1985); in economic groupings the benefits of economies of scale, larger markets and cumulative causation are that states tend to join the bandwagon. Whereas in foreign policy terms the British initiative in setting up a rival alliance to the EC, the European Free Trade Association, was very sensible, maintaining a balance of power in Europe, in economic terms it was not, since the benefits depended on the total size of the market, and Britain reversed this policy.

One difficulty in the economic sphere emphasised in Kindleberger (1986), and discussed earlier, is that the system which the regime is supposed to regulate evolves faster than the regime can be reformed or even codified. In these circumstances the need for long-term rules and principles can conflict with the demands of short-term crisis management. This has been a major problem in the financial arena where the provision of a co-ordinating regime to provide the quasi-state function of a world central bank is needed to prevent financial collapses. The details of these arrangements are discussed later, but as Strange (1986, p. 173) points out: 'in recent international monetary history, it is the crises that central banks have been particularly good at dealing with. It is the chronic problems that have always been dodged and avoided.'

One of the most influential explanations of how the world central banking functions come to be fulfilled is given by Kindleberger (1973). He attributes them to a hegemonic power, though he avoids the term and refers to leadership. Essentially the United States acted as the world central bank after the Second World War just as Britain had done before the First World War. In the interwar period when neither could do it there was general chaos; as there was after 1971 when US dominance of the system was eroded. The role of hegemony is discussed further below as is the need for a world central bank, but first we consider the other method of providing quasi-state functions, international organisations.

International organisations

The need to regulate the internationalising economic activities and to provide quasi-governmental structures at a global level has spawned a whole set of multinational organisations. Of particular importance were the set of supra-national legal structures set up under the Bretton Woods system after the Second World War, including the International Monetary Fund (IMF), the International Bank for Reconstruction and Development (IBRD or World Bank), neither of which were world central banks, and the General Agreement on Tariffs and Trade (GATT). The status of such supra-national negotiating and legal or quasi-legal structures is controversial. They have substantial influence over governments, firms and economic processes, but limited power. They are prone to become bureaucratised and fall victim to the veto powers that member states preserve. They may merely be conduits for the transmission of the instructions of the hegemonic power. Governments have varied motives for joining or boycotting them (Jacobson et al., 1986).

Much of the co-ordinating discussion takes place within international organisations. These institutions have proliferated in layers, from the grand designs like the UN, NATO, EC, GATT, IBRD and IMF, to the equally important but more prosaic technical organisations, whose initials are unknown to all but specialists. Most are merely negotiating forums designed to facilitate a deal, which once negotiated becomes binding, to a greater or lesser extent, on the participating states. To get such deals agreed requires that the institution operates at the right level, in terms of the expertise and the political influence of the individuals involved, and includes a set of states likely to share a common interest in the matter at hand.

The requirements of a co-ordinating institution can demand a different gathering for virtually every problem. The revival of the Western European Union (WEU) is indicative in this respect: it provides a compromise between NATO and EC membership, neither of which were suitable for the defence discussions the French envisaged. The development of a 'variable geometry or 'à la carte' EC represents a response to similar problems. The composition of the gathering can be a very sensitive matter. Traditionally, some economic matters were discussed by the Group of Five (G5), composed of the countries whose currencies were widely used in international trade (the United States, Britain, Japan, West Germany and France); others were discussed by the Summit Seven: G5 plus Italy and Canada, whose heads of state met at the economic summits. Italy strongly opposed this division, particularly since (on some figures) it has displaced Britain as the fifth richest state, and consequently disrupted these meetings, with the consequence that the crucial currency decisions have moved to G3 (the United States, Japan and Germany). Membership is one aspect, leadership is another. The G (3, 5, 7)'s action on exchange rate at the 1985 Plaza and 1987 Louvre meetings were largely dependent on the willingness of the United States to act.

The line between the international organisations being an independent entity or a set of mechanisms at the disposal of nation states is very blurred. Co-ordinating institutions may not require formal organisations, but may be more informal arrangements such as the Paris Club, which is responsible for debt renegotiation. The Paris Club is an international forum for the rescheduling of service payments on debts granted or guaranteed by official bilateral creditors. It has neither a fixed membership nor an institutional structure. Rather it represents a set of practices and producers that have been developed over thirty years since the first ad hoc meeting was convened for Argentina in 1956. Meetings are traditionally chaired by the official of the French Treasury and were all open to all official creditors that accept Paris Club practices and procedures. In 1985 twenty-one reshedulings providing $18m dollars in debt relief were concluded (IMF survey, 1986, p. 297).

While many international institutions can be regarded as being like the Paris Club, a forum to agree a deal, like NATO and the EC in particular, have more ambitious aspirations. Not merely does each in its different sphere aim to provide its members with greater power and influence by the concentration of forces that would be otherwise dispersed, but each was impelled by a strong ideology or vision, and explicitly infringes sovereignty.

In the case of the EC the concentration of forces argument is clearly put by Lord Cockfield. He argues that one of the major reasons for Europe's indifferent economic performance 'is the continued fragmentation of the Community market. Instead of acting as a single economic unit of 320m people – almost as big as the US and Japan combined – we still act essentially as a dozen separate markets, a dozen individual economies, divided from one another by different laws, regulations and currencies, and often conflicting economic policies' (*Financial Times*, 22 July 1987).

Fortunately for its survival, the Community is held together by factors other than economic advantage.

Shared political commitments, to democratic governments within Western Europe and to an open and stable international order outside, shared concerns about the Atlantic Alliance and American leadership and about the Soviet threat, shared advantage in acting as a caucus in international negotiations both on economic and security issues, now provide the real cement of European co-operation. (Wallace, 1982)

Against this Padoa-Schioppa (1988, p. xi) comments that 'the Community's scope for economic action and successful development is, rather paradoxically, limited by the strictly economic nature of the Community itself. This is because the Community, unlike fuller political systems, is not responsible for the provision of essential "public goods" such as defence, justice and social security.'

The vision of President Jacques Delors of a more 'cohesive' Europe, with both a barrier-free internal market by 1992 and a greater central power, may be discounted as pious hopes by some and infringement of national sovereignty by others, but however little they inspire EC member governments, they appear to be inspiring others to rethink their attitudes to the Community. The United States and Japan have responded, in different ways, to a perceived threat of a fortress Europe. The peripheral states are trying to develop closer links. MNCs are changing their strategies and the EC is having to respond by developing its competition policy.

Whatever the potential of an integrated Europe, longer-term supranational visions are blurred by the shorter term pre-federal reality with its intergovernmental disputes over the budget and the Common Agricultural Policy, and deadlock over many detailed policies. The speed of economic change leaves the bureaucratic pace of EC initiatives far behind, and it has proved difficult to adjust Community policies except in crisis conditions. Thus the optimistic visions are replaced either by a more resigned recognition that there is no alternative to trying to create a more effective Community or by the stalemate, boredom and bitterness so characteristic of international negotiations (Strange, 1986, p. 45).

Hegemony

Constructing co-operative cartels, whether to price products, defend freedom, to co-ordinate macro policy or to construct a regime, is difficult and expensive. It helps to have a leader, who can move first, provide direction and perhaps enforce compliance with the regime. In game-theory terms leadership can move the system from a Nash to a Stackleberg solution, with potentially higher welfare (Artis and Ostry, 1986). In the international economic system the leader is commonly referred to as a hegemonic or hegemonial power or as a hegemon.

Hegemony is not a straightforward concept, even in this well-defined context, i.e. the role of Britain in the international economy before the First World War and the United States after the Second World War. There are, of course, quite different contexts: the Maoist code for Soviet activities or Gramsci's ideological dominance, for instance. The elements of hegemony can be military, economic, ideological or political. At the military level it corresponds to traditional dominance: the ability to project power, defend the system and act as a world policeman. At the economic level, it depends on the country's power in production, trade or finance, three elements which may not be congruent, and the ability and willingness of the country to take actions of the appropriate type and magnitude to sustain the system. At the ideological level it can involve being able to promulgate ethics, beliefs and aspirations favourable to the maintainance of the system, and perhaps favourable to the hegemonic power itself. At the political level it can involve pure leadership, moving first to establish a focal point in an uncertain environment that will provide a basis for co-ordinated action. Thus there are both subjective and objective elements in the creation of hegemony; hegemonic power may differ between issues; and different hegemons may be qualitatively different.

Gill (1986), for instance, argues that the order established by the United States after the Second World War was qualitatively unique.

This organic alliance was itself based on the congruence or 'fit' between interpenetrating political, economic and military structures. Central to this was the compromise between the gradual liberalisation of the world capitalist economy and the interventionist imperatives of domestic social democracy, and a general military commitment to contain the spread of Soviet Communism. This congruence enabled the institutionalisation of US hegemony, and the careful construction and maintenance of international regimes embodying principles and values favourable to the US. (p. 322)

The status of a hegemon is related to but qualitatively different from the traditional notion of a 'great power'. Kennedy (1989) charts the rise and fall of great powers since around 1500 and discusses the relative industrial decline and strategic overstretch of the United States without using the term hegemony. While the conventional wisdom is that US hegemonic power has declined and that, as a result, aspects of the regime have disintegrated, creating disorder in international capitalism, this interpretation is disputed by Strange (1988, p. 235) who argues that the United States has not in fact lost power, but rather misused it.

In the controversy about the nature and status of the concept of hegemony and the extent to which the United States was, or is, a hegemonic power, a central question is the relation between the economic and military dimensions of hegemony. There are very different balances between the willingness of the United States to lead and the other capitalist states to follow, in the military and economic spheres. Whereas US economic dominance has been eroded, its military dominance among the capitalist states remains unchallenged. The United States accounted for 43 per cent of OECD GNP in 1983, but 63 per cent of its military expenditure. In fact these proportions understate the asymmetry. US economic power was exaggerated by the then high dollar, its military dominance understated by the expenditure figure. Since economies of scale are more important in military forces than economic production, it matters more for relative power that US military expenditure was concentrated, while that of the other OECD states fragmented. More significantly, the hegemon's position has traditionally depended on its role as banker to the system, a role the United States will not be able to play now that it is the world's largest net debtor.

The regime of hegemonic stability may have ended in the economic sphere but it still remains the foundation of Western security policy. The linkage and tension between the two spheres remain problematical. For instance, Europe, recognising the end of the hegemonic stability in the global economy as a whole, might attempt to decouple and create a European Currency Unit zone of protected regulation within it, with Germany as the hegemon. But to do so would immediately raise the spectre of military decoupling from the United States, given the US deficit and its perception that it is carrying an unfair burden in defending Europe. More generally, the willingness of other capitalist states to accept US economic leadership has been influenced by the perceptions of the danger of a Soviet threat, perceptions which are being re-evaluated in the light of Gorbachev's initatives and change in other Warsaw Pact countries.

One interesting theoretical question is the extent to which hegemony is contradictory: the costs, particularly military, undermining the economic dominance on which it is based (Smith, 1977). There are clearly costs associated with operating a hegemonic regime. These include the transactions costs associated with arranging and defending the system, monitoring compliance and enforcing the rules. These costs fall, primarily, on the hegemonic power. The hegemonic power does gain some economic benefits from its position, such as 'seignorage' (the benefits from issuing money).

Although not strictly seignorage, the ability of the United States to run chronic balance of payments deficits, paying for its imports with paper rather than goods, is an immediate though eventually contradictory benefit.

Although the United States is widely seen as exploiting its power under neo-colonialism for its own economic benefit, just as Britain was seen as exploiting its colonial position in an earlier age, it is not clear that becoming a hegemon is a good investment in economic terms (Stein, 1984). The motivation is more likely to be political or ideological; the status and influence it brings is valued; power, not money, is the attraction.

TRENDS

This section examines the trend towards economic integration in a little more detail, under the headings of transport and communications; trade; production; and finance. In describing the process of internationalisation it tries: to identify the major policy problems that the process poses in each area; to consider the degree to which the autonomy of national states has been reduced; and to assess the extent to which a regime of international regulation has been constructed.

Transport and communications

The quantitative change in the speed, ease and cost of communications, whether the travel of people, the transport of goods or the telecommunication of information, needs no emphasis. However, this change has had qualitative consequences, not all of which are obvious. National policies depend on the existence of relatively impermeable boundaries which are eroded by enhanced communications (Cooper, 1986, ch. 4). Many economic and social policies depend on the ability of governments to control the range of products available within those boundaries. Mobility increases the cost of such regulation as cheap transport raises the profitability of evasion of controls over products such as drugs, pornography and official secrets. This is an area where economic opportunities and social changes are very closely linked.

Telecommunications unite fragmented markets, the globalisation of financial markets is largely a creation of electronic transmission and information technology. The advances in communications permit the centralised control vital to the development of MNCs and allows the development of international media, such as satellite television which make national controls on the information and entertainment available less effective. The companies, media and personal mobility create psychological interdependence, and foster common tastes, not only for Coca Cola, but also for a range of other global products which are eroding national differences in consumption patterns. Reduced transport costs bring competition to goods and services previously sheltered from international trade. Personal mobility, whether immigration, brain drains or just tourism, impacts on social structure and cohesion. Provision of abortions to foreigners provides an example of how reduced transport costs have not only made what was once a purely local service tradable, but reduced the effectiveness of governments' legal powers to restrict the choices of their citizens. Likewise, capital mobility limits the state's capacity to enforce its writ in taxation and regulation.

Partly because of the existence of natural monopolies and externalities, governments are heavily involved in the regulation and provision of communications facilities. Post Offices and PTTs were often state owned as were carriers such as railways and airlines. Since competitiveness can depend crucially on access to the advanced facilities of modern communications and to nodal gateway positions in global networks, provision of suitable infrastructure and internationally compatible standards becomes a major national concern. Internationalisation has increased competition in communications and encouraged the privatisation of national communications enterprises. The uncertainty and large fixed costs often associated with communications projects means that private enterprise faces problems of financing and efficient pricing. The Channel Tunnel may show that private provision is possible in such cases, but it is too early to judge how well Eurotunnel will overcome the financial obstacles.

Transport and communications projects are also often international, which requires negotiation between states to regulate the terms on which the transfers of goods or information take place. Strange (1988, ch. 7) examines the political economy of the quite different forms of regulation used in sea and air transport. Within Europe the regulation and control of communication (for example, airline pricing and landing rights) and the establishment of network standards (for example, to achieve compatible cellular radio systems) are a recurrent source of conflict. Technological and market trends mean that traditional forms of national provision and regulation are less feasible. In the case of direct broadcasting by satellite (DBS), provision (launch vehicles) and regulation (control of the material transmitted) need to be co-ordinated at a European level. However, national governments have resisted the European Commission's claim to be the appropriate body to regulate such broadcasting.

At a more down-to-earth level, telecommunications equipment production was once effectively protected in most major markets. In Britain the Post Office ran a cartel, with GEC, Plessey and STC being given fixed market shares. The poor export performance of these companies in telecommunications equipment would question the validity of any mercantilist justification for such protection. In any event, increasing R&D costs, the application of electronics and business demand for the most advanced communications infrastructure made this cosy arrangement unsustainable even without the privatisation of British Telecom. Similar trends are apparent in the telecommunications provision of other industrial countries, but attempts to create a European market or industry have not yet been successful (Morgan, 1987), though Community Competition Policy has targeted telecommunications equipment.

The reduced time and cost of transport and communication are central to all the forms of integration discussed below, and are instrumental in the creation of a new international division of labour. There are also some general points to be made about such trends. Firstly, they are not new, but have been progressing for centuries. Nor is it obvious that the rate of change is greater now than it was, for instance, in the third quarter of the last century when it allowed the expansion of the transatlantic grain trade. However, steady predictable trends can pass unexpected thresholds, when reduced costs make possible new opportunities, and thus have unpredictable consequences. The uses to which micro computers would be put was not something that could be predicted, even on the basis of the well-established trends in semiconductor technology. Interactions between well-understood trends (for example, in computers and in telephones) may also produce surprising results.

Secondly, the response to such trends is complicated by the fact that institutions have to adjust to the changes and provide new legal structures, accounting systems and regulatory frameworks, which take time to develop. While this is happening there is usually inadequate data, poor statistical coverage and considerable technical uncertainty. Nor will those involved have mastered the changing environment. In these circumstances, investment choices tend to be particularly risky (for example, cable or DBS?). The evolution of the trend reveals new constraints or bottlenecks within the social infrastructure which the authorities are unprepared to handle. The trends create new communities, unsocialised outsiders become involved and stable working relationships (the Post Office cartel) and shared values (public service broadcasting) are disrupted.

These features are characteristic of all the trends examined below. They pose difficult policy problems. The authorities must be sufficiently flexible to allow rapid adjustment and the exploration of the variety of possibilities

Table 5.1. *Percentage growth rates, 1953–85*

	1953–63	1963–73	1973–79	1979–85
World trade	6.5	8.9	4.7	2.1
World GDP	3.7	5.2	3.1	2.1
Ratio	1.76	1.71	1.52	1.00

Source: Boltho and Allsopp, 1987.

raised by new developments. Yet they must also provide clear direction that will minimise uncertainty and conflict while maximising positive interactions.

Trade

For most of the post-war period trade grew much faster than output, implying a rising share of exports and imports in national income (see table 5.1). In the early 1980s, trade seems to be growing at only about the same rate as output, whereas it grew faster in the later 1980s. The growth of protectionism, structural imbalance in the world economy or disturbances in the international monetary system can all produce a change in the relationship between output and trade. The Less Developed Countries were particularly badly hit by the debt crisis and the steep decline in primary product prices. The share of developing countries in world exports fell from a third in 1980 to just under a quarter in 1986 (IMF Survey, 1987, p. 227). The contrast between the period after 1973 and the 1930s is very striking. In the previous period of major international troubles (trough of the long-wave?) trade contracted abruptly. Maddison (1982) provides data on the phases of capitalist development. The maintenance of trade growth through the recent period of turbulence must be seen as a major achievement of the system: though it is not obvious what aspect of the system should be given credit for the achievement.

Explanations for the trend to increasing trade emphasise such factors as: declining transport costs; removal of protective barriers; diversification of production location by firms, partly to evade trade barriers; and the interaction of the demand by consumers for increasing variety of goods with the desire by firms to centralise and standardise production to take advantage of economies of scale. Whether these are structural trends or merely rationalisations for the observed growth in trade is difficult to tell. It is interesting to contrast these theories with those that were once put forward in the light of the experience of the 1930s. Then it was argued that industrialisation, rising incomes and technological diffusion were forces that would actually tend to diminish trade (Kenwood and Lougheed, 1983, p. 233).

There have been very substantial changes in the structure of world trade and Britain's trade. In the case of Britain, the traditional picture was that it exported manufactures and services to buy raw materials and food. It is now a net importer of manufactures and has a rough balance on non-manufactures (food, materials and fuel), though it remains a net exporter of services. In the United States the traditional picture has been found equally wanting. Political concern was expressed over a comparison of the top ten goods exported to Japan and imported from Japan. Whereas Japan exported high-technology manufactures to the United States, the USA, with one exception (civil airliners), primarily exported food and raw materials to Japan.

At a world level the growth of manufacturing exports by the Newly Industrialised Countries (NICs) of Latin America and the Far East represents another major structural change, symbolised perhaps by the RAF's purchase of a Brazilian designed basic trainer. Developing countries' exports of manufactures grew from $24bn in 1973 to $149bn in 1985, with three-quarters of the total accounted for by Taiwan, South Korea, Hong Kong and Brazil. Of course, over the longer term world economic growth has always been characterised by the appearance of a succession of newly industrialised countries.

Alongside the change in what we sell, there have been changes in who we sell to: away from Empire towards Europe, which now accounts for over half our trade. At the same time, Britain has steadily lost export share, from over 20 per cent of the world total in 1953 to less than 8 per cent now. Britain tended to do better during recessions since it sold relatively low-quality, low-tech goods. But this niche is being eroded by the entry of the NICs into the market. At home we have seen rising import penetration, particularly in manufactures. The flood of Japanese imports has been restricted to some extent by Voluntary Export Restraints (VERs) negotiated with exporters, but the gap has just been filled by imports from EC countries. The significance of this process, by which Britain has become 'deindustrialised', is a matter of dispute (Rowthorn and Wells, 1987).

Trade transmits variations throughout the world economy. A depression in other countries reduces our exports, lowering our demand, output and employment. Increasing trade creates increased economic interdependence. To an individual country its net position on trade is recorded in the balance of payments accounts, which portray nations as economic agents trading with each other. The position on international trade acts as a symptom of the health of the economy, any underlying structural weakness is manifested through the balance of payments and the exchange rate. The balance of payments itself used to be seen as an independent constraint, enforcing 'stop–go' policies and preventing that dash for sustained growth that would have solved all Britain's problems. Then the balance of payments constraint was removed by the discovery of North Sea oil. But rather than living happily ever after, the exchange rate was forced up and manufacturing output and employment reduced. Nor is the process symmetrical. There is no reason to believe that just because having found North Sea oil was bad, causing de-industrialisation, having it go away should be good. It can appear that to the British economy all blessings are problems in disguise. To some traditional Keynesian economists who say Britain's unusual position in 1987 of being the fastest growing European economy as a cyclical, electorally induced fluke, the recurrence of severe balance of payments troubles in 1988 seemed to confirm that the pessimism suggested by past experience was still justified.

Britain is a very open economy, in the sense that trade accounts for a large proportion of economic activity; imports and exports account for about a third of GDP. This acts as a constraint on the effectiveness of fiscal policy, in the sense that a large part of any reflationary boost is merely spent on imports and does not generate income or employment at home. In the United States the proportion is much smaller, less than 10 per cent and it was around 5 per cent ten years ago. This made US politics relatively insensitive to international repercussions of its actions, and it means that American economic theories, like monetarism, tended implicitly to assume a closed economy. The political response in the United States to increased domestic sensitivity to international economic developments is a matter for concern.

When the world moved from fixed to floating exchange rates in the early 1970s, it was suggested by some economists that balance of payments imbalances would be self-correcting because of exchange rate adjustments. This has not happened. Whether because exchange rate movements are destabilising or because governments have distorted their movements, the floating rate regime has been characterised by recurrent volatility and misalignment. There is a vast economic literature on the determination of exchange rates (Goodhart, 1988), which is beyond the scope of this review, but for most purposes they can be treated as a random walk.

The misalignment of exchange rates is reflected in substantial and persistent balance of payments imbalances. In 1987 the US trade balance was in deficit to the tune of \$154 billion while Japan and Germany had surpluses of \$87bn and \$45bn respectively, imbalances which persisted in subsequent years. Pairwise deficits, such as those of Britain and the United States with Japan, tend to attract the most attention; but because much trade is triangular or multilateral, trying to eliminate pairwise deficits may be counter-productive – the deficit with one country being the counterpart of a surplus with another.

As a result of running persistent balance of payments deficits, caused in part by large budget deficits, the United States has moved from being the world's largest net creditor (assets owned abroad less liabilities owed to foreigners) to being the world's largest net debtor, with a net external debt projected to reach over \$1,000bn by the early 1990s. Although there are statistical problems with the valuation of the assets, this is a debt of the same order of magnitude as that of the fifteen largest LDC debtors together. Unlike them the United States has the advantage that the debt is denominated in its own currency and the debt is smaller as a percentage of its GDP. The United States also earns a higher rate of return on its assets abroad than it pays on its debts, but it will still require interest payments of around \$35bn annually to foreigners in the 1990s. The politics of such payments by the United States to the rest of the world are difficult to imagine, and the reduction in American living standards required to effect the adjustment may be politically destabilising, fuelling protectionist or isolationist tendencies. The alternative, the acquisition of large parts of the US economy by foreigners, has also provoked political outrage. Neither candidate in the 1988 Presidential election seemed willing to confront the crucial economic issues, since to do so would involve a commitment either to tax increases or to cuts in the defence or social security programmes, commitments which were seen as politically damaging. The expectation was that, sooner or later, reality would persuade President Bush to renounce his explicit election pledge not to increase taxes.

Governments are heavily involved in the regulation of trade and in the international negotiations on tariffs and quotas partly through GATT, the framework designed after the Second World War to liberalise trade. Trade liberalisation has been sought in successive 'rounds', the current one being the 'Uruguay round'. Trade disputes are complex, fragmented, well studied and a major source of international acrimony. Jacques Pelksman (in Tsoukalis, 1986) characterises GATT as a bickering bigemony. GATT traditionally focused primarily on manufactured goods, but the central issue in the Uruguay round is its extension to agriculture and services. In most of these negotiations, Britain operates with or through the EC. This provides both the benefit of extra leverage in the negotiation and the costs that arise when British and EC interests do not coincide. As always, agriculture is a problem. The failure of the Montreal negotiations on the Uruguay round in December 1988 was followed by a fresh outbreak of fighting in the farm war between the EC and the United States, before negotiations were resumed.

High unemployment and the adverse effects of structural change and industrial decline have generated strong domestic pressures for protection and a more inteventionist trade policy in the United States and Europe. Developing countries, however, are tending to liberalise their exchange and trade regimes. Traditional disputes between mercantilist and liberal conceptions of the role of the state in international economic relations have become fashionable once more. In many cases, it is difficult to distinguish protection from certain types of domestic policies which may create non-tariff barriers against imports or subsidise exports through industrial support such as for R&D, say, in the development of Airbus. There are a range of economic arguments in favour of protection: micro, macro and strategic (in the game-theoretic sense) (Krugman, 1986) and protection has historically played a major role in successful industrialisation strategies. In this area, as in many others, the Japanese example has been closely scrutinised. In particular, it is argued that Europe can only generate the necessary volume to establish low costs of production in high-technology areas by creating a 'walled city' within which innovation and expansion would be profitable.

Economists have traditionally questioned the benefits of protection. British Treasury estimates of the costs of protection can be found in their *Economic Progress Report* of May 1985. The objection to protection is based partly on the argument that free trade maximises choice and welfare and partly on the grounds of second round effects. An import restriction may be followed by retaliation from the exporting country, or may lead to a breakdown in the general standard of rule observance which hits our exports elsewhere. Between 80 and 90 per cent of exports from both Britain and the United States are associated with MNCs and just under a third of the 100 largest British exporters in 1986 were foreign owned (*Financial Times*, 26 August 1987). Many of them have 'good citizen' policies which involve adjusting their sourcing to ensure rough balance between imports and exports. To the extent that they suffer the restriction on imports they are likely to reduce exports to compensate. The imports may also be components in exports (semiconductors, for instance) and the import tariff then raises the prices and reduces the competitiveness of the country's exports of assembled equipment. Protection itself may allow firms to become inefficient and uncompetitive, and foreign competitors may set up plants within the country to avoid a protective barrier. Pearce and Sutton (1985) for instance, discuss the issues associated with protection and industrial policy in Europe.

There are also military strategic arguments for intervention in trade. On the import side, protection, or prohibition on foreign ownership of particular firms or industries, such as parts of the Defence Industrial Base, may be seen as necessary to avoid dependence. GATT and EC rules on free trade have traditionally excluded defence equipment; however, fears of an EC tariff on imports of weapons provoked US concern. The high cost, fragmentation and over-capacity characteristic of the European arms industry is a cause for concern (Hartley et al., 1987). The Vredeling report to the Independent European Programme Group (IEPG) 'Towards a Stronger Europe' made recommendations for reform, but implementation has been slow. While the political pressures are for cross-Channel collaboration, the commercial pressures favour cross-Atlantic links, and acquisitions of US subsidiaries by British companies and of British by American companies have been common.

On the export side, transfers of arms or high-technology equipment may be restricted for security reasons. NATO and Japan co-ordinate their export restrictions through the co-ordinating committee, COCOM. Restraint of exports to the Soviet Union has been controversial, both between governments, where United States and European perceptions of the threat differ, and within governments, where Defence and Commerce departments may have different objectives. The restrictions can be quite severe (the ban on exports of 8 bit micros was only removed in the summer of 1987); have implications for the diffusion of information in science, technology and industry; and raise issues of the extra-territorial application of US laws. Toshiba's export through Norway to the USSR of milling machines which could be used to reduce submarine propellor noise, caused the US Congress to propose a ban on all Toshiba products.

Production

British industry has always been very internationally oriented and by international standards very concentrated (the 100 largest firms account for over half of production). This has meant that overseas production was always an opportunity available to large British multinationals, whereas in economies dominated by smaller, domestically oriented firms, operation on a national scale is emphasised. British multinationals traditionally were very large, though now they have have dropped down the league table, losing ground particularly to the Japanese.

These MNCs (or Trans National Enterprises) have been extensively studied (Hood and Young, 1979; Dunning and Robson, 1988). The largest 600 industrial companies account for between a fifth and a quarter of manufacturing value added in the market economies, and the service-oriented MNCs are rapidly expanding (United Nations, 1988). They integrate production on a regional, if not global scale: multi-sourcing components and transferring assembled products between countries. The integration is not merely through direct investment in subsidiaries but through franchising, collaborative joint ventures and subcontracting with independent firms or state organisations. There is a real sense in which the MNCs have been more successful at creating truly European institutions, integrated on a continental scale like Ford Europe, than have the European political bodies. Ford centralises European R&D, strategic planning and finance; the EC has not been able to co-ordinate, let alone centralise, any of these functions. *Business Week* (31 August 1987) in a cover story on 'Creating Europe Inc' claims that 'Corporate chieftains have eclipsed governments in the quest for an integrated Europe' (p. 28). Of course, these corporate chieftains integrating Europe are as likely to be American or Japanese.

With MNCs the nationality of the product becomes ambiguous. 'Foreign' cars with a large proportion of British-built components, for example, may be more British than apparently British ones. Ford for instance, was for long Britain's largest car importer, the foreign- and domestic-produced models being almost indistinguishable. As a result complex 'rules of origin' have developed informally, and under EC rules sometimes illegally, to establish criteria for product nationality (Holmes, 1987), and these rules provoked the dispute between Britain and France about the treatment of British-built Nissan cars.

As components are transferred between subsidiaries of the company, they are priced by the company. The 'transfer price' that Ford uses to value components and assembled cars shipped between countries will determine the value of the country's exports and imports, the flows of foreign exchange, the profitability of each national subsidiary and the liability to taxation in each country. Since there is no arm's-length valuation, no real market in such items, the company has considerable leeway to choose the prices. This has implications for taxation, balance of payments and exchange control which have been the source of much concern. It is not clear that Britain necessarily suffered from transfer pricing, because it had a sophisticated regulation system and its low corporate tax rate made it an attractive place to declare profits.

To help countries, particularly less developed ones, deal with transfer prices, specialised consultants (pre-shipment inspection companies) provide valuations and price comparisons of the goods transferred. American exporters have begun to litigate and lobby against such companies and the Department of Trade and Industry was under pressure from British exporters to outlaw such price comparison checks (*Financial Times*, 21 July 1987). One British exporter complained that 'HMG quite willingly permits a private concern acting as the agent of the Government of a foreign power to demand confidential information on a British company's profit margins, establishment costs and pricing policy'. The DTI submitted the issue to the European Commission which intended to take it to the Uruguay round of GATT talks.

This small example raises a range of illustrative issues. The problems of control of multinational companies; the development by the market of solutions, like the consultancies, to policy problems; the limits to sovereignty; the ambiguous national interest of Britain (control MNCs or help British exporters?); the need to co-ordinate actions through multilateral institutions; and the technical complexity of most of the issues.

The role of governments in trying to deal with MNCs is never as straightforward as the 'sovereignty at bay' approach portrays it. The governments will use incentives and regulations to attract internationally mobile capital in competition with other countries, to defend their own companies and to maximise the benefits the country gains from MNC decisions. In some areas Britain has done quite well in this competition. In pharmaceuticals eight of the fifty top-selling drugs are reported to be made in Britain (*Financial Times*, 28 July 1987), second only to the United States. But the attractiveness of Britain as a place to locate research and production may be at the expense of higher prices to the National Health Service which the government has used as an incentive. Nor are the companies sovereign states, they are dependent on their relationships with host governments, hence the good citizen policies, and they are themselves subject to global market forces.

Multinational companies pose an extreme problem of nationality. At first sight, their nationality may appear identifiable in terms of ownership and head office location; though there are exceptions where the company has dual nationality, like Unilever and Shell, or where the company head office is internationally mobile. But formal nationality cannot be identified with corporate national interest. Foreign-owned companies may produce and invest more in Britain than British-owned ones whose prime concern is to diversify overseas. The outflow of long-term investment overseas by British companies increased; being matched by an inflow from foreign companies. The growth of British-owned assets located overseas in the last decade has been phenomenal. Total net external assets grew from £12.1bn at end 1979 to £113.2bn at end 1986, before dropping to £89.5bn at end 1987 as a result of the strong pound and the October 1987 crash. Britain returned to the position at the beginning of this century when over half of its investment flowed overseas. Much of this is portfolio investment, rather than foreign direct investment, and is partly explained as an adjustment to the removal of exchange controls in 1979. But there has also been a heavy investment in expansion and acquisition, particularly in the United States where Britain is the largest foreign investor. Not all of these acquisitions have been successful: the experience of Midland Bank with Crocker, or Ferranti with ISC, are examples. Although there have been a number of European acquisitions and joint ventures, quantitatively the main thrust of British companies has been expansion in the United States rather than in Europe.

For policy purposes, criteria for corporate nationality may be based on ownership, or location of production, or the amount of employment in Britain. It may be invidious to offer attractive grants to foreign companies to locate in Britain, when such grants are not available to indigenous companies. Should one distinguish between 'good foreigners', such as the European consortium as Heseltine argued over Westland, and 'bad foreigners', such as the United States or Japanese? In some cases strategic arguments can be made. However, the restrictions on foreign ownership of privatised defence companies (15 per cent of the shareholding of BAe and Rolls Royce) was successfully challenged by the European Commission and the proportion was increased. In other cases, commercial and strategic arguments operate in different directions. The government seemed to be grateful initially for the support Kuwaiti purchases provided for BP shares when their price was so depressed immediately after the 1987 crash and privatisation issue. Once the shares were firmer, strategic issues seemed more important, and the Kuwaitis were forced to reduce their holding. In general, it is not clear that it matters whether companies are foreign owned if the result is a more successful producer. Nor, given that owners are motivated by profits and constrained by market forces, should we expect large British-owned companies to be any more patriotic than foreign-owned companies with substantial interests here. Issues of nationality also arise at a European level, for instance over whether IBM should be allowed to join the EC Esprit high-technology research project. IBM is one of the largest European electronics companies, Britain's fifth largest exporter, and holds 35 per cent of the market for computers in Europe; but many in Europe saw the whole point of the project as challenging IBM.

There have been various attempts to create a European industrial policy, and to foster the development of European champions, many of whom were earlier promoted as national champions. So far they have foundered on national regulatory obstacles, lack of commercial logic and the difficulties of combining competition with collaboration. Such corporatist visions are also now less fashionable outside the defence sphere. Industry is also developing cross-border links through initiatives such as the European Roundtable of industrialists established by Volvo President Pehr Gyllenhammer, as well as by mergers and joint ventures, but progress is slow and beset with difficulties.

It may not make any sense to try to create such European champions since there is a fundamental sense in which the large MNCs are 'denationalised' in the sense of being non-national. They accept obligations to host countries, but plan on the basis of global profitability, with little special concern for their parent country. This raises nice ironies. In Angola, Cuban troops protected the assets and profits of an American multinational (Chevron's Gulf Oil subsidiary) from attack by American-financed guerrillas. The State Department position was that it wanted Chevron 'to take into account US interests'; the Pentagon wished to take stronger action by withholding oil contracts (*Financial Times*, 2 May 1986).

The idea that the economic interest of Britain is associated with the economic interest of British-owned companies no longer holds. Corporate nationality is undefined and economic interest ambiguous.

Finance

London has always been a major financial centre and it has played a major role in the globalisation and rapid growth of the financial markets. The dominance of the City plays an important role in some explanations of Britain's poor economic performance, both in terms of the international orientation and the contrast between market-based financial systems like London and those organised around industrial banking like the European continent and Japan. The latter are regarded as having a longer-term strategic vision towards national investment particularly in R&D, in contrast to the myopic short-termism of stock market oriented systems.

Even when the production side of the British economy was not doing well, finance blossomed in London. Banking, Eurocurrency, Foreign Exchange, Securities, Insurance and Commodities remain important activities in London. In the longer run it is possible that liberalisation in the trade in services pressed for by the United States and the growth of new competitors may threaten London's position, or leave it dominated by foreign companies taking advantage of the time difference with New York and Tokyo. Because Britain earns a lot of money from the City and because governments must be sensitive to the repercussions of their actions on capital flows, national policies are constrained to preserve the City's health. On occasion Britain has been an obstacle to international monetary reforms, such as regulation of the Eurocurrency market, that might threaten London's position.

The capital flows in the foreign exchange market dwarf the trade flows; 89 per cent of Foreign Exchange transactions are purely between banks, and an estimated 95 per cent are not related to any trade or direct investment transfer, but result from swaps, speculation, hedging against risk, and the like. Partly as a result of the volatility of these markets there has been a growth in the importance of the Treasury function within companies over the last decade. Companies can make or lose more money on financial management, such as coverage of foreign exchange exposure, than they do on their main activity of production. The case of GEC, which for long earned more by investing its £1.5bn cash mountain in the money markets than in productive investment, is illustrative. The integration of short-term capital markets has gone much further than that of long-term capital markets, and different national regulatory structures still constitute important barriers to the international trade in securities. However, these barriers are being eroded both by financial innovation and by policy changes such as the move towards a single EC market by 1992.

The growth of the international financial markets, the trend to deregulation, the succession of 'Big Bangs' in different countries, the proliferation of new instruments (swaps, options, and the like) and the volatility of interest and exchange rates, can be seen in many ways. On the one side it is 'Casino Capitalism' (Strange, 1986), speculative roulette which distorts the real economy. On the other side the markets are seen as a flexible and essential adjustment mechanism which share risks and have enabled the system to cope with severe shocks. The British Treasury, commenting on an OECD report, says: 'Increased internationalisation and deregulation of financial markets has already produced significant benefits through increased competition and more efficient resource allocation' (Economic Progress Report, August 1987, p. 4).

A financial system should contain mechanisms to promote adjustment, provide liquidity, maintain confidence and supply an anchor that stabilises prices (Rybczynski, 1987). The claimed weaknesses of the current system, or non-system as some would have it, are the volatility and unpredictability of exchange rates and interest rates; the large and persistent misalignments among major currencies; the lack of discipline and co-ordination of macro policies among major countries; and the asymmetric adjustment it imposes on some countries. Managed exchange rates, it is claimed, would reduce uncertainty, impose some discipline on policy-makers and keep rates closer to fundamentals. Whether such targeted rates are possible given the structure of economic power, the high degree of capital mobility and the desire for national autonomy is another matter.

The claimed strengths of the system are that it increases the efficiency of capital markets by lowering intermediation costs, narrows cost differences between countries and between instruments, and spreads risks associated with exchange rate and interest rate uncertainty. Of course, procedures that reduce individual risk, through pooling or switching to shorter-term investments, may increase system risk and the danger of a total collapse like that of the 1930s (Portes and Swoboda, 1987). Some co-ordinating regime is needed to offset that risk.

The provision of a co-ordinating regime to provide the quasi-state functions discussed in the second section is particularly important in the financial arena, where central bank activities are needed to prevent financial collapses. From the start of the expansion of capitalism, the trade cycle slumps were preceded by a financial crisis. The exact definition of a financial crisis is a matter of dispute (Eichengreen and Portes, in Portes and Swoboda, 1987) but from the Mississipi and South Sea Bubbles of 1720 onwards, there was a succession of 'Manias, Panics and Crashes' (Kindleberger, 1978) at roughly ten-year intervals. In Britain, these ended with the Baring Crisis of 1891, in the United States with the Great Crash of 1929.

This tendency of the system to crash recurrently was ended by the intervention of the national central banks. The central bank did two things: it provided Lender of Last Resort (LLR) and similar protective facilities such as deposit insurance; and it established preventative Prudential Regulation. Both were necessary for stability, neither sufficient.

LLR facilities for illiquid financial institutions maintain confidence, thus stopping contagion, withdrawal of deposits, and the failure of strings of banks and firms because of domino effects. But alone, they are not enough. If banks know that the central bank will always bail them out, they are encouraged to lend on more dangerous but more profitable investments, since the central bank absorbs the downside risk. Thus LLR facilities have to be combined with prudential regulation to ensure that the banks remain solvent. This is done by restricting the type of investments that banks can make, and requiring reserve-asset and capital-adequacy ratios to be maintained. Prudential regulation alone is not enough because even if a bank is solvent, with assets greater than liabilities, it might become illiquid. Then it would not have the cash to meet its immediate liabilities, either because of unexpected shocks or because of the dangers created by its function of borrowing short and lending long. Thus LLR facilities, or deposit insurance, are also needed.

The problem is that although national regulation and LLR facilities were established, the system became international, much of it 'offshore' to any particular country, so that it was unclear which central bank was responsible for either supervision or support, nor was there a world central bank to fulfil these roles at a global level. The International Monetary Fund (IMF) is a bank for countries; the World Bank a development institution; the Bank for International Settlements (BIS) a clearing house. Thus financial crises recurred but at an international not national level. The failures of the Herstatt in 1974, and Ambrosiano in 1982 prompted central bankers, through the Basle Concordat of 1975 and subsequently the Cooke Committee, to attempt to clarify responsibility for bank supervision, if not support. But many ambiguities remain, in part because the distinction between banks and other financial institutions has become very blurred and the relation of the foreign branch or subsidiary to the parent ambiguous.

What constitutes a bank differs internationally with implications for the stability of the financial system, because it can be unclear who is responsible for it. The failure of Banco Ambrosiano Holdings (BAH) in Luxembourg left bankers with unsatisfied claims asking why the Bank of Italy was not responsible, whereas the Bank of Italy did not regard BAH as a bank (Guttentag and Herring, in Portes and Swoboda, 1987, p. 175). In 1987, the granting of British deposit-taking licences to two Japanese securities companies enabled them to undertake banking business in London which they could not do in Tokyo. The January 1987 agreement by the United States and Britain to have a common regulatory framework to determine a bank's capital adequacy was thus 'a major step forward in international convergence' (Bank of England Quarterly Bulletin, May 1987), which has since been extended to other countries.

Some saw the move to floating exchange rates as removing constraints on domestic economic policy. In fact, contrary to what was expected, the combination of floating exchange rates and extreme short-term capital mobility has not increased the scope for an autonomous monetary policy (Thygesen, in Tsoukalis, 1986). World events impinge on money supply and interest rates, stopping them being set freely by the government. Thus relatively fixed exchange rates appear more attractive. Even if there is still no scope for a complete system of fixed exchange rates, the exchange rate mechanism of the European Monetary System offers a substantial degree of stability, despite the regular realignments. In addition, the ECU, which is quite widely used for private financial transactions, could play a useful role in the reform of the international monetary system (Strange, 1986, p. 187). The British government is now issuing ECU-denominated Treasury bills. Given that it is not possible to establish a stable global financial system using the IMF Special Drawing Rights, a European system using the ECU might be second best, and might be easier to negotiate.

Britain's extended refusal to join the exchange rate mechanism of the EMS thus constitutes an interesting political question. There were economic issues: the appropriate rate at which to join the suitability of the intervention arrangements, the extent to which Britain's high real interest rates reflect a risk premium for sterling's volatility, the effect of the oil price on the British exchange rate, and the extent to which monetary policy would be further constrained, or would need to converge. None the less, at heart the refusal appeared political, associated as much with sovereignty as economic policy; a perception that membership constituted a recognition of deutschmark dominance and a constraint on independent action.

Conclusion

This part of the review has examined trends, and trends are designed to be extrapolated. However, it is important to bear in mind the warnings at the end of the first section, and to remember that the most interesting developments and most difficult policy problems arise not from the direct effects of the trends themselves, which may be foreseeable, but from processes which are *ex ante* inconceivable such as threshold effects and second-order interactions between trends.

The debt crisis provides an example of interaction effects. In 1970, despite the long history of international debt defaults, it would have been inconceivable that the developing countries would, in 1986, have an external debt, mainly to private banks, of over $1bn. As Kindleberger (1970, p. 167) says: 'Apart from Mexico, few if any such countries have the credit standing that entitles them to sell bonds to private investors.' For them to acquire that debt required a whole chain of unlikely events: the oil crisis and the massive flows to OPEC; the failure of the international community to develop any official system of recycling those funds; the expansion of the Eurocurrency markets and the development of syndicated credits; the willingness of bankers to believe in the safety of sovereign debt; the willingness of the borrowers to accept vast obligations subject to currency and interest rate uncertainty; and the unwillingness of the international community to take early remedial action when the risks were so apparent (Kindleberger, 1978). *Ex post*, the chain is clear. *Ex ante* many of the links would have appeared inherently improbable and their conjunction quite unthinkable. Eichengreen and Portes (in Portes and Swoboda, 1987) discuss the role of linkages in the generation of financial crises.

Threshold effects arise when a smooth quantitative trend passes a crucial boundary and produces a qualitative transformation of the system into something quite different. The events of August 1971, when President Nixon's economic package transformed the international economic system, might be such a boundary. The difficulty is that the threshold is difficult to identify in advance; by definition we have no observations on it, and the structure of the successor system is likely to be a matter for imagination. Economic theorists preoccupied with models that exhibit a unique stable equilibrium path have given such processes comparatively little attention, though there may be hope in more recent models which exhibit multiple equilibria, 'chaotic' patterns or path-dependent probabilities.

POLICIES

This final section will not consider the specific options for British policy, many of which have already arisen and are discussed extensively in the literature. In particular, Tugendhat and Wallace (1988) and Treverton (1985) consider the international economic dimension of foreign policy in some depth. Instead, we shall return to the general questions about the appropriate framework to use which were raised in the introduction. In providing a framework for policy formation, one can focus on problems, polarities or processes; each will be examined in turn.

Problems are the primary concern of policy, the detailed day-to-day issues that occupy the bulk of government time, the sensitive, often technical, questions that require resolution. This chapter has tried to emphasise the range and complexity of these questions, and any daily paper will provide scores more examples of international economic issues that require a governmental position. A general argument in this review is that the international policy issues that concern governments, either because they are involved in negotiations or because they have to respond to foreign developments, have increased in quantity and heterogeneity. Thus the policy-making apparatus is fragmented into specialist groups dealing with complex questions, without general foreign policy co-ordination. Traditional diplomacy, involving bilateral exchanges between professionals conducted on the basis of mutual confidence, has been supplanted by detailed technical, political and sectoral exchanges contaminated by domestic interests and conducted by issue specialists unaware of diplomatic implications. Other countries will then infer British attitudes from such detailed responses. If Britain fails to co-ordinate these responses, other countries may make misleading inferences about British attitudes, creating uncertainty and complicating international relations.

Polarities are used to characterise such general attitudes and to provide the political representations of the alternative approaches. The list of familiar polarities is long, including: 'state intervention' or 'market forces'; 'growth' or 'conservation'; 'protectionism' or 'free trade'; 'efficiency' or 'distribution'; 'national sovereignty' or 'international community'; 'Atlanticist' or 'European'. Dispute about the location of policy along such polarities is central to political debate. In a parochial context it is tempting to project such positions on to a Conservative–Socialist axis. In a comparative context, location on the Left–Right axis tends to be a poor predictor of positions on such polarities. Consider a right-wing military dictator, fearful of the disruptive effects of market forces, following a protectionist policy, which gives priority to maintaining the economic position of his power base, emphasising national sovereignty and close links with the United States. He is followed by a Socialist government, which frees markets, opens up the economy and emphasises efficiency within a European Community. While this is an oversimplification of the Iberian experience, that and a range of other examples could be used to indicate the lack of correlation.

The process of decision-making by which national position on such polarities is determined can be characterised in many different ways. Rather than examine the realities of process, consider the economist's idealised account. This involves the government:

- specifying national interests and objectives, the ends to which policy is directed;
- identifying the appropriate instruments: the means by which policy can be effected;
- assessing the capability of those means to achieve the desired ends, given the environment it faces;
- devising a strategy, which uses the means available in the most effective way to achieve the desired ends; and
- implementing that strategy.

In this account position on a polarity is the outcome of the process, not a determinant of policy. Such a decision-making process is not, of course, a description of how policy is actually made. The issues are rarely even structured in that way, except, perhaps, for some types of technical economic management. None the less it poses a range of important issues.

The primary one, and in many ways the most difficult, is the specification of national objectives or interests. Lord Palmerston's view that Britain had no eternal allies or enemies, only eternal interests, which it was his duty to follow, may once have been true; the difficulty now is lack of clarity about interests and perhaps a reluctance to change accepted views about allies and enemies. While Mrs Thatcher's foreign policy has been characterised by its resolute, and often acrimonious, defence of British national interest, the interests involved have tended to be defined in terms of narrow, short-run, economic advantage: contributions to the European Community, trading concessions, foreign orders, and the like.

Unlike domestic economic policy, where the Medium-Term Financial Strategy provided a long-run framework and monetarism provided a philosophy, there has been little concern in foreign policy with defining either long-term interests or general philosophy. The five guiding principles set out in Mrs Thatcher's Bruges speech are a shopping-list rather than a philosophy. They were:

- Willing and active co-operation between independent sovereign states is the best way to build a successful European Community.
- Community policies must tackle present problems in a *practical* way.
- The need for Community policies which encourage enterprise.
- Europe should not be protectionist.
- Europe must continue to maintain a sure defence through NATO.

Nor are the British government's four, first-order, foreign policy objectives (cited in Wallace, 1980, p. 187) operational principles. They were:

- to ensure the external security of Britain;
- to promote the country's economic and social well-being;
- to honour international commitments; and
- to work for a peaceful and just world.

The dilemma is that while clear objectives are necessary to co-ordinate policy, avoid conflicts and stop the transmission of misleading signals to other countries, yet circumstances may be such that it is impossible to provide a coherent operational philosophy of national economic interest which is suitable for policy purposes. This is not a new problem. Frankel (1970), for instance, distinguishes four uses of the term 'national interest', which he calls 'aspirational, operational, explanatory and polemical', and comments that foreign policy is generally pursued without any clear purpose (p. 26).

There does seem to be a case for some aspirational-polemical conception of the national interest in foreign policy, comparable to monetarism in domestic economic policy. It might, at least, provide operational guidance to the specialists negotiating their international deals, and help explain

Britain's actions to the world. Without such a philosophy, other characterisations will appear plausible.

> Britain has had the same foreign policy objective for at least the last five hundred years – to create a disunited Europe. In that cause we have fought with the Dutch against the Spanish, with the Germans against the French, with the French and Italians against the Germans, and with the French against the Italians and Germans … In other words, divide and rule. And the Foreign Office can see no reason to change when it has worked so well until now … It was necessary for us to break up the EEC, so we had to get inside. We had previously tried to break it up from the outside but that didn't work. Now that we're in, we are able to make a complete pig's breakfast of it. We have now set the Germans against the French, the French against the Italians, the Italians against the Dutch, and the Foreign Office is terribly happy. It's just like old times. (Lynn and Jay, 1981, p. 117)

Acknowledgements

I am grateful to a large number of people who made comments on earlier versions, in particular Jerry Coakley; the discussants at the Conference: DeAnne Julius and Loukas Tsoukalis; and the many generations of students at the Civil Service College who interrupted my lectures on Britain and the World Economy to put me right.

6 ～ Towards a theory of state and sovereignty in contemporary Britain

Ellen Kennedy

'The British State in the Contemporary World' assumes a distinction central to modern political theory: the government is not the state. An earlier generation was inclined to dispense with the notion of the state altogether, or at least deny it any analytical status. Agreement among English political thinkers on this point cut across political orientations, but wherever the 'anti-state' attitude appeared, it concurred with T. D. Weldon's view. 'The state ... has a vague but ordinary' meaning and a 'precise, legal, technical, usage' – anything else tends to end in an irrationalism born of 'unconscious addiction to the mustical residue' in the concept itself.[1]

I want to argue here against that view on two grounds. Throwing out the state doesn't help us with empirical analysis nor can we understand the conceptions that are crucial to political life in democracies unless we have some notion of the state as a thing different from governments of the day. Yet it would be foolish to assume that 'the state' is an obvious concept at any level above the 'vague and ordinary'. While generating an abstract conception of the state is at most a logical problem and the ordinary notion of the state can easily be found on the Clapham omnibus, these are not really what concerns us.

We are after something more elusive, what Hegel would have recognised as a true concept. We want to know what this familiar word in the vocabulary of political theory has to do with the actions and responsibilities of states in the world we live in towards the end of the twentieth century.

Sovereignty has been the keystone of our thinking about political authority and power since the seventeenth century. But in a political world so interdependent as ours the ordinary meaning of sovereignty sounds increasingly archaic – even if British foreign policy in the 1980s did much to revive it. It remains important for reasons that also make it difficult to discuss adequately in abstract terms: 'What is argued about in the history of sovereignty is the concrete application' (Schmitt, 1976, 1985). The Falklands War of 1982 illustrates the truth of that better than any other incident in recent British history. Should it prompt revision of our assumptions about the state and sovereignty? Or does it confirm the major premises of traditional theory? Whether there must be any substantial modifications of these concepts and if so, the direction our thinking should take, depends of course on what has been claimed about the state.

Sovereignty can be defined simply as 'the idea that there is a final and absolute authority in the political community', but there are always two sides to the doctrine (Hinsley, 1986, p. 1). Considered internally, it asserts that for the sake of domestic peace and legal security government as an office of the state must enjoy the 'final and absolute authority' to which F. H. Hinsley's definition refers. In foreign affairs, sovereignty implies precisely the opposite: there is no final and absolute authority above nations. That division defines the boundary of two European traditions of political thought. Positivists sharply distinguish between the state's internal and external spheres and stress its material reality. Idealists justify the state as an articulation of public values. Both traditions can be read as an attempt to mediate the dualism inherent in the reality of the state itself, resolving it as a dialectic of power and authority. Together they provide all the important elements of our conception of political life in the modern state.

THE POSITIVIST LINE: FROM HOBBES TO AUSTIN AND DICEY

Arguably the most influential test in English for a theory of the state is Hobbes's *Leviathan* (1659). Written in the context of civil war, it offers two models of political reality: one dangerous and anarchic, the other peaceful and secure. Before sovereignty (the state of nature) men are free and equal with natural rights to whatever interests them. The laws of nature (morals) oblige only when they would not endanger the individual and are thus left to private judgement. No system of rules (law) or enforcement (courts) stands over the individual's natural right to self-preservation and the pursuit of interests. Since this is the condition of life ('the desire for power after power ceasing only in death') natural freedom cannot produce felicity but results in constant insecurity.

Hobbes's *Leviathan* develops an hypothesis about human nature that allows us to understand how governments come into existence and why sovereignty is necessary to peace in political societies. The most irrational factors (fear and self-interest) function to release men from their original circumstances. In constituting a sovereign power, individuals surrender all their natural liberties (except the right of self-preservation) absolutely in exchange for protection from each other and those outside the commonwealth. This act means more than consent to government – 'it is the real unity of them all' (Hobbes [1659] 1972, p. 227). Through men's natural constitution-giving power their collective representation is authorised and the artifice of sovereignty which is the state comes into being. Only this device allows the laws of nature to become the substance of positive law and thus binding on men's actions.

The state of nature model also suggests a conceptually powerful starting-point for international relations theory because it seems to fit the reality of politics among nations so closely, as Hobbes himself recognised (p. 187). But its relevance lies less in Hobbes's analysis of anarchy than in its model of politics in an uncertain world. The implication of his suggestion that sovereign states are in a position analogous to natural men is not developed. These were first explored by J. L. Austin's *The Province of Jurisprudence Determined* (1832) which develops the consequences of a plurality of sovereign states for British jurisprudence.

For Austin 'sovereignty' and 'independent political society' were inextricably linked. It made no sense to talk about the former if the latter did not describe the actual conditions of a given people, and it was equally illogical to conceive political society without a notion of sovereignty. The mutual relation existing between sovereign and subject is defined by reference to 'dependence or subjection' (the position of the subject) and 'independence or superiority' (the sovereign's position). All sorts of societies with various forms of rule-governed conduct exist, but only those characterised by relations between sovereign and subject constitute 'independent political society' or 'an independent and sovereign nation' for Austin (Austin, [1832] 1954, p. 195).

Societies can be political or natural but not both, and the marks of sovereignty and independence are uncertain. The varieties of societies existing in the world cannot be distinguished solely by reference to independence (or sovereignty), and to avoid the uncertainties that would follow, Austin suggests the simple measure of size. Only societies of a certain size and habitually obeying a sovereign power are genuinely political societies according to that test. 'Natural societies' which are very small, even if they are independent, cannot be regarded as political societies; primitive peoples such as those who live by 'hunting or fishing in the woods or coasts of New Holland' and 'the ordinary state of the savage and independent societies which range in the forests or plains of the North American continent' are thus excluded from the community of nations (p. 209).

Sovereignty thus depends on a capacity in the relations of states. No society can be regarded as political and independent, unless, he argues with Hobbes, 'it can maintain its independence, against attacks from without, by its own intrinsic or unaided strength' (p. 213). Recognition by other states is the sign of sovereignty. When should a given society be recognised by others? Austin's test case for recognition – Mexican independence from Spain – has often repeated itself in our century. If members of the society habitually obey an instance (the sovereign) and that society is independent in the specifically Austinian sense of having its laws made only by itself, then it should be recognised. *The Province of Jurisprudence Determined* is also important for another reason. Austin held that law originates as a command carrying sanctions. This definition serves as a criterion for distinguishing 'law' from other sorts of rules such as moral rules, codes of conduct, manners, the rules of a game or club. Similarly norms of international law and what H. L. A. Hart calls 'fundamental constitutional laws' are rules but not law in Austin's sense. The laws of God, or natural laws, are laws only because God commanded them.

If command and sanction define law, why do men obey? From fear or duty? Austin's answer is clear: laws are obeyed by individuals because they are in the habit of doing so. Following Hobbes, Austin recognises that a variety of specific considerations motivate obedience, but these fall into two categories of types of obligation: *moral* obligation. (I obey because I think it right to do so) or *prudential* (I obey because I am afraid of the consequences of disobedience). The sovereign is both the source of law and the reference point of obedience in political society and thus crucial to an analysis of law. If the criterion of command and obedience tells us what 'law' is, how can we recognise sovereignty? Austin's analysis shifts the question to established custom and convention as elements defining a constitution and makes the case of 'clear, hard, empirical terms' (Austin, [1832], 1954, p. ix). He thought this would make identification of 'sovereignty' like the notion of law itself, easy and practical.

This notion became the centre of legal theory in nineteenth-century England, and a generation later, A. V. Dicey made it the foundation of constitutional law.

Hobbes conceived 'the unity of them all' as representation in the state, but representation is a fiction and the state is an artifice. Dicey's *The Law of the Constitution* realised this theory in British consitutional law: 'The sovereignty of Parliament is, from a legal point of view, the dominant characteristic of our constitution' (Dicey, [1885] 1982, p. xviii). It means no more or less than that Parliament has 'the right to make or unmake any law whatever; and further that no person or body is recognised by the law of England as having a right to override or set aside the legislation of Parliament' (p. xviii). Dicey's is still the classic expression of the internal aspect of sovereignty in British constitutional law, defining it simply as 'all rules which directly or indirectly affect the distribution or the exercise of the sovereign power in the state' (p. 22).

Dicey used Austin's notion of political conventions to restate the doctrine of sovereignty in moden England, but the implications of his argument could not be developed through a functionalist approach to political conventions. Dicey's theory of conventions as intended to ensure that law expresses 'the will of that power which in modern England is the true political sovereign of the State – the majority of the electors or (to use popular though not quite accurate language) the nation' assumes a concept of democractic legitimacy developed more fully by the idealists (p. 424).

THE IDEALIST LINE: FROM HEGEL TO GREEN AND BOSANQUET

Traditional conceptions of legitimacy referred primarily to historic title that was typically at issue in disputed succession. Although historic claim can be entered in evidence in an international court of law and may be construed in its judgement, other and more political claims play a larger part in the definition of legitimacy today. Appeals to higher values today 'trump' purely historic or procedural claims about legitimacy (Dworkin, 1982). Customs of international law, its conception of a 'civilised nation' and of 'principles of humanity, the standards of international law and the conscience of mankind' are part of the international legal order (Falk, 1985, p. 263). Many treaties in this century, beginning with the Hague Conventions on the Laws and Customs of War (1907), try to define the normative aspects of international relations as binding rules for the signatory nations. Trials of 'war criminals' based on these treaty obligations, as well as exercise of the extraordinary sovereign power of *ex post facto* legislation followed the world wars. Such notions now belong to the ordinary expectations of the mass or people when it comes to international affairs. The abstract concepts that guide international legal thinking about the world order will be discussed at greater length in the next section. It is enough for now to note their role in the global public constituted by vast systems of news-gathering and commentary.

One might think that no two positions could be further apart than those of empiricism and idealism, yet English political thought in the last century provided a striking synthesis of them. How are they combined? What are the implications of their synthesis for our perceptions of world order?

Positivism says little about the political or ethical values on which the normative case for the state and politics rest, although the argument for prudent government suggests limits on the sovereign power of the state. Hobbes, for example, accepts that equity binds the sovereign as much as it does the private man, but its rule is conceived as a procedure. While concern for equity might check power, no institutional restraints are placed on it, and sovereignty continues to exhibit its definitive characteristics – unity of decision and finality of judgement. This is still the central idea behind the British tradition of an unwritten constitution, but when democratic values of participation are taken into consideration, such limitations seem inadequate.

The limitations on sovereignty implicit in the positivist theory of prudent government are political and cultural – they assume a criterion of legitimate government in evaluation of competing political claims. Austin considered that habit and obedience justified sovereignty. Hobbes thought it justified by the needs of individuals. These philosophers generate a theory of the state through considerations of individual interest. Questions about the purpose of the state as such, or the role a political commonwealth might play in the realisation of goals above individual interests, are not raised.

But precisely those questions are implicit in the idea of democracy. Hegel's *Philosophy of Right* changes our perspective dramatically while retaining essential features of the Hobbesian world of international relations. Like Hobbes, Hegel too understood them as insecure and unpredictable but unlike Hobbes, Hegel conceived the state as more then representation of particular interests in 'the unity of them all'. In its constitution the state becomes more than the agglomeration of interests in civil society; it is the agent and rational structure of the nation. *The Philosophy of Right* postulates an ideality of representation in the relationship between nation and transcendent being in universal spirit. A nation is the particular and concrete representation of the universal spirit in time. As the agent of a nation, the state's ends are not self-justifying but can only be justified as representing the goal of world history. This is what elevates the state above mere force or material existence and gives its claims their hold on individuals.

The late Victorian revolt against empiricism incorporated such ideas into an English theory of the state. T. H. Green's *The Principles of Political Obligation* (1882) reinterpreted Austin's notion of 'habitual obedience' as the psychological ground of sovereign power and tied it to a theory of democracy as the common interest of the nation. 'Austin's doctrine seems diametrically opposite to one which finds the sovereign in a "volonté générale"', Green writes, but 'perhaps it may be by taking each as complementary to the other that we shall gain the truest view of sovereignty as it actually exists' (Green, [1882] 1948, p. 96). Only on the basis of some ethical evaluation and the positive marks of sovereignty, according to Green, can we arrive at a true concept of the state.

This allows for a democratic modification of sovereignty. By restating Rousseau's argument in the *Social Contract* that democracy is the identity of rulers and ruled as 'a sense of possessing common interests, a desire for common objects on the part of the people' (p. 97), Green weds the ideal of the state to the modern idea of democracy, identifying the General Will with 'the hopes of the people'. Adding this conception of democracy to the positive theory of sovereignty provided a practical criterion and a normative theory of law. This conception of the General Will is not only a criterion for the legitimacy of government and the state, it also indicates the signs of constitutional decay. It can be a negative mark of sovereignty as well as a positive one. Should the sense of sharing a common interest cease to come into conflict with the (positive) sovereign's commands, 'the habitual obedience will cease also' (p. 97).

The positivist theory recognised conquest as a legitimate source of sovereignty. The only question concerned the success of the occupation. Green's analysis of the circumstances in which sovereignty as command and obedience are exercised, justifies the right of self-determination and thus removes the legitimacy of colonial domination. No principled arguments for self-determination have been added to Green's since the end of the nineteenth century.

The elements of a now familiar view can be found in *The Principles of Political Obligation*: command and habitual obedience may be necessary to rightful rule, but they are not sufficient indicators of legitimate government. The practical and moral questions that arise after military occupation, or when government has been changed by force, or in the circumstances of colonialism fall into three categories according to the intention of the occupier: 'tax-collecting', where the occupying power has no intention of more than economic exploitation; transformational occupation of a developed people in which the occupier has more far-reaching aims such as cultural domination, or eventual integration of the subject lands and people into his own territory; and hegemonial relationships in which the occupier becomes the 'leading power' of a bloc including the people originally subjected. The first case has little bearing on the argument for Green. The others offer schematic possibilities for the genesis of a new 'sovereignty' or the persistent tension between the people's own continuing sovereign identity and the command and obedience relationship which the occupier establishes.

In every case, power can be distinguished from right as a negative mark. Where right (as consent to rule or identification with a new regime) is missing, there is no sovereignty. Domination alone – command and obedience without an identity between the positive law and the people's values and traditions – is not sovereignty.

The conception of sovereignty based on values instead of domination enlarges the claims that can be made on behalf of the authority of the democratic state. Bernard Bosanquet developed Green's synthesis of positive claims about sovereignty and idealist criteria for its use in the most influential statement in English political thought of the idealist theory. Bosanquet's *The Philosophical Theory of the State* (1899) owed its conception of institutions as ethical ideas to Hegel. We acknowledge the state's sovereignty, Bosanquet argues, because we see in it our 'representative and champion in the affairs of the world outside', but like Hobbes, Bosanquet too argues that the logic of power determines the unity of sovereign power, 'so far as the world is organised' (Bosanquet, [1899] 1965, p. 298).

Bosanquet suggests that the political principle of the nation state is like the principles of family, district and class – it engenders an identity beyond the particular and individual. If we read this notion less in the ethical terms of the nineteenth century, and more in the collectivist ones of our own, Green and Bosanquet together develop a theory of democracy that better explains political experience towards the end of the twentieth century than in late Victorian Britain. The definitive experiences of our times have been collective experiences in a new sense. The immediacy of 'the global village' gives our attitude towards political reality a distanced and voyeuristic quality at odds with classical liberal conceptions of the rational individual. At the same time, the state appears to us as an agent that acts in and creates that reality, in ways that are minimally rational – 'the hopes of the people' in Green's sense are open to manipulation on a once-unimaginable scale (Green [1882] 1948, p. 95). No democratic state (and here familiar distinctions between liberal-democratic democracies and others seem to be less important than the mass character of both kinds of societies) can afford to ignore the capacity of the people to be moved by interpretations of those events. The essence of politics as a way of giving meaning to events beyond individual interpretations is captured in Bosanquet's assertion of the nation state as having 'a faith or a purpose – we might say a mission, were not the word too narrow and aggressive' (Bosanquet, [1899] 1965, pp. 298–300).

This idea of the state leads Bosanquet to the most vexed question of 'high politics': *Staatsräson*, or reason of state. If we ask whether the state is a moral agent, that misses the point at issue. Of course the state can make promises and fulfil obligations, and much of international relations is concerned with just such acts of state. The issue is rather 'does an interest of state justify what would otherwise be immorality or wrong-doing on the part of an officer of the state?' (p. 302). Bosanquet's answer depends on separating the immoralities of the state's agents in 'the alleged interest of the State' from the state itself (p. 305).[2]

FROM THEORY TO REALITY IN INTERNATIONAL RELATIONS

The elements of sovereignty identified in traditional political theory are part of contemporary international relations. Through incorporation into international law and the constitutional law of most countries, the ideas of state and sovereignty became postulates of the international system. Much political dispute focuses on the interaction of domestic political considerations with the state's international existence. The politics of alliances since 1945 offers innumerable examples of this. One such was Adenauer's decision in favour of NATO membership. It resulted not just from defence considerations, but the alliance with the West was also and perhaps more importantly a means of establishing Western political values in a reconstructed Germany. The goal of national unification which might have been achieved through German neutrality in the 1950s was forfeited for the sake of constituting the Federal Republic of Germany as a liberal democracy with political and social institutions characteristic of its Western partners. Recognition of the two Germanies by their respective blocs after 1949 provides further examples of the impact of foreign policy events on the domestic system. Recognition, intervention, legitimacy and the justification of particular actions all feature in a theory of the state that informs our sense of 'right and wrong' in world politics, and remain the basis of normative judgements even when they do not fully describe the real circumstances of international politics.

As we move away from grand theory towards political practice, four aspects of the vast body of work on a philosophical concept of state and sovereignty have defined the practice of diplomacy and foreign relations:

(a) The essence of the state consists in the freedom and superiority of its decisions. The principle of the *clausula rebus sic stantibus* is derived from that definition.

(b) The state enjoys a monopoly of authoritative decision-making power within a territory where that authority is recognised and obeyed by the populace.

(c) The sovereign state is a subject in international law. Its agency consists of (i) the freedom to determine its own interests and pursue those; (ii) the autonomy of its decisions: in the realm of international politics, the state has no superior and is not responsible.

(d) The legitimacy of the modern state depends on the congruence of *de facto* sovereignty with the general will of the people. This principle gives rise to criteria for recognition by other states. As a negative mark it may justify intervention or the use of force against the state in question.

The first three of these belong to the world of ninteenth-century diplomacy and seem increasingly less typical of the reality of world affairs, even when 'state' and 'sovereignty' remain underlying assumptions in an international legal order. The fourth principle, democratic legitimacy, increases in importance as the nineteenth-century model of European nation states diminishes. As we shall see in the case of the Falklands, it is a crucial factor in the instability of international relations today.

The British–Argentinian war of 1982 for the Falkland Islands conformed more to the pattern of 'cabinet wars' of previous centuries than the mass confrontation of the twentieth. It was short, it was limited in scope and aims – and it was militarily decisive. It was a classic example of Clausewitz's dictum that war is politics carried on by other means. The Falklands War was anomalous in that respect, but in other ways it demonstrated some of the most characteristic features of the contemporary world: the impotence of international organisations and of 'normative restraints', and the impotence of the superpowers to affect a conflict into which they were necessarily drawn by events.

In the Falklands context, sovereignty was not inherently vague although it was difficult to conceptualise because it belongs to the 'outermost sphere' of the state's reality. The question of sovereignty arises in the extreme moments of the state's life – the constitution of order, or its preservation in armed struggle, or in its disappearance (Schmitt, 1985, pp. 5–6).

Force and sovereign decisions determined the beginning of the crisis in spring 1982 and its outcome, and although both sides construed normative arguments to justify their actions these were neither coherent nor did reference to norms cause Britain or Argentina to take the steps they did. If we begin with analyses of the Falklands War as a case in international law it poses two issues: the concrete application of the principle of sovereignty; and the self-determination of a people. The formal perspective leaves us with two principles in unresolved conflict. A narrative vision begins to dissolve the static construction of the case, leaving the Falklands as a story that can be read on many different levels, and at least one story can be told around each of the four main elements of a theory of sovereignty. Was the outbreak of war deliberate? Or did 'mixed signals' intended to produce a quite a different result lead both sides into armed conflict?

Freedom of decision

Like most wars the story of the Falklands could be called 'force vs. negotiation'. Both parties were signatories of the United Nations Charter, and it is a first source of legal argument about the conflict. Appeal to the

Charter did not end the Anglo-Argentinian dispute, but provided different normative justifications for action taken by both sides. One set of relevant articles in the charter deals with renunciation of force as a means of international relations (Arts. 103, 23, 24, 39 and 40). Anther article (Art. 51), however, specifically authorises use of force in self-defence, but also obliges nations in conflict to bring their dispute to the Security Council. A third set of articles (Arts. 73 and 74) deal with the right of self-determination and is relevant to the status of the Islands' present inhabitants (Grieg, 1983; Weber, 1982, pp. 77–82). Although Britain and Argentina had been engaged in negotiations under UN auspices since 1965 that were intended to resolve the question of sovereignty over the Islands, neither felt bound ultimately to the course of negotiations alone.

We can look at the Falklands War of 1982 as yet another example of two parties claiming their right to what only one of them can have – but that tells us little about how war broke out over this remote bit of territory in the first place. Each side tells a different story with the same theme: 'mixed signals'. Basically about power and its exercise at both levels of state activity, domestic and international, it raises the question of intentionality. Here the link between the state's internal and external existence and between its normative and power-political aspects is dramatic. Margaret Thatcher's campaign image as 'the Iron Lady' was realised in the minds of many observers, and no other policy decision made her so popular with the British electorate. On the Argentinian side, the war destabilised the junta and ushered in a democratic regime there. Another story is legal and conceptual, but here too the Falklands War carries important implications for the use of force in international politics and the ability of law to structure the outcome of conflicts. With some two hundred border disputes of the Falklands type lurking on the world's agenda, that aspect of the war takes on considerable importance (Hassan, 1982; Snyder, 1961; Jervis, 1970).

Much international diplomacy goes on in an elaborate system of 'signalling' that fuses image and reality. Its language ranges from such apparently trivial symbols as the shape of the negotiating table, the subject of long negotiation at the start of talks to end the Korean and Vietnam Wars, to more serious symbols sent by military manoeuvres, extension of diplomatic recognition or its withdrawal, and a variety of other signals such as the exchange of cultural or scientific delegations (Socarras, 1985).

Interpreting British signals to Argentina between November 1980 and April 1982 depends on what the Argentinians claimed they understood as opposed to what the British claimed they intended. Over this period, the British repeatedly accepted Argentinian actions asserting its authority over the Falklands and Dependencies:

(1) In November 1980 there were reports that the Argentine State Petroleum Company had bid to drill for oil in an area straddling the British-declared boundary between the Falklands and Tierra del Fuego. The British had also carried out geological exploration of the area. There was an official protest by the British to the Argentine government on 9 December 1980 and in April 1981 the British published a newspaper advertisement warning companies against tendering bids for the Argentine contract to drill. The Argentinians refused the British note as 'flatly unacceptable' and went on to say 'there does not exist any boundary dispute in the area in question, for the simple reason that the whole area corresponds to Argentine sovereignty'. In the mean time the Argentinian government had signed a contract with the Soviet Union for joint exploration and exploitation of the region's fishing waters (Socarras, 1985, p. 370).

(2) At the end of June 1981 the British decommissioned *HMS Endurance* with effect in March 1982. It was the only Royal Navy ship stationed in the south Atlantic.

(3) On 27 July 1981 a statement by the Argentine Ministry of Foreign Affairs warned that the question of sovereignty could no longer be postponed. The British did not respond.

(4) In December 1981 a party of 'scrap dealers' from Argentina landed on South Georgia allegedly to inspect a disused British whaling station for salvage. On 31 December 1981 the Governor of the Falklands informed the British Foreign Office that the party had not obtained permission for their activities and was in violation of the Islands' laws. The Foreign Office reply warned the Governor not to take action against the Argentinians that might 'risk provoking a most serious incident which could escalate and have an unforeseen outcome' (Franks, 1983, p. 164). On 6 January 1982 the British Ambassador contacted the Argentine Foreign Office about the South Georgia incident, but made no protest. When the British note was presented, on 9 February 1982, it was rejected.

A series of notes followed and in late March 1982 additional men landed at the South Georgia site apparently from an Argentine ship. Having ordered *HMS Endurance* to confront the invaders on 20 March, and after alerting the British Base Commander to tell the Argentinians to lower the flag they had raised, the British Foreign Office three days later cancelled *HMS Endurance*'s orders. On the 25th the Foreign Office in London learned that Argentina had dispatched warships to the Falklands and that another Argentine ship had brought landing craft and a helicopter to Leith Harbour. There were still no orders to *HMS Endurance* to intercept the invaders.

On 26 March the Argentines declared their intention of giving 'all necessary protection' to the men on South Georgia. Apparently in response to demonstrations against the junta, General Leopoldo Galtieri announced that 1982 was not the most 'propitious' year to solve the fundamental problems of the nation's economic and social order.

All these events in the winter and early spring – including the British government's refusal on budgetary grounds to reverse the decommissioning of *HMS Endurance* – 'signalled almost consistently that the United Kingdom was not serious about keeping control of the disputed area' (Socarras, 1985, p. 357). Moreover, after talks in New York on the sovereignty issue had broken down British intelligence repeatedly warned Mrs Thatcher during March 1982 that military confrontation appeared inevitable.

(5) The Argentinians invaded on 2 April 1982; the next day Mrs Thatcher told the House of Commons that a naval task force would be sent to the south Atlantic. Negotiations to end the armed conflict led to nothing, the British received support from its European Community partners, and the war ended in British victory on 14 June.

Argentina's decision to invade and the British response seem to confirm the traditional notion of sovereignty as freedom and unity of action, but only in the specifics of invasion and counter-force. The months leading up to the actual conflict are characterised by hesitation, confusion about the direction of central British policy and general confusion in British–Argentine relations. The outcome of one story that can be told about events leading up to the outbreak of war seems clear. While this narrative appears to confirm Argentina's claim that it acted in response to signals encouraging its actions in March and April 1982, the British response on 3 April indicates that, whatever the other side might have understood, the Thatcher government had not intended to renounce sovereignty in the Falklands. The 'mixed signals' thesis is confirmed.

Right vs. might

The other stories about the Falklands are less precise, but just as important. Situated on the 'mythological' level of the conflict, they are the stories each state tells about its interests in the South Atlantic to justify policy decisions domestically and internationally (Grieg, 1983, p. 70; Hasson, 1982; Dolzer, 1986, Fisch, 1983; Dicke, 1983). One story is 'historical', the other 'idealist'. Both are less about facts than about the meaning of experience over long periods of time.

(1) Argentina's rationale for the invasion(s) of early 1982 rests, like its

claim to sovereignty over the Islands and Dependencies itself, on the history of European exploration in the region. It claims legitimate title on the basis of succeeding to Spanish imperial possessions. Legal justification for the Portuguese and Spanish empires in South America rested on the Papal Bull 'Inter caetera Divinae' (1493) that demarcated the world into areas of European exploration. Papal authority for the division of the non-Christian world was based on his position as Christ's Vicar on earth and on St Augustine's interpretation of God's 'property' in the earth as a whole. It followed from this construction of the Church's authority that the Pope had the right to allocate lands which did not already belong to Christendom. This is the original legitimacy of title, confirmed in the Treaty of Tordesillas (1494) and other treaties to which Britain was party, including the Treaty of Utrecht (1713).

(2) Spanish, Portuguese and now Argentinian interpretation of these grants and treaty obligations rests on historic obligations by France and England to recognise Spanish and Portuguese trading rights and dominion over their South American territory. This included the Falkland Islands.

(3) Britain recognised these rights in the eighteenth century and withdrew from the Islands in 1774. By withdrawing, the British forfeited all claim to the Falklands Islands.

(4) After the revolt against Spain the settlement on the Falklands, was abandoned, and the Argentines only returned to the Islands in 1820.

(5) The British seized the Falklands in 1833 claiming that it was *terra nullius*. This was a pure fabrication (Grieg, 1983, p. 39).

(6) Argentina never recognised British title to the Islands and protested regularly throughout the intervening years.

(7) After creation of the United Nations, the Falkland Islands came under Article 73e of the Charter, and were also included under the Declaration on the Granting of Independence to Colonial Peoples (G. A. Res. 1514 [XV]) of 1960. This supported Argentina's interpretation of their status: in 1810 they were an integral part of Argentine territory through succession to the Spanish empire; Britain's presence there is a colonisation without further claims to legitimacy.

The British story also interprets events reaching back to the fifteenth century. It denies that Britain had ever recognised Spanish sovereignty under the Papal Bull of 1493. It denies, too, that discovery alone gave rise the title, but if it did, Britain could point out that its sailors had been the first to visit the Islands and had landed on them long before 1833 and before Argentina came into existence as an independent state.

The crucial elements of the British story refer to their 'continuous and peaceful exercise of sovereignty' in the Islands for more than a century and thus to the main principle of the positivist theory. The other aspect of the British view stresses the principle of self-determination for the Islanders. The non-democratic character of the Argentine government played an equally important role in British political argument. A plebiscite provided evidence for the view that Argentine sovereignty would violate the 'general will' of the Islands' population. In 1980, Falkland Islanders had voted to remain British. At the same time, however, Britain was signalling its willingness to negotiate a settlement devolving sovereignty to Argentina (thus ignoring the Islanders' preferences). The plebiscite caused obvious embarrassment to the Thatcher government's diplomatic line but that was forgotten two years later. Mrs Thatcher's speeches in Parliament and her statements to the press during the crisis stressed idealist reasons for Britain's response. Rhetorical appeals to the defence of freedom were made, and the popular press conjured up images of British resistence to Nazism, including the evacuation at Dunkirk.

Although 'historical' vs. 'idealist' characterise the respective stories Argentina and Britain told about the Falklands dispute, both mixed power-political and normative-legal argument in their appeal to world public opinion and international organisations.

International law had little effect on the outcome of the crisis. Both sides construed principles of sovereignty historically and democratically, and these arguments belonged to the rhetoric of British and Argentine politics in spring 1982. Each treated law and right as means to influence world public opinion and as devices for achieving publicity outcomes in the United Nations and Organisation of American States. Serious legal discussion only started after the war, when international lawyers focused on the classic methodological question, Which principle takes precedence: historic title of self-determination?

Argentina's interpretation of its rights to the Falklands depended on the original legitimacy of Spanish territorial sovereignty in South America. Only if that title were accepted as valid, could their claim to have succession be persuasive. While the overt appeal to 'historic title' seems purely positivistic, then, its underlying logic depended on a different sort of argument about legitimacy. The normative claim was dissipated, however, by the Argentine invasion. Before April 1982, they could persuasively claim that Britain was in possession of the Islands only by use of force – in fact that interpretation had been widely accepted by outside parties and even tacitly by the British themselves since the 1960s (Socarras, 1985; Green, 1986).

It remained theoretically as valid afterwards as before, but the political consequences of the Argentine invasion allowed the British to tell another and much more effective story in the circumstances. One of the curiosities about the Argentine case was that, while condeming the British claim as 'colonialism', it rejected the corollary to the anti-imperialist case, popular self-determination. The Argentine Ambassador to the Organisation of American States declared in 1982 that 'self-determination was one of the ways to get out of the colonial situation, but ... the principle of self-determination was not applicable in this case, whereas the principle which should apply is territorial integrity' (American Society for International Law, 1982, p. 281). Argentina ultimately used the principle that best fitted its own decision to take the Islands from Britain. The British case was also supported by the logic of power. When international lawyers finally met to reflect on the implications of the Falklands War, they agreed that 'There is no such thing as a perfect title in international law' (American Society, 1982, p. 269). Leslie Green commented on the original British use of force in the Falklands that this aspect of the matter should not be examined too closely as 'it would ill behoove any of us to look deeply into how we had achieved a title to territories' (American Society, 1982, p. 269).

International lawyers also agreed that in the conflict of principles at issue – territorial sovereignty vs. self-determination – historic title does not trump the people's will. Two previous cases (the *Western Sahara* case of 1975 and the *Palmas Islands* case of 1928) offered precedents for the Falklands dispute and affirmed the supremacy of self-determination. One way of looking at that view might see it as the affirmation of an idealist conception of sovereignty. Certainly it undermines the positivist case for state sovereignty, conforming to a trend in international law evident since the end of the First World War when the American President Woodrow Wilson asserted that self-determination must be the basic principle of a democratic world order. Equally obvious about the construction of the self-determination argument (then and now) is that it too relies, as much as the historic title argument, on force to back it up. That might take the form of 'revolution' or – as in the case of the post-war conferences in 1919 and 1945 that redrew the European political map – it might come in the shape of great power interventions justified by appeal to normative principles.

The case of the Falkland Islands indicates that sovereignty includes the freedom to interpret actions, as well as freedom to act even when the results are not successful. In an international system where open conflict between members of the two major power blocs is rare compared to the covert involvement in various conflicts not directly affecting alliance members, this is a significant addition to the state's available modes of enacting its sovereign freedom.

What are the general lessons of the Falklands?

The structure of events points to the relative decline of superpower influence over events involving their spheres of interest. Both the United States and the Soviet Union were involved on the sidelines of the conflict, but had relatively little power to shape its outcome. In the American case, the Falklands finally put to rest the Monroe Doctrine, already weakened by Castro's revolution and Soviet influence in Cuba. The crucial test of the Falklands conflict for American foreign policy is obviously Central America. British independence in the Falklands War was pursued despite American interests in Latin America as a whole. One superpower could not influence the actions of its closest ally in its own sphere of hegemony, an outcome symptomatic for the weakening of American's overt power since Suez in 1956. While small and medium powers can still afford to use force in the way Argentina and Britain did during 1982, the superpowers seem increasingly less able to do so.

The old model of sovereignty as decisive unity which was part of both the positivist and idealist theories of it does not fit the events here. Indecision, failure to recognise a vital interest and failure to pursue it consistently because there were competing domestic policy considerations (budgetary restraint) characterises British policy in the relevant weeks prior to the outbreak of hostilities. Traditional concepts of the state stressed its 'agency'. Political philosophers as divergent as Hobbes and T. H. Green thought the crucial feature of representation in the state was its constitution of political authority as a unity of action. The state's efficacy in domestic and foreign politics and its legitimacy derived from its representativeness.

The Falklands War appears to confirm that view, but its results for Britain and Argentina demonstrated how little they were in control of the circumstances. The junta fell from power. Mrs Thatcher ended up with a policy in the south Atlantic which is expensive and dubious in its ultimate consequences for Britain and the West's broader interests in the region. Having escaped from the prolonged dilemma of decolonisation in the Falklands, the British are now burdened with a situation far worse. The Argentinians' traditional claims – as much a matter of national pride as was the British response to the invasion – will also have to be shelved for the foreseeable future. A British government so deeply committed to defending British sovereignty, and thus to justifying policy choices and the loss of life in a war, is unlikely to compromise with the new regime in Argentina however democratic it now is.

The Falklands War does, however, seem to confirm the most significant aspect of the traditional notion of sovereignty: the final irresponsibility of

Britain and Argentina towards an international system of norms and organisations. Calls for an end to the hostilities were consistently ignored in 1982.[3] Negotiations had been carried on without binding commitments for nearly two decades – only to have the dispute resolved ultimately by resort to force when both sides considered their vital interests at stake.

Despite all the qualifications of normative restraints and international law, the state remains the most important political organisation in the modern world. Its sovereignty is manifest in the ability to take decisions about friend and foe which characterise the sphere of the political.

A DEMOCRATIC *REALPOLITIK*? SOME QUESTIONS FOR FURTHER RESEARCH

If we move away from the particular incident of the Falklands War, towards the level of general theory, are there any implications for the future work on Britain's place in the world? What other incidents of British policy, foreign or domestic, might guide a theory of the state today?

A revised theory of state and sovereignty should not try to describe reality, though it must tell us something about what reality is like. It cannot be just any collection of assumptions, neither will it be a collection of facts. Its purpose is to help us understand the object of our enquiry. It will be useful or not; its conclusions may be tested (as its assumptions might be) for their truth-value. Even when a theory does not produce predictive or causal explanations, it might still be a good theory because it tells us something important about the world. 'The state', like 'power' and 'interest' or 'justice' or 'right' belongs to a specific kind of theory that tries to account for occurrences in the international system in *purely political terms*. That does not mean there are not other factors in the reality of international relations. Economics, moral goals and values, even aesthetics, play their part and it would be foolish to think these are completely irrelevant to a conception of the state and its actions. But they are secondary.

Machiavelli's invention of the political theory of the state still has much to tell us about what the task of rethinking it would entail. To explain and justify have always been the goals of political theory, and Machiavelli revealed why we should try to theorise such a practical matter at all.[4] *The Prince* and *Discourses* are the first books of modern political theory precisely because they dispensed with appeals to transcendent causes and theological justifications for the state. Machiavelli assumed that politics occupies an autonomous sphere and that explanations for it must be found in its own terms.

The typically modern notion of the state is secular and immanent.

Neither transcendent causes nor transcendent reasons concern it. The modern European state postulates the basic rationality of political practice, not in the sense of there being only reasons in politics and no interests and passions, but by assuming that reason can control and direct those. The starting-point of all political knowledge, von Rochau wrote a century-and-a-half ago, is 'the study of those powers that form the state, support it and change it' (Rochau, 1972, p. 25).

Contemporary political theory must accept those assumptions. The state belongs at the nexus of our conception of 'social forces' in a particular place and time and the legal order that governs them. According to this account the state exists as a continual integration of forces in society which constitute or threaten the order it represents (Smend, 1968). Power is the fundamental law of its existence; however just or noble a cause it can only be realised through the state if the relationship between right and power is not to be reduced to the equation 'might-equals-right', or the reverse. This postulate of *realpolitik* can be amended by including the further assumption that the concept of the state assumes the concept of the political. The state creates right, but independent forces constitute an autonomous realm of politics (Schmitt, 1976).

These reflections should be the starting-point of a theory of the state in its internal and external relations. Further components of such a theory would include human nature (as a constant in the theory of politics) and the corollary conceptions of reason, prudence, interest and will. The purpose of such a theory, like Machiavelli's own, would be to reduce the effect of fortune on men's lives through the discovery of principles of politics that enhance the power of political will over events. This is the driving force of politics as the pursuit of interest and advantage but also as the impetus for 'action on principles that reason had discovered' (Waltz, 1976).

Such a political theory would not reduce politics to power games and force alone – though it would acknowledge that 'right only governs as power' (Rochau, 1972, p. 26). In the relationship between political ideas and reality, the former can be as significant as brute force. Political judgement, according to this theory, is always a prudent calculation of means and ends aware of the circumstances. The purpose of a political science, and the justification for theorising about the state at all is to marshall reason and will for the preservation of the democratic state.

Sovereignty allows us to conceptualise the fusion of power and right within a general theory of the state that locates institutions of decision about the public good and procedures for its legitimate realisation. In a secular universe of means and ends government's first duty is to protect the state from internal disintegration and outside threat. The only criterion for judging it is the success of its policy. The basis of sovereignty in political theory is the belief that 'Politics has its own laws, discernible by reason and rooted in political interest, in circumstances and in the necessities they give rise to' (Waltz, 1976, p. 35).

Must *realpolitik* be inimicable to the purpose of democratic states – government by and for the people? I do not think so, but I do think that a democratic *realpolitik* would have to address the following questions:

(1) How can sovereignty as the unity of the state be conceptualised in a pluralist world?

Pluralism is now a force for the domestic disintegration of the state as T. H. Green understood it: 'as a sense of possessing common interests, a desire for common objects on the part of the people'. Where 'adversarial pluralism' fosters private greed at the expense of public good are there conceptual limitations on diversity that do not violate criteria of democratic legitimacy such as participation and equality? What institutional reforms would such a conception require? (Hirst, 1986; Mansbridge, 1985). Two areas of British public policy could provide points of theoretical departure, the regulation of trade unions and markets, and integration in the European Community.

(2) What do contemporary theories of personality tell us about how we could more plausibly conceive the public agent that is the state?

The agency of the state in traditional political theory is a convenient fiction that allowed conceptualisation of sovereignty after the sovereign was no longer indentified with a single person. In a world after Freud and Nietzsche do our political theories depend on an anachronistic notion of human personality? A different account of agency need not sacrifice the conceptual unity of the constitution, and it might allow us to see the pluralism of the international system as an integral part of the more complex network of 'normative restraints' that foster peace.[5] The formal and informal policy processes of international organisations would certainly produce a more varied picture of agency of states that could be incorporated into a theory of the post-modern state.

(3) Could democratic homogeneity be conceived, not as the prelude to a totalitarian theory, but as the precondition of a functioning set of normative restraints in domestic and foreign affairs?

Constitutional law as a political science assumes the constant reproduction of similarities and differences. Political discussions about reforming the system of justice in Britain or about the introduction of a bill of rights and democratic electoral reform are obvious places to start rethinking fundamental institutions.

Together these questions seem an appropriate focus for a modified theory of the contemporary European state, whose central dilemma remains that of a democratic polity. How can public power be represented in a world of greater diversity than assumed by traditional theories of the state without falling into one of the traps that have always bedevilled the democratic state – an all too appealing utopianism or a dangerous pursuit of power for its own sake?

Notes

1 T. D. Weldon, *The Vocabulary of Politics* (Harmondsworth, Penguin, 1953), pp. 46–7. Cf. Harold Laski, *Studies in the Problem of Sovereignty* (New Haven, Conn., Yale University Press, 1917), and *Studies in Law and Politics*, (London, Allen & Unwin, 1932). For an excellent general discussion of the concept, W. J. Rees, 'The Theory of Sovereignty Revisited', in P. Laslett, *Philosophy, Politics and Society*, vol. 1 (1956).

2 While British theorists were justifying the absolute sovereignty of Parliament, constitutional lawyers in Germany after 1871 tried to limit it within the federal structure of the German empire. Although their solution to the paradox of Bodinian sovereignty and constitutional monarchy was the formal one of 'auto-limitation', at least the question of how to limit sovereignty was recognised in Germany unlike England. Rupert Emerson, *State and Sovereignty in Modern Germany* (New Haven, Conn., Yale University Press, 1928), pp. 47ff. Wilhelm Hennis sees the loss of 'a sense for what the state and politics mean' as a fundamental element in our contemporary disorientation. In Hennis's view having a sense of the state is part of public-mindedness. Not this 'sense of the state' is the prelude to totalitarianism, but its loss: 'the total emptying out of the state and politics opened the way for total domination of every sphere of social and intellectual life'. Hennis, 'Zum Problem der deutschen Staatsanschauung', in *Politik und praktische Philosophie. Schriften zur politischen Theorie* (Stuttgart, Klett-Cotta, 1981), p. 159. French and German thought on sovereignty in the period before the end of the Holy Roman Empire is analysed in Helmut Quaritsch's masterful study, *Souveränität. Entstehung und Entwicklung des Begriffes in Frankreich und Deutschland vom 13. J. bis 1806* (Berlin, Duncker & Humboldt, 1986).

3 'When a Great Power considers its interests are at stake it will only use the United Nations so long as it considers that body is likely to support it in its action or reactions.' Leslie C. Green, 'The Rule of Law and the Use of Force – the Falklands and Grenada', *Archiv des Völkerrechts*, 24 (1986), 173–4. The United Nations' precursor, the League of Nations, was similarly regarded: 'Wherever there is a self-confident sense of the state and a clear feeling for national honour, especially in great states such as England, France or Italy, one doesn't need to ask if [the concept of] sovereignty still belongs to international law. It consists in the fact that in a decisively critical case each state that is sovereign will decide all questions affecting its existence and honour for itself. The English government will gladly use the League of Nations ... but as long as England is a Great Power, it will not permit an international institution to prescribe what the English navy shall fight for. In the critical moment it will always remain the judge in its own case, and precisely that is sovereignty.' Carl Schmitt, *Die Kernfrage des Völkerbundes* (Berlin, F. Dümmlers, 1926), p. 11. See also, W. M. Reisman, 'The Struggle for the Falklands', *Yale Law Journal*, 93 (1983), and G.A. Res. 2065,

20 U.N. GAOR Supp. (No. 14) at 57, U.N. Doc. A/6014; O.A.S. Doc. OEA/Ser. F/II.20, Doc. 28/82 rev., 28 April 1982, and Doc. 80/82 rev. 1, 29 May 1982.

4 Before the Renaissance, 'explanation' and 'justification' of political power and authority in Europe went on in theological terms. Not only did political thinkers such as St Augustine praise and blame worldly leaders by reference to God's will, the Deity also provided a transcendent cause for what happened in the world. In *The City of God* Augustine tells us that God is the sole creator of every nature and form, and distinguishes between the external form given by craftsmen to objects and their internal form, or purpose: 'This form supplies the efficient causes, and it derives from the hidden and secret decision of a living and intelligent nature, which, being itself uncreated, is responsible for the creation not only of the natural, physical forms, but also of the souls of living creatures.' Augustine, *Concerning the City of God against the Pagans* (Harmondsworth, Penguin, 1972), p. 505. Creative power belongs to God alone. This is the basis on which Augustine argues at the conclusion of *The City of God* that man's supreme good is peace and that everything is directed towards peace, even war. God, who made man, has also given him a purpose which he, in so far as he acts in accordance with God's will, carries out in politics. On that basis state policy could be justified or condemned.

The rationalist and secular culture of the Renaissance changed that in Europe, but not everywhere. Certain primitive societies still depend on magical or quasi-theological explanations, and world politics is now dramatically affected by the reappearance of a theological politics in the Arab world. It would be hard to understand either the dynamic of Iranian actions in the Middle East or their justification by Islamic fundamentalists without recourse to the political theology once familiar to European states. And it would be foolish in the extreme simply to dismiss the transcendental factor as 'irrational' and therefore irrelevant for Western states. See Peter Winch, 'Understanding a Primitive Society', in Winch, *Ethics and Action* (London, Routledge & Kegan Paul, 1972), p. 25.

5 On the normative dimensions of the Falklands War and for an assessment of Britain's gains and losses, see Lawrence Freedman, *Britain and the Falklands War* (Oxford, Basil Blackwell, 1988). In general, see also Richard Falk, 'The Interplay of Westphalia and Charter Conceptions of the International Legal Order', in C. Black and R. Falk (eds.), *The International Legal Order*, vol. 1 (Princeton, N.J., Princeton University Press, 1969). A subtle and complex theory of norms which tries to move away from the coherence perspective of Locke and Hume, and seems to fit the case at hand better, is advanced by Friedrich V. Kratochwil, 'Anarchy and the State of Nature: The Issue of Regimes in International Relations', in his *Rules, Norms and Decisions. On the Conditions of Practical and Legal Reasoning in International and Domestic Affairs* (Cambridge, Cambridge University Press, 1989). He points out that rules and norms are more often 'enabling' than constraining: 'actors are not only programmed by rules and norms ... they reproduce and change by their practice the normative structures by which they are able to act, share meanings, communicate intentions, criticize claims, and justify choices.' Kratochwil, *Rules, Norms and Decisions*, p. 61.

APPENDIX

Contributors to the 'Britain in the World' Conference held at King's College, London, on 12–13 November 1987.

Introduction to the Conference

Lawrence Freedman   *King's College*

Interdependence and Britain's External Relations

Barry Buzan   *University of Warwick*
Discussants
Charles Reynolds   *University of Durham*
Alasdair Smith   *University of Sussex*

Foreign Policy Analysis and the Study of British Foreign Policy

Steve Smith   *University of East Anglia*
Discussants
Chris Hill   *London School of Economics*
Sir John Thompson   *Foreign and Commonwealth Office (rtd)*

The Political Economy of Britain's External Relations

Ron Smith   *Birkbeck College*
Discussants
DeAnne Julius   *Royal Institute of International Affairs*
Loukas Tsoukalis   *St Antony's College, Oxford*

Towards a Theory of State and Sovereignty in Contemporary Britain

Ellen Kennedy   *Queen Mary College*
Discussants
William Wallace   *Royal Institute of International Affairs*
Michael Akehurst   *University of Keele*

REFERENCES

Allison, Graham (1971) *Essence of Decision* (Boston, Mass., Little, Brown).
Allison, Graham, and Morton Halperin (1972) 'Bureaucratic Politics: A Paradigm and Some Implications', in R. Tanter and R. Ullman (eds.), *Theory and Policy in International Relations* (Princeton, N.J., Princeton University Press).
American Society for International Law (1982) 'The Falklands/Malvinas Crisis: A Panel', *Proceedings of the American Society for International Law*, 76.
Artis, M., and S. Ostry (1986) *International Economic Policy Coordination* (London, Routledge/Royal Institute of International Affairs).
Austin, John, [1832] (1954) *The Province of Jurisprudence Determined and the Uses of the Study of Jurisprudence* (London, Everyman).
Axelrod, R. (ed.) (1976) *Structure of Decision* (Princeton, N.J., Princeton University Press).
Baldwin, D. A. (1980) 'Interdependence and Power: A Conceptual Analysis', *International Organization*, 34 (4).
Barber, James (1976) *Who Makes British Foreign Policy?* (Milton Keynes, Open University Press).
Baylis, John (1986) '"Greenwoodery" and British Defence Policy', *International Affairs*, 62 (3).
   (1989) *British Defence Policy: Striking the Right Balance* (London, Macmillan).
Bentinck, Marc (1986) 'NATO's Out-of-Area Problem', *Adelphi Papers*, 211 (London, International Institute for Strategic Studies).
Berridge, Geoffrey (1980) 'The Political Theory and Institutional History of State Systems', *British Journal of International Studies*, 6 (1).
   (1981) 'International Relations', *Teaching Politics*, 10 (1).
Boardman, Robert, and A. J. R. Groom (eds.) (1973) *The Management of Britain's External Relations* (London, Macmillan).
Boltho, A., and C. Allsopp (1987) 'The Assessment: Trade and Trade Policy', *Oxford Review of Economic Policy*, 3 (1).
Booth, Ken (1979) *Strategy and Ethnocentrism* (London, Croom Helm).
   (1990) 'Steps Towards Stable Peace in Europe: A Theory and Practice of Coexistence', *International Affairs*, 66 (1).
Bosanquet, Bernard, [1899] (1965) *The Philosophical Theory of the State* (London, Macmillan).
Boulding, Kenneth (1956) *The Image* (New York, Galaxy Books).
Brecher, Michael (ed.) (1979) *Studies in Crisis Behaviour* (New York, Transaction Books).
Brecher, Michael, B. Steinberg and J. Stein (1969) 'A Framework for Research on Foreign Policy Behaviour', *Journal of Conflict Resolution*, 13.
Bull, Hedley (1977) *The Anarchical Society* (London, Macmillan).
Burgess, P. (1966) *Elite Images and Foreign Policy Outcomes* (Columbus, Ohio, Ohio State University Press).

Burgess, P., and Geoffrey Edwards (1988) 'The Six Plus One: British Policy-Making and the Question of European Economic Integration, 1955', *International Affairs*, 64 (3).

Buzan, Barry (1983) *People, States and Fear: The National Security Problem in International Relations* (Brighton, Wheatsheaf).

(1984) 'Economic Structure and International Security: The Limits of the Liberal Case', *International Organization*, 38 (4).

(1987) *An Introduction to Strategic Studies: Military Technology and International Relations* (London, Macmillan).

Cable, James (1985) 'Out of Area But Under Control', *Defence Analysis*, 1 (1).

(1987) *Political Institutions and Issues in Britain* (London, Macmillan).

Callaghan, P., L. Brady and M. Hermann (eds.) (1982) *Describing Foreign Policy Behaviour* (Beverley Hills, Calif., Sage).

Clarke, Michael (1979) 'Foreign Policy Implementation: Problems and Approaches', *British Journal of Political Studies*, 5 (2).

(1989) 'The Foreign Policy System', in Michael Clarke and Brian White (eds.), *Understanding Foreign Policy: The Foreign Policy Systems Approach* (Aldershot, Edward Elgar).

Clarke, Michael, and Marjorie Mowlam (eds.) (1982) *Debate on Disarmament* (London, Routledge & Kegan Paul).

Clarke, Michael, and Brian White (eds.) (1981) *An Introduction to Foreign Policy Analysis* (Ormskirk, Hesketh).

Clarke, Michael, and Brian White (eds.) (1989) *Understanding Foreign Policy: The Foreign Policy Systems Approach* (Aldershot, Edward Elgar).

Cohen, Raymond (1981) *International Relations: The Rules of the Game* (London, Longman).

Coker, Christopher (1986) *Nation in Retreat?* (Oxford, Pergamon).

(1987) *British Defence Policy in the 1990s* (London, Brassey's).

Cooper, Frank (1990) 'Economists and Defence: The Views of a UK Practitioner', *Defence Economics*, 1 (1).

Cooper, Richard N. (1968) *The Economics of Interdependence: Economic Policy in the Atlantic Community* (New York, McGraw-Hill).

(1972) 'Economic Interdependence and a Foreign Policy in the 1970s', *World Politics*, 24.

(1986) *Economic Policy in an Interdependent World: Essays in World Economics* (Cambridge, Mass., MIT Press).

Croft, Stuart (1989) 'The Impact of Strategic Defences on European–American Relations in the 1990s', *Adelphi Papers*, 238 (London, Brassey's).

Dando, Malcolm, and Paul Rogers (1984) *The Death of Deterrence* (London, CND Publications).

Dicey, A. V., [1885] (1982) *Introduction to the Study of the Law of the Constitution* (Indianapolis, Liberty Classics).

Dicke, Delter Christian (1983) 'Der Streit um die Falklands-Inseln oder Malvinen', in Norbert Achterberg et al. (eds.), *Recht und Staat im Sozialen Wandel. Festschrift fur Hans Ulrich Scupin* (Berlin, Duncker & Humboldt).

Dillon, M. (1988) 'Thatcher and the Falklands', in Richard Little and Steve Smith (eds.), *Belief Systems in International Relations* (Oxford, Basil Blackwell).

Dolzer, Rudolf (1986) *Der Völkerrechtliche Status der Falkland-Inseln (Malvinas) im Wandel der Zeit* (Heidelberg, R. v. Decker & C. F. Muller).

Downs, G. W. (1989) 'The Rational Deterrence Debate', *World Politics*, 41 (2).

Dunning, John H., and Peter Robson (eds.) (1988) *Multinationals and the European Community* (Oxford, Basil Blackwell).

Dworkin, Ronald (1982) 'Rights and Trumps', in J. Waldron (ed.), *Theories of Rights* (Oxford, Oxford University Press).

Dziedzic, Michael J. (1989) 'The Transnational Drug Trade and Regional Security', *Survival*, 31 (6).

East, Maurice, S. Salmore and C. Hermann (1978) *Why Nations Act* (Beverley Hills, Calif., Sage).

Edmonds, Martin (ed.) (1986) *The Defence Equation* (London, Brassey's).

Falk, Richard (1985) 'The Decline of Normative Restraint in International Relations', *Yale Journal of International Law*, 10 (2).

Finlayson, J. A. and D. G. Haglund (1987) 'Whatever Happened to the Resources War?', *Survival*, 29 (5).

Finnis, John, Joseph M. Boyle and Germain Grisez (1987) *Nuclear Deterrence, Morality, Realism* (Oxford, Oxford University Press).

Fisch, Jorg (1983) 'The Falkland Islands in the European Trading System 1493–1833', *German Yearbook of International Law*, 26.

Flowers, M. (1977) 'A Laboratory Test of Some Implications of Janis's Groupthink Hypothesis', *Journal of Personality and Social Psychology*, 35 (12).

Frankel, Joseph (1970) *National Interest* (London, Pall Mall).

(1975) *British Foreign Policy 1945–1973* (London, Oxford University Press).

Franks Report (1983) *Falklands Islands Review*, Cmnd 8787 (London, HMSO).

Freedman, Lawrence (1981) *The Evolution of Nuclear Strategy* (New York, St Martin's Press).

(1985) 'Strategic Studies', in Steve Smith (ed.), *International Relations: British and American Perspectives* (Oxford, Basil Blackwell).

(1986) *Arms Control: Management or Reform?* (London, Routledge/Royal Institute of International Affairs).

(1989a) 'General Deterrence and the Balance of Power', *Review of International Studies*, 15 (2).

(1989b) 'The Politics of Conventional Arms Control', *Survival*, 31 (5).

Gardner, Richard N. (1980) *Sterling-Dollar Diplomacy: The Origins and Prospects of Our International Economic Order* (New York, Columbia University Press).

George, A. (1969) 'The "Operational Code": A Neglected Approach to the Study of Political Leaders and Decision-Making', *International Studies Quarterly*, 13 (2).

Gilbert, M. (1971–86) *Winston Churchill*, vols. 3–7 (London, Heinemann).

Gill, Stephen (1986) 'American Hegemony: Its Limits and Prospects in the Reagan Era', *Millennium*, 15 (3).

Gill, Stephen, and David Law (1988) *The Global Political Economy: Perspectives, Problems and Policies* (Baltimore, Md.: Johns Hopkins University Press).

Gilpin, Robert (1987) *The Political Economy of International Relations* (Princeton, N.J., Princeton University Press).

Goodhart, Charles (1988) 'The Foreign Exchange Markets: A Random Walk with a Dragging Anchor', *Economica*, 55.

Gordon, David (1988) 'The Global Economy', *New Left Review*, 168.

Green, Leslie C. (1986) 'The Rule of Law and the Use of Force – the Falklands and Grenada', *Archiv des Völkerrechts*, 24.

Green, T. H. [1882] (1948) *Lectures on the Principles of Political Obligation* (London, Longman).

Grieg, D. W. (1983) 'Sovereignty and the Falklands Islands', *Australian Yearbook of International Relations*, 8.

Halperin, Morton H. (1987) *Nuclear Fallacy: Dispelling the Myth of Nuclear Strategy* (Cambridge, Mass., Ballinger).

Handrieder, Wolfram (1978) 'Dissolving International Politics: Reflections on the Nation-State', *American Political Science Review*, 72 (4).

Hartley, Keith, Farooq Hussein and Ron Smith (1987) 'The UK Defence Industrial Base', *Political Quarterly*, 58 (1).

Hassan, F. (1982) 'The Sovereignty Dispute over the Falkland Islands', *Virginia Journal of International Law*, 23.

Hermann, Charles, C. Kegley and J. Rosenau (eds.) (1987) *New Directions in the Study of Foreign Policy* (London, Allen & Unwin).

Herspring, Dale R. (1989) 'The Soviet Military and Change', *Survival*, 31 (4).

Hinsley, F. H. (1986) *Sovereignty* (Cambridge, Cambridge University Press).

Hirshleifer, J. (1985) 'The Expanding Domain of Economics', *American Economic Review*, 75 (6).

Hirst, Paul (1986) *Law, Socialism and Democracy* (London, Allen & Unwin).

HMSO (1989) *Statement on the Defence Estimates 1989*, vol. 1, Cmnd 675-1 (London, HMSO).

Hobbes, Thomas [1659] (1972) *Leviathan* (London, Penguin Books).

Holmes, Peter (1987) *Rules of Origin in Intra-EC Trade*, Discussion Paper 87/46, International Economic Research Centre, University of Sussex.

Holsti, O. (1969) 'The Belief System and National Images', in J. N. Rosenau (ed.), *International Politics and Foreign Policy* (New York, Free Press).

Hood, N., and S. Young (1979) *The Economics of Multinational Enterprise* (London, Longman).

Hopple, Gerald W. and Gene Gathright (1987) 'International Security Policies', in Gavin Boyd and G. W. Hopple (eds.), *Political Change and Foreign Policies* (London, Frances Pinter).

Howard, Michael (1986) 'The Future of Deterrence', *Royal United Services Institute Journal*, 131 (2).

 (1989) 'IISS – The First Thirty Years: A General Overview', in International Institute for Strategic Studies, 'The Changing Strategic Landscape', Adelphi Paper 235 (London, IISS).

International Monetary Fund (1986) *Survey* (Washington, D.C., IMF).

 (1987) *Survey* (Washington, D.C., IMF).

Jacobson, H. K., W. M. Reisinger and T. Mathers (1986) 'National Entanglements in International Government Organisations', *American Political Science Review*, 80 (1).

Janis, Irving (1972) *Victims of Groupthink* (Boston, Mass., Houghton Mifflin).

 (1982) (2nd edn) *Groupthink* (Boston, Mass., Houghton Mifflin).

Janis, Irving, and L. Mann (1977) *Decision-Making* (New York, Free Press).

Jervis, Robert (1970) *The Logic of Images in International Relations* (Princeton, N.J., Princeton University Press).

 (1976) *Perception and Misperception in International Politics* (Princeton, N.J., Princeton University Press).

Jones, R. (1974) *The Changing Structure of British Foreign Policy* (London, Longman).

Jones, R. J. Barry, and Peter Willetts (1984) *Interdependence on Trial* (London, Frances Pinter).

Kaiser, Karl, and R. Morgan (1971) *Britain and West Germany* (London, Oxford University Press).

Kay, J. A., and M. V. Posner (1989) 'Routes to Economic Integration: 1992 in the European Community', *National Institute Economic Review*, 129.

Kennedy, Paul (1981) *The Realities Behind Diplomacy* (London, Allen & Unwin).

(1989) *The Rise and Fall of the Great Powers* (London, Fontana).

Kenwood, A. G., and A. L. Lougheed (1983) *The Growth of the International Economy 1820–1980* (London, Allen & Unwin).

Keohane, Robert (1984) *After Hegemony: Cooperation and Discord in the World Political Economy* (Princeton, N.J., Princeton University Press).

(1986) *Neorealism and Its Critics* (New York, Columbia University Press).

Keohane, Robert, and Joseph Nye (1977) *Power and Interdependence* (Boston, Mass., Little, Brown).

Kindleberger, Charles (1970) *Power and Money* (London, Macmillan).

(1973) *The World in Depression 1929–30* (London, Allen Lane).

(1978) *Manias, Panics, Crashes: A History of Financial Crises* (London, Macmillan).

(1981) 'Dominance and Leadership in the International Economy', *International Studies Quarterly*, 25 (2–3).

(1986) 'International Public Goods Without International Government', *American Economic Review*, 76 (1).

Krugman, Paul R. (ed.) (1986) *Strategic Trade Policy and the New International Economics* (Cambridge, Mass., MIT Press).

Leites, N. (1951) *The Operational Code of the Politburo* (New York, McGraw-Hill).

Levene, Peter (1987) 'Competition and Collaboration: UK Defence Procurement Policy', *Royal United Services Institute Journal*, 132 (2).

Little, Richard (1981) 'Ideology and Change', in Barry Buzan and R. J. Barry Jones (eds.), *Change and the Study of International Relations* (London, Frances Pinter).

Little, Richard, and Steve Smith (eds.) (1988) *Belief Systems in International Relations* (Oxford, Basil Blackwell).

Longley, J., and D. Pruitt (1980) 'Groupthink: A Critique of Janis's Theory', *Review of Personality and Social Psychology*, 38 (1).

Lynn, Jonathan, and Anthony Jay (1981) *Yes Minister*, vol. 1 (London, BBC Publications).

MccGwire, Michael (1986) 'Deterrence: The Problem not the Solution', *International Affairs*, 64 (1).

McKibben, Bill (1989) *The End of Nature* (New York, Viking Press).

McNamara, Robert (1987) *Blundering Into Disaster* (London, Bloomsbury).

Maddison, A. (1982) *Phases of Capitalist Development* (Oxford, Oxford University Press).

Malcolm, Neil (1989) 'The "Common European Home" and Soviet Foreign Policy', *International Affairs*, 65 (4).

Manning, C. A. W. (1962) *The Nature of International Society* (London, Oxford University Press).

Mansbach, Richard, Yale Ferguson and Don Lampert (1976) *The Web of World Politics* (Englewood Cliffs, N.J., Prentice-Hall).

Mansbach, Richard, and J. Vasquez (1981) *In Search of Theory* (New York, Columbia University Press).

Mansbridge, Jayne (1985) *Beyond Adversarial Democracy* (Chicago, Chicago University Press).

Mathews, R. (1986) 'Economic Institutions', *Economic Journal*, 96.

May, E. (1973) *'Lessons' of the Past* (New York, Oxford University Press).

Medlicott, W. N. (1968) *British Foreign Policy Since Versailles 1919–1963* (London, Methuen).

Moon, B. (1977) 'Political Economy Approaches to the Comparative Study of

Foreign Policy', in Charles Hermann, C. Kegley and J. N. Rosenau (eds.), *New Directions in the Study of Foreign Policy* (London, Allen & Unwin).

Moravcsik, Andrew (1990) 'The European Armaments Industry at the Crossroads', *Survival*, 32 (1).

Morgan, Kevin (1987) 'Monopolies Under Siege in Western Europe: Challenge and Deregulation in Telecommunications', *IDS Bulletin*, 18 (3).

Morgenthau, Hans J. (1948) *Politics Among Nations* (New York, Knopf).

Myers, Norman (1989) 'Environment and Security', *Foreign Policy*, 74.

Neustadt, Richard, and Richard May (1986) *Thinking in Time* (New York, Free Press).

Newsome, David D. (1989) 'The New Diplomatic Agenda: Are Governments Ready?', *International Affairs*, 65 (1).

Nicholson, Michael (1989) *Formal Theories in International Relations* (Cambridge, Cambridge University Press).

Northedge, F. S. (1974) *Descent From Power* (London, Allen & Unwin).

Nye, Joseph (1989) 'The Contribution of Strategic Studies: Future Challenges', in International Institute for Strategic Studies, 'The Changing Strategic Landscape', Adelphi Paper 235 (London, IISS).

Organisation for Economic Co-operation and Development (1987) *Economic Progress Report* (Paris, OECD).

Padoa-Schioppa, Tommaso (1987) *Efficiency, Stability and Equity* (Oxford, Oxford University Press).

Pearce, Joan, and John Sutton (1985) *Protection and Industrial Policy in Europe* (London, Routledge & Kegan Paul).

Portes, Richard, and A. K. Swoboda (eds.) (1987) *Threats to International Financial Stability* (Cambridge, Cambridge University Press).

Powell, Enoch (1987) 'Return to an Older Pattern of Europe', *Guardian*, 7 December 1987.

Prins, Gwyn (ed.) (1983) *Defended to Death* (Harmonsworth, Penguin Books).

Renner, Michael (1989) 'The Drain of a Permanent War Economy', *USA Today*, July.

Rhoads, Steven E. (1985) *The Economist's View of the World* (Cambridge, Cambridge University Press).

Richards, Peter (1967) *Parliament and Foreign Affairs* (London, Allen & Unwin).

Roarty, Michael J. (1987) 'The Impact of the Common Agricultural Policy on Agricultural Trade and Development', *National Westminster Bank Quarterly Review*, February.

Roberts, Adam (1987) 'Rethinking Deterrence', *Royal United Services Institute Journal*, 132 (1).

Rochau, Ludwig August von (1972) *Grundsätze der Realpolitik* Frankfurt, Ullstein).

Rowthorn, Robert E., and John Wells (1987) *Deindustrialisation and Foreign Trade* (Cambridge, Cambridge University Press).

Rybczynski, Tad M. (1987) 'The Approaches towards the Reform of the International Monetary System', *National Westminster Bank Quarterly Review*, February.

Safer World Project (1990) *New Thinking About Security* (Bristol, Safer World Project).

Schelling, Thomas C. (1963) *The Strategy of Conflict* (Oxford, Oxford University Press).

Schmitt, Carl (1976) *The Concept of the Political* (New Brunswick, N.J., Rutgers University Press).

(1985) *Political Theology* (Cambridge, Mass., MIT Press).

Segal, Gerald (1984) 'Strategy and Ethnic Chic', *International Affairs*, 60 (1).

Sen, Gautam (1984) *The Military Origins of Industrialisation and International Trade Policy* (London, Frances Pinter).

Sheehan, Michael (1988) *Arms Control: Theory and Practice* (Oxford, Basil Blackwell).

Shlaim, A. (1983) *The United States and the Berlin Blockade* (Berkeley, Calif., University of California Press).

Shlaim, A., P. Jones and K. Sainsbury (1977) *British Foreign Secretaries Since 1945* (Newton Abbot: David and Charles).

Smend, Rudolf (1968) *Staatsrechtliche Abhandlungen* (Berlin, Duncker & Humboldt).

Smith, Michael, Steve Smith and Brian White (eds.) (1988) *British Foreign Policy: Tradition, Change and Transformation* (London, Unwin Hyman).

Smith, R. P. (1977) 'Military Expenditure and Capitalism', *Cambridge Journal of Economics*, 1 (1).

Smith, Steve (1980) 'Allison and the Cuban Missile Crisis', *Millennium*, 9 (1).

(1982) 'Berridge on International Relations', *Teaching Politics*, 11(1).

(1985a) 'Policy Preferences and Bureaucratic Position: The Case of the American Hostage Rescue Mission', *International Affairs*, 61 (1).

(1985b) 'Groupthink and the Hostage Rescue Mission', *British Journal of Political Studies*, 15 (1).

(ed.) (1985c) *British and American Approaches to International Relations* (London, Allen & Unwin).

Smith, Steve, and Michael Clarke (eds.) (1985) *Foreign Policy Implementation* (London, Allen & Unwin).

Snidal, D. (1985) 'Coordination versus Prisoners' Dilemma: Implications for International Cooperation and Regimes', *American Political Science Review*, 79 (4).

Snyder, Glen (1961) *Deterrence and Defense: Towards a Theory of National Security* (Princeton, N.J., Princeton University Press).

Socarras, M. P. (1985) 'The Argentine Invasion of the Falklands and International Norms of Signalling', *Yale Journal of International Law*, 10.

Stein, A. A. (1984) 'The Hegemon's Dilemma: Great Britain, the United States and the International Economic Order', *International Organization*, 38.

Steiner, Zara (1969) *The Foreign Office and Foreign Policy, 1898–1914* (Cambridge, Cambridge University Press).

Strange, Susan (1986) *Casino Capitalism* (Oxford, Basil Blackwell).

(1988) *States and Markets* (London, Frances Pinter).

(ed.) (1984) *Paths to International Political Economy* (London, Allen & Unwin).

Taylor, Trevor (1990) 'Defence Industries in International Relations', *Review of International Studies*, 16 (1).

Taylor, Trevor, and Keith Hayward (1989) *The UK Defence Industrial Base: Issues and Future Policy Options* (London, Brassey's).

Tetlock, P. (1979) 'Identifying Victims of Groupthink', *Journal of Personality and Social Psychology*, 37 (8).

Thorne, C. (1972) *The Limits of Foreign Policy* (London, Hamilton).

(1978) *Allies of a Kind* (London, Hamilton).

Timberlake, Lloyd (1988) 'The Greatest Threat on Earth', *Independent*, 12 September 1988.

Treverton, Gregory F. (1985) *Making the Alliance Work* (London, Macmillan).

Tsoukalis, Loukas (ed.) (1986) *Europe, American and the World Economy* (Oxford, Basil Blackwell).

Tugendhat, C., and W. Wallace (1988) *Options for British Foreign Policy in the 1990s* (London, Routledge/Royal Institute of International Affairs).

Tunander, Ola (1989) 'The Logic of Deterrence', *Journal of Peace Research*, 26 (4).

United Nations (1988) *Transnational Corporations in World Development* (New York, United Nations).

United States Information Service (1989) 'Baker Outlines Blueprint for a New Era in Europe', USIS Press Release, 13 December 1989.

Vasquez, J. (1979) 'Colouring It Morgenthau: New Evidence for an Old Thesis on Quantitative International Politics', *British Journal of International Studies*, 5 (3).

Vital, David (1968) *The Making of British Foreign Policy* (London, Allen & Unwin).

Walker, Brian (n.d.) *Peace, Environment and Development*, OPPS Paper 16 (Oxford, Oxford Project for Peace Studies).

Walker, S. (ed.) (1987) *Role Theory and Foreign Policy Analysis* (Durham, N.C., Duke University Press).

Walker, William, and Philip Gummett (1989) 'Britain and the European Armaments Market', *International Affairs*, 5 (3).

Wallace, William (1975) *The Foreign Policy Process in Britain* (London, Royal Institute of International Affairs).

(ed.) (1980) *Britain in Europe* (London, Heinemann).

(1982) 'Economic Divergence in the European Community', in J. M. Letiche (ed.), *International Economic Policies and Their Theoretical Foundations* (New York, Academic Press).

(1984) *Britain's Bilateral Links with Western Europe* (London, Routledge/Royal Institute of International Affairs).

(1986) 'What Price Independence? Sovereignty and Interdependence in British Politics', *International Affairs*, 62 (3).

(1989) 'European Security: Bilateral Steps to Multilateral Cooperation', in Yves Boyar, Pierre Lellouche and John Roper (eds.), *Franco-British Defence Cooperation* (London, Routledge).

Walt, Stephen M. (1985) 'Alliance Formation and the Balance of World Power', *International Security*, 9 (4).

Waltz, Kenneth N. (1970) 'The Myth of National Interdependence', in Charles Kindleberger (ed.), *The International Corporation* (Cambridge, Mass., MIT Press).

(1976) 'Theory of International Relations', *Political Science Yearbook*, 8.

(1979) *Theory of International Politics* (Reading, Mass., Addison-Wesley).

Watt, D. C. (1965) *Personalities and Politics* (London, Longman).

Weber, Hermann (1982) 'Recht und Gewalt im Südatlantik. Der Streit um die Falklandinseln (Malwinen) als Völkerrechtsproblem', *Vereinte Nationen*, 3.

White, Brian (1988) 'Macmillan and East–West Relations', in Richard Little and Steve Smith (eds.), *Belief Systems in International Relations* (Oxford, Basil Blackwell).

Wight, Martin (1986) (2nd edn) *Power Politics* (Harmondsworth, Penguin Books).

Wiles, Peter (1986) 'Whatever Happened to the Merchants of Death?', *Millennium*, 15 (3).

Wilkenfeld, J., G. Hopple, P. Rossa and S. Andriole (1980) *Foreign Policy Behaviour* (Beverley Hills, Calif., Sage).

Windass, Stan (1985) 'Nuclear Guidelines: Next Steps', in Stan Windass (ed.), *Avoiding Nuclear War* (London, Brassey's).

Young, J. W. (1984) *Britain, France and the Unity of Europe* (Leicester, Leicester University Press).
Young, Oran (1969) 'Interdependencies in World Politics', *International Journal*, 24.

INDEX

For EU product safety concerns, contact us at Calle de José Abascal, 56–1°,
28003 Madrid, Spain or eugpsr@cambridge.org.

www.ingramcontent.com/pod-product-compliance
Ingram Content Group UK Ltd.
Pitfield, Milton Keynes, MK11 3LW, UK
UKHW010047140625
459647UK00012BB/1654